AFFIRMATIVE ACTION FOR WOMEN:
A Practical Guide for Women and Management

Dorothy Jongeward
President, Transactional Analysis Management Institute
Interpersonal Relations and Communication Consultant

Dru Scott
President, Dru Scott Associates
Management Communication Consultant

ADDISON-WESLEY PUBLISHING COMPANY
Reading, Massachusetts · Menlo Park, California
London · Amsterdam · Don Mills, Ontario · Sydney

Fifth printing, May 1979

ISBN 0-201-03275-9
ABCDEFGHIJ-AL-79

PREFACE

Many organizations are faced with the problem of establishing affirmative action programs. They are seeking practical, workable steps to help them in their own move toward equal opportunity for women. For most, it may be confusing or uncertain as to exactly what these programs should be in order to be effective. It is the purpose of this collection of comments, programs, and articles to give some insight and guidelines as to what would be a useful course for organizations to take.

The term *affirmative action* is used in this book in both a specific and general sense. It means progress that is particularly related to an Equal Employment Opportunity program, and also any other progress that helps women move toward equality of opportunity. It is our hope that the articles and programs contained in this book will serve both individual women and management well.

In addition to the positive programs designed for and about women, we have included (1) a clear interpretation of the laws affecting organizations and women, (2) the current place of women in organized religion and in government service, (3) the unique problems of black women in organizations, and (4) insights into selecting a professional counselor for a woman.

We included this last contribution for those women who feel upset enough to seek outside help and as a guide for those who may counsel women into psychotherapy. It has been our experience that many women have received messages in childhood that cause them to restrict their life goals and negate their own potentials. Such experiences influence many women's motivation to succeed in organizations.

Both of us have had considerable experience designing, coordinating, and instructing courses to meet the new needs of women and to establish effective affirmative action. Two very successful models included here are the Bank of America's Affirmative Action Seminar and A Training Model of Seminars for Career Women.

We hope this book will serve a vital need for organizations now. We also hope that within the next five to ten years the need for such a guide will be part of history.

Acknowledgments

We wish to extend our sincere appreciation to the people who have contributed their professionalism toward the goals and purposes of this book. In addition, we thank those organizations which have been generous enough to share their programs.

We want to give special thanks to those women who assisted us in researching the current facts on women's personal lives and organizational lives: Madelyn Burley, Marilyn MacGregor, Debra Smith, and Pat West, research assistants; and also for the fine secretarial assistance contributed by Glenda Robinson and Sandy McPartlon.

Dorothy Jongeward
Pleasant Hill, California

Dru Scott
San Francisco, California

June 1975

CONTENTS

1. How do new laws and government regulations affect
   employers and working women?

   Fair Labor Standards Act?
   Equal Pay Act of 1963?
   Title VII of the Civil Rights Act of 1964?
   Education Amendments of 1972?
   Executive Order 11246 as amended?
   Department of Labor's Revised Order 4?

2. What can employers do in response to these regulations?

3. What can working women do who feel discriminated
   against?

1. How does the Federal government rate as an
   employer of women?
2. How high can women go in the Federal service?
3. How can women get started?
4. How can women best prepare themselves?

1. What part has religion played in the oppression or
   liberation of women?
2. What changes are taking place in organized religion
   today?
3. How do these changes affect the role of women?

2. How do the following patterns hold women back?
   The visibility system?
   The property-value system?
   The sponsor-protégé system?
   The legal system?
3. How can people identify, confront, and adjust to
   these systems?

1. What are the specific steps followed in one
   successful short session?
2. Why present a short seminar for managers and
   supervisors on affirmative action for women?
3. How can you select and develop leaders for
   these half-day seminars?

1. What kind of job-related training can help women
   better understand what motivates their behavior?
2. How can transactional analysis be combined with
   special training for women?
3. How can a short course be organized?
4. What are the results of such training?

1. What can a woman who has been a capable
   executive secretary for 15 years, with a B.A.
   degree, do next?

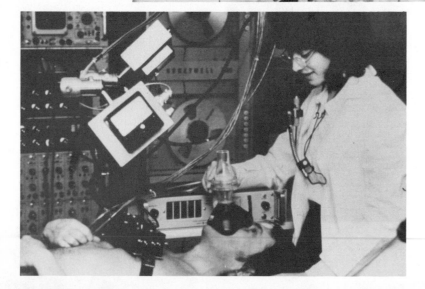

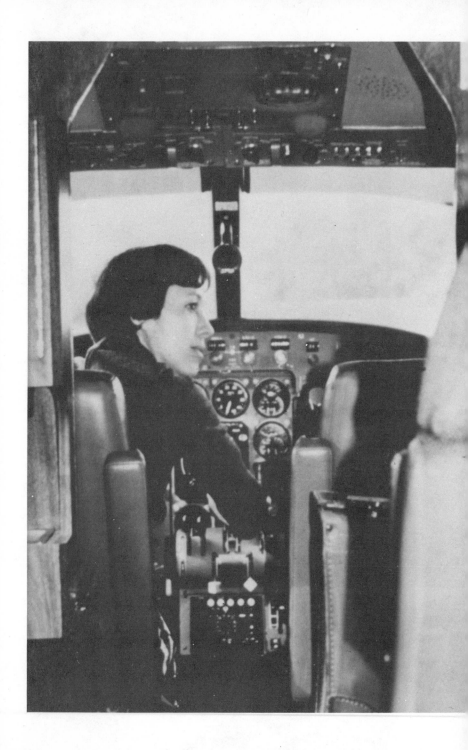

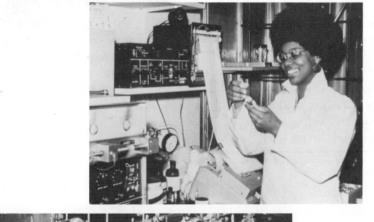

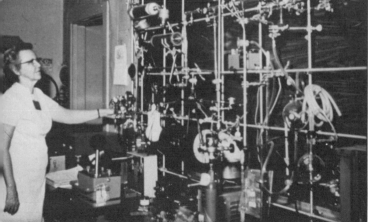

All the preceding pictures, except for the second one — which is of an Addison-Wesley executive — were compiled and presented as part of the U.S. Civil Service Commission's San Francisco Regional College Relations Program. Don Robbins, Regional Recruiting and College Relations Officer, headed this project. The pictures are used in recruiting programs for the Federal government as well as training programs for men and women within the Federal service itself.

1

THE ORGANIZATION WOMAN: THEN AND NOW

Life styles are changing.

Women's lives are changing.

Women will work.

New faces in new places.

Women need models.

Women need mentors.

In summary.

Let's listen in on a Monday morning staff meeting. The executive officer shakes up the staff with: "We're under new pressure now to hire women." Three different staff members immediately jump in with:

> "Why do we need affirmative action? I haven't discriminated against women, and I don't think most employers do. If a qualified woman comes along, I'll hire her, if I think she can do the job, and if it looks as though she won't go running off to get married or have a baby. But we can't let down standards, or then where will we be?"

> "Oh, I think you're wrong. Women have been discriminated against for years, and the only way we'll ever catch up and make things fair is to hire nothing *but* women for a while till things even out."

> "Nuts! You're both wrong, and you've got your heads in the clouds. We ought to fire all the women who are working now and give their jobs to men who have families to support. That way we'd get a lot of people off welfare and the women would be at home where they belong."

Similar comments crop up in meetings across the country. These ideas can be overheard in gatherings ranging from the executive dining room to the warehouse lunch area to the ladies' lounge.

Working women are no longer just a matter of discussion. They are a fact of life. Companies will pay over $72,000,000 in awards for violations of equal opportunity — mostly because of discrimination against women. [1] The $72,000,000 stems from only one of the pieces of powerful legislation and court decisions outlining changing organizational responsibilities. In light of these new government regulations, organizations are now compelled to examine any practices that discriminate against women.

The time for new patterns of opportunity for women is now. The challenge to change is now. However, this challenge is only one of the many changes confronting all men and women in their organizational and personal lives.

LIFE STYLES ARE CHANGING

Our society is floundering amidst a sea of sweeping change. These changes force all of us to look at and evaluate our nostalgia toward long-accepted traditions. Alvin Toffler highlights this in *Future Shock*. He points out the rapid acceleration of the rate of change we are caught in right now.

It has been observed, for example, that if the last 50,000 years of man's existence were divided into lifetimes, lifetimes of approximately sixty-two years each, there have been about 800 such lifetimes. Of these 800, fully 650 were spent in caves.

Only during the last seventy lifetimes has it been possible to communicate effectively from one lifetime to another — as writing makes it possible to do. Only during the last six lifetimes did masses of men ever see a printed word. Only during the last four has it been possible to measure time with any precision. Only in the last two has anyone anywhere used an electric motor. And the overwhelming majority of all the material goods we use in daily life today have been developed within the present, the 800th, lifetime. [2]

As the environment changes, organizations must evolve that reflect new faces of the new environment. Let's see how this relates to one small organization: the family. When men and women lived in caves, it was good management for them to divide the work on the basis of sex. With threats to bodily survival, and with the male's superior strength, it was logical that men should be the ones to forage for food and protect women and the young. Because of the state of the art of family-planning technology, women's mobility was limited by frequent pregnancies. It was then logical for women to stay in the caves and care for the young and the sick and the elderly. In addition, someone had to keep a fire going at the mouth of the cave to ward off hostile animals. Survival depended on it. Since women were already at "home," it was reasonable to assign them the task of keeping the home fires burning.

Here's an organizational chart that might have been scratched on the cave wall.

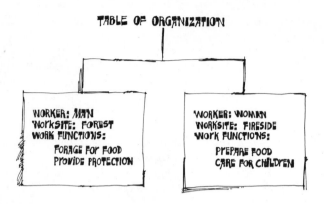

If we were to see the cave wall today, we could add "relevant" only for the first 650 lifetimes in human history. During more than the first three-quarters of the history of people, this table of organization accurately reflected the most practical division of labor between men and women.

Today's lifestyles, however, are far removed from the cave. Yet even though we have physically moved, many people still mentally cling to the image of women "keeping the home fires burning." They continue to see women's only rightful place as near the hearth.

Whether the organization is the family or the corporation, to be successful today it must produce something relevant to the environment. For example, early family organizations focused on physical survival. While this level of operation is still necessary for most of the world's people, it is not true for many families in America where survival needs are often easily met.

Today's family organization needs to center on producing a healthy psychological climate. People growing up today must cope with drastic new changes affecting their emotions — overcrowded cities, pressures for education, high standards of living, rootlessness, frequent moves, temporary relationships, computer-shaped lives, and nuclear power. An effective family organization today could help people survive these pressures without going crazy.

If the energies of the organization are not related to the "now," that organization becomes obsolete. Its energies are then spent in maintaining the organizational structures and not in maintaining contact with the needs of the environment. The degree of obsolescence can be measured by the distance between what is produced and what is actually needed.

Railroads in America are an example of companies that have failed to keep up with changing demands. John F. Stover writes of this obsolescence:

They have faced increasing competition from new highway, barge, air and pipeline facilities; and the slow response of the railroads themselves to changing conditions has worsened their predicament. [3]

An organization that continues to provide a product no longer needed must spend energies in suppressing creative problem solving, selling the public something that is useless or harmful, and searching for plausible reasons for self-perpetuation.

In order to better judge what best suits the current reality of the environment, it is important to be in touch with what is happening now. Let's look at the changing circumstances and patterns in the lives of today's women.

WOMEN'S LIVES ARE CHANGING

American women are marrying earlier, having fewer children, buying more services, and living longer than ever before.

At the turn of the century, the median marriage age for women was 22. It is now closer to 20. [4] More women will marry at age 18 than at any other age. [5] At the turn of the century, many children meant many hands to work the land, to gather the crops, to make the cloth. Families were big, and children were an economic asset.

Today, families average about 2.5 children, [6] and these children are likely to be an economic liability. The birthrate is decreasing in all ages of women, except for teenage women, where it is still on the increase. People's lessening interest in having large families is reflected in polls. In 1965 the average desired family size was 3.03 children. Only six years later this figure diminished to 2.5. [7] At the turn of the century, women stopped childbearing when their bodies were no longer able to produce children, usually in their forties. In startling contrast, today's average woman is still in her twenties when she bears her last child.

Another interesting change is the increasing number of women who choose to remain single. In 1960 a third of women 21 years of age and over were single, while in 1970 the number had increased to one-half. [8]

Today's homemakers are no longer using their time baking bread, making cloth, churning butter, or sewing all the family garments. Most of these things are now done by others outside the home. In addition, many family members seek pleasure and relaxation outside the home.

However, the greatest pressure for change comes from the added number of years women are living. Today, women can expect to live some 75 years. In contrast, their counterparts in 1900 could expect to live only to the age of 48. [9]

The following chart vividly portrays this difference.

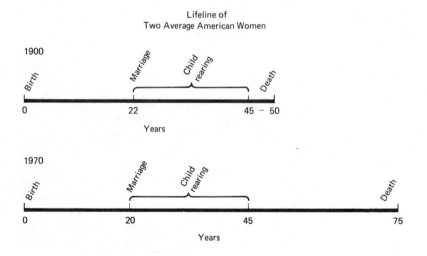

Lifeline of
Two Average American Women

As a consequence of these changes, what happens to a married woman today who reaches her late thirties or early forties? Her child-rearing time is over. She may receive a mandatory retirement from the need for full-time homemaking. If so, often vague feelings of depression and uselessness settle over her. Her doctor frequently prescribes antidepressants or tranquilizers. If not tranquilizers, she may turn to alcohol. For some, the dull realization comes that there are 30 to 40 more years to live with no dominant purpose in life. (See "What Do You Do When Your Script Runs Out" in Appendix A at the end of the book.)

With a longer life expectancy, with fewer children, and with less time spent producing the physical necessities of life, today's women literally have more of their life's time available to work outside the home. And that is exactly what women are doing. Even though most women will work, they often face special problems. The following examples portray three typical situations in which women may find themselves. In each situation the woman is unprepared for what the work world demands. History speaks for thousands of other women who have patterned themselves in similar ways.

Illustration 1

Edith J. did not enter college with the idea of developing herself or learning a profession; she entered college because it was such a "good place to meet the right kind of man." Her goal was met. She was pinned as a junior, engaged as a senior, and married shortly after her graduation. Her first child was born a year and a half after her marriage, and the second child two years after that. As the children grew and as her husband progressed in his company, they moved to a comfortable home in the suburbs. Much of Edith's time was spent taking care of her children and furnishing the house the way she felt it should look. As Edith's children entered school and as the house was finally decorated, she found herself with time on her hands. The idea began to occur to her that a job would be a good thing. She found, however, when applying to various companies, that they were not impressed with her ten-year-old degree in the humanities and her lack of any definite job preparation. They were also not impressed when she said, "Well, I don't know what I want to do, but I like working with people and helping others."

Illustration 2

Yvonne H. knew when she started high school that all she really wanted was to get married. During high school she was very interested in the social activities, the football games, and the dances. She often complained that classes in algebra or history had little to do with her life, because she was "just going to get married." Yvonne married shortly before high-school graduation and had her first baby within a year. Although her husband was a capable high-school graduate, his job did not work out the way he expected and money was scarce. Shortly after her second baby arrived, Yvonne found herself as a 21-year-old divorcée and the mother of two small children. The only job she was able to get was as a relief waitress in a coffee shop.

Illustration 3

Betty E. was born and reared in the South on a small farm. When only 16, she married and moved with her husband to Los Angeles. Her husband tried his hand at a number of jobs, and Betty and their three small children followed him from one location to another. The moves, the children, and their lack of money became the subjects of many arguments, and they eventually separated. Even though a reconciliation was attempted, Betty was soon deserted by her frustrated, young husband. She found herself alone with three small children, the sole source of income for her family. The only job her background qualified her for was that of a presser in a laundry, earning $1.65 an hour. Betty held her job for several months. However, the cost of babysitting, plus food and housing and transportation, soon forced her to seek county aid.

These three women have widely differing backgrounds, yet they share a common problem of many women — lack of preparation for earning a living.

WOMEN WILL WORK

Prepared or not, nine out of ten American women will work. [10] A single woman can expect to work 45 years outside her home. A married woman can expect to work 25 years outside her home. [11] * Even in the face of these facts, women are shocked to learn the number of years they will probably devote to paid employment. Most of them do not plan this work carefully. They often learn to think of their vocational training only as a backup — an insurance policy — "just in case" they should have to work.

For example, teenage women who have seen their mothers go through a difficult time finding employment after divorce are often motivated to learn some kind of skill to sell in the market place. Many, however, are still not motivated to think of this work as a career.

In light of the facts, it is no longer appropriate for most women to ask, "What can I do just in case?" It would be much more useful to ask, "What would I enjoy doing?" and "For how many years?" and "Where?"

The belief that employment is optional has been particularly true of white middle-class women who may expect someone else to earn the income. In case of divorce or a husband's death, many such women find that they have been just one man away from welfare. More frequently lower-income women expect to do some kind of work, even though their aspirations may be low and they have little, if any, training.

One out of nine households is headed exclusively by a woman. [13] Almost 40% of these households headed by women exist at or below the government-defined poverty level. (The U.S. Department of Labor defines poverty as less than $3,968 a year for an urban family of four.) [14] During the last ten years the number of poor families headed by women stayed the same — 1.9 million. However, during the same period the number of poor families headed by men has been cut in half — to 3.3 million in 1970. [15] In addition, black women face even graver money problems.

---

* The expected worklife of a woman is closely related to her marital status and the number of children she has. In the large group of women who enter the labor force by age 20, the relatively small number who never marry have a worklife expectance of 45 years. This is about 10 years longer than for those women in the group who marry but have no children and about 2 to 3 years longer than for those who become widowed or divorced. For the large number of married women with children, worklife expectance declines with the higher number of children and the later timing of the last child. A woman marrying at age 20 has a worklife expectance ranging from 25 years if she has just one child to 17 years if she has four or more children. [12]

One out of four black families is headed by a woman. Almost two-thirds of these are poor. The median wage for black women is the lowest for all groups. [16]

At least part of these problems can be attributed to the lack of thought and preparation most women give to their money-making skills. Because of a lack of preparation and failure to set long-term goals, many women find themselves in jobs which are unfulfilling, unchallenging, and underpaid. Two-thirds of the 31 million women who work are in dead-end, menial jobs. Half of all employed women earn less than $5,323. This compares to $8,966 for men. Looking at the top end of the scale, only 7% of women earn over $10,000. In contrast, 40% of men earn over this amount. (For more information, see "What You May Not Know About Women" in Appendix B at the back of the book.)

NEW FACES IN NEW PLACES

Women are beginning to take new roles in many organizations. Some are even stepping into jobs traditionally labeled "man's work." They are climbing poles for the telephone company, piloting jets for the Navy, selling cars on lots, examining pathological tissue, running data-processing departments, and directing traffic at busy intersections. Although these changes are coming all too slowly for many women, nonetheless, changes are happening.

The Federal government is leading the way in putting new faces in new places. The pictures at the beginning of this book illustrate actual women who are members of the Federal service working in new roles. Even though they represent a minority of women in the Federal service, they serve as powerful models to women aspiring to higher levels and wider horizons.

In spite of these discouraging statistics about where most women are now, some women are moving ahead. They are discovering that work within an organization can fulfill and enrich their lives. As we get in touch with the current environment, it's exciting to see women moving into jobs that they have not held before.

WOMEN NEED MODELS

It is unrealistic to think that these women are typical of all women now employed by either the public or the private sector. However, they serve as effective models to others in lower levels of employment. Models have been lacking in the lives of working women ever since the nation's women left their houses to work in offices and factories. Seeing and working with women taking professional responsibilities gives other women more options. They can then begin to make new judgments and set new goals about their own capabilities and careers. Until now such opportunities have been rare in most organizations.

Illustration

One training division contained 19 professional training officers. Seventeen were men and two were women. The manager of the training office was holding a counseling session with Sharon M., a 20-year-old typist. When asked what her career goals were, Sharon answered that she would like to do the kind of work Nancy and Carol, the only two women, were doing. It didn't occur to her that she could have patterned her career after the men. However, the two women served as effective models. As a result, Sharon now has a better chance of contributing her full capacities on the job.

Many women have trouble modeling themselves after men. Such women find it easier to identify with other women managers. This is especially true if they are trained to think of themselves as subordinates or helpmates.

Even some career women justify their vocation by saying they are only helping other people. Few women easily see themselves as the person "out front" with someone else backing them up. It's common to hear "behind every successful man is a good woman," yet if we say "behind every successful woman there's a good man," it sounds strange.

As a consequence, many women cannot picture themselves as having supporters behind them. A woman who is succeeding professionally in an organization needs the help of many competent people, whether it is a secretary on the job or a housekeeper at home.

In some cases women have moved into executive jobs by acting out a helpmate role. For example, a woman who keeps the books for her father's small store may end up running the store. A woman starting as a secretary may end up the administrative officer. A woman helping her politically minded husband may end up holding the office. Maureen Neuberger and Margaret Chase Smith are examples. Many women feel more comfortable moving up this way. This pattern fits the concept of women succeeding as helpmates rather than as primary up-front people. Even so, such women eventually serve as models.

Similar models were not available to women in previous generations. Women in new positions today may lead to future generations of women having wider career choices and better career plans. Women of tomorrow will be more likely to invest their talents in areas that better match their unique abilities.

WOMEN NEED MENTORS

For women to achieve equal opportunity, they not only need models, they also need mentors. One of the most powerful forms of management education is the mentor system. This system has been traditional for men in organizations. Usually a senior man promotes a junior man that he sees as "up and coming." The mentor may say, "Mr. Smith is coming in to go over the new contract. Why don't you sit in on our discussion?" Or, "Let's have a drink and talk over your presentation." Or, "I'm having lunch with the man in charge of the Henderson building contract. Why don't you come along with us?"

This kind of management education cannot be gained in any school or university. It takes place on the job. It is very practical. It is watching people who already function well, and learning their skills — the skills of closing a deal, handling and working with other people, making a contact, persuading a committee, confronting a problem. The mentor may also provide visibility for the protégé. For example, he may invite the junior man to serve as recorder on an important executive planning committee. This kind of management training opportunity is rarely open to women.

Most women have to seek their management education simply by keeping their own eyes and ears open or taking what management training courses are available to them. Some women will not aspire to the next rung of the ladder without having someone in the company encouraging, supporting, and training them. Yet many women feel uncomfortable being helped by a sponsor or mentor, or are not even aware that the system exists.

Managers can help motivate women who demonstrate potential. Among the most useful questions a manager can ask an unmotivated woman is, "Where do you expect to be in this organization within five years? What are your next two job spots?" A good share of women will not have thought about it.

The lack of on-the-job management training for women is intensified by the fact that traditionally women who have "made it" in organizations don't help other women. Because women executives are rare, they often think of themselves as something special. They set themselves apart from other women as unusual. This behavior results in the Queen Bee Syndrome. Such women covet their position. They often display little interest in and may even show disapproval of other working women.

Women's lack of models and mentors often cause them to set psychological limits on the use and development of their own talents. This can be changed.

IN SUMMARY

- The lifetimes of women have drastically changed.

- Most women now will work.

- Most women are working for the same reason as most men — they need the money. Two-thirds of all working women head households or are married to men who earn less than $7,000.

- Some women need models and mentors.

- Many women today are job-oriented just in case they have to work. They see their jobs as insurance rather than as a career.

- However, more women are seeking paid employment as a meaningful way to invest their life's time.

- More women will also be working in jobs that have been traditionally labeled "men's work," picking up hard hats as well as brief cases.

- As a result, younger women will have more career models.

- In the future it is likely that more women will think of work as an expression of their own uniqueness, rather than as only something to fall back on in an emergency.

REFERENCES

1. James C. Hyatt, "Women, Government, Unions Increasingly Sue Under Equal Pay Act," *Wall Street Journal*, 89 (No. 37, August 22, 1973): 1,25.

2. Alvin Toffler, *Future Shock* (New York: Random House, 1970), p. 15. Reprinted by permission.

3. John F. Stover, *The Life and Decline of the American Railroad* (New York: Oxford University Press, 1970) from the book cover. Reprinted by permission.

4. Paul H. Jacobson, *American Marriage and Divorce* (New York: Rinehart, 1959), p. 75.

5. U.S. Department of Labor, Wage and Labor Standards Administration, *1969 Handbook on Women Workers*, Women's Bureau Bulletin 294, U.S. Government Printing Office, 1969, p. 7.

6. John D. Rockefeller, III, "Population Growth and America's Future," *Britannica Book of the Year, 1972* (Chicago: Encyclopaedia Britannica, 1972), p. 569.

7. *Ibid.*, pp. 569 and 573.

8. George E. Delury, Managing Editor, 1973, *The World Almanac and Book Of Facts* (New York, Newspaper Enterprise Association, 1972), p. 955.

9. *Ibid.*

10. U.S. Department of Labor, Wage and Labor Standards Administration, *1969 Handbook on Women Workers*, Women's Bureau Bulletin 294, U.S. Government Printing Office, 1969, p. 7.

11. *Ibid.*, pp. 7-8.

12. *Ibid.*

13. U.S. Department of Labor, Employment Standards Administration, *Why Women Work*, U.S. Government Printing Office, 1973 (rev.), p. 2.

14. U.S. Department of Labor, Employment Standards Administration, *Fact Sheet on the American Family in Poverty*, U.S. Government Printing Office, 1971 (rev.), pp. 1-3.

15. *Ibid.*

16. "What You May Not Know About Women," Unitarian Universalist Women's Federation, 25 Beacon Street, Boston, Mass., p. 1. (See Appendix B.)

2

WOMEN'S LACK OF ACHIEVEMENT: THEN AND NOW

Both men and women follow scripts.

Many women have self-negating scripts.

Different cultural attitudes are held toward men and women.

Have you heard what they say about women?

Some women achieve anyway.

Cultures have scripts.

Women learn organizational scripts.

Scripts can be changed.

In summary.

Morton Hunt writes:

The mechanism of modern women has many outmoded and archaic parts, and runs haltingly toward its future. A major difficulty, for instance, is woman's — and her employer's — poor opinion of her capacity. Everyone knows that aside from the occasional great women of history, the female sex has simply never amounted to much outside the home. James Cattell, an experimental psychologist, once calculated that of all persons who had ever become eminent only 3.2 percent had been women; even in our own emancipated age, only 6 percent of the celebrities in Who's Who in America *are women. No matter that woman has had exceedingly little opportunity for achievement of the sorts recorded by history; the record stands, and convinces both sexes that she is not very good at man's kind of work.*

Many beliefs and notions crystallize around this tradition. [1]

Why have women achieved so little and contributed so little to those things considered precious enough to preserve for all of mankind?

BOTH MEN AND WOMEN FOLLOW SCRIPTS.

What people achieve in life is often motivated by a *psychological script.** Self-concept, life goals, and attitudes about other people are set in the minds of most of us by the eighth year. Feelings about self are expressed as I'm OK or I'm not-OK; feelings about others as You're OK or You're not-OK. These positions and patterns crystallize into an individual's psychological script. [2] [3] [4] [5] A script is a predetermined, ongoing life plan based on early childhood experiences. Although a psychological script powerfully shapes a life, it usually operates at an unconscious level. A psychological script can open or close people's doors to the future, and can squeeze or stretch people's potential.

Psychological scripts bear a striking resemblance to theatrical scripts. People play roles, rehearse and deliver dialogue, wear costumes that suit their character, and are involved in living out a plot. Some people's life dramas are like sagas. Others are comedies,

---

*   The description of the phenomena of psychological scripts was first developed by the late Dr. Eric Berne in his writings on transactional analysis.

or even farces. Some portray dull, plodding plots, while still others move toward a tragic ending — suicide and/or murder.

All script dramas have a theme. These themes cover a wide spectrum of human theatrics. Do you know people whose life themes are like the following?

Almost making it	Killing oneself
Being oneself	Working hard
Trying hard	Going nowhere
Enjoying life	Being nobody
Being boring	Making money

Scripts are formed by the messages a child receives from the outside environment. A warm, protective, nourishing, realistic climate contributes in a positive way to a child's destiny. Lack of care and nutrition, or a severe or brutal emotional climate, all contribute in a negative way to a child's sense of worth and purpose.

However, the most important influence on a person's script is someone else's opinion, evaluation, and response. The attitudes, injunctions, and permissions displayed by significant authority figures (i.e., parents, grandparents, and older siblings) send messages to a child that eventually form that child's identity and preconceived destiny.

Messages are conveyed many ways. The messages may be communicated by examples such as a child never seeing a mother or father stop busily working for a time of relaxation and fun.

Or the message may be communicated in a three-handed manner. For example, mother says to a neighbor while daughter stands by, "This child has never given us a moment's trouble."

Or the messages may be communicated directly in words such as an oft-repeated, "You stupid kid, you'll never amount to anything."

The child who sees an always busy parent year after year will probably work busily through adult life and feel out of place at a picnic.

The child who gets approval for always being quiet and compliant may later be praised for "never causing trouble on the job."

The child who hears "You stupid kid!" over and over will, later in life, probably feel stupid and not-OK and may feel uncomfortable if praised as bright.

Most of us realize, without being students of psychology, that children who decide they are stupid by the age of four, will begin to act stupid when they reach school and will still be doing "dumb things" at the age of 40. The tendency is to reinforce any not-OK feelings.

Such children experience a distortion of their possible selves. Rather than pursuing and developing the resources they were born with, they begin to manipulate their own behavior and that of others to make themselves look dumb. They learn to become losers instead of winners.

As grownups, people experience scripts as compulsions. Both men's and women's scripts will always involve three questions. [6] [7] [8]

> Who am I?
>
> What am I doing here?
>
> Who are all those other people?

Think about the life dramas that might develop from each of these sets of assumptions made in early childhood.

I'm stupid and ugly.

I'll never get anywhere.

You can't trust anyone.

or

I'm confident I can figure it out.

I can do most of the things I want.

Most people are pretty fair.

or

I have the right answers.

I could do OK, if it weren't for this rotten society.

People are no damn good and should listen to me.

or

I'm helpless and dependent.

I can't make it on my own.

Other people seem to know how to do everything.

Many women are scripted to feel:

I'm cute and dumb.

I should have a family but to do anything else well is "unfeminine."

Other people will take care of me.

The suppression of intelligence and talents has long been traditional among myriads of American women.*

MANY WOMEN HAVE SELF-NEGATING SCRIPTS

Frequently, women set limits on their own achievements because of the messages they received in early childhood from significant authority figures. These messages are internalized and eventually form self-images, life goals, and attitudes toward other people. The messages a woman receives and the decisions she makes about them form her script — the life plan she feels compelled to fulfill as an adult.

Scripting messages are often sent around various subject matters. Take a few minutes and work through the following exercise. Jot down a few answers to each question. If another person or two is available, you might want to work on these questions together.†

---

* Men also receive messages that distort their unique possibilities. For example, many men are scripted to be stoic and repress their emotions. While this kind of scripting is equally unrealistic, our book is designed to help men and women understand women. The same questions could be asked of men.

† We have used this exercise with thousands of men and women in training about women. The exercise starts people actively thinking about and questioning script messages.

What is a little girl likely to hear about the importance of her intelligence?

About the intelligence of women in general?

About her ability to solve problems?

About her ability to deal with mechanical things?

About her education?

About her vocation?

About marriage?

About children?

About her relationship to men?

About her own sexuality?

About feminine behaviors?

About masculine behaviors?

About leadership?

About her ability to drive cars, buses, and trucks?

About working mothers?

About her future duties?

About her physical agility and grace?

And what is she likely to hear about the importance of her appearance?

You may be interested in taking this exercise one step further. See what pattern evolves when you rank these various subjects in the order of importance they might be taught a little girl.

It may also be interesting to contrast the kinds of messages little boys typically hear about the same subject matters. Compare the kinds of scripts that would be likely to develop as a consequence.

A significant number of women hear that they should be smart, but should not show their brains in front of men they expect dates from; and that their major emphasis should be on how they look, not on who they are. They also hear that feminine behaviors are passive, sweet, clean, pure, good; that respectable vocations for women are nursing, teaching, secretarial work, and being a social worker; that women are bad drivers; and that women are not innately capable of abstract thinking or balancing the checkbook or operating mechanical equipment.

Appearance is often thought of as so important to women that if they are not really acceptable looking, their only alternative is to have a career.

Illustration

As one woman reported, "My family said to me over and over again, 'Jane, you're so plain looking that you'll have to have a career'." Jane is at this time 42, single, and an accomplished engineer. Even now she finds it difficult to feel good about her job success. Her career, to her family, indicates a failure rather than a success — to be successful as a woman, she should have been pretty enough to attract a man and not have to work. Even now her mother often remarks to Jane's more attractive sisters, "It's really too bad about Jane that she's so dedicated to her career. If only some man could have gotten to know Jane and discovered how nice she really is, she wouldn't have to be knocking herself out with that job today."

Women who have learned patterns of downgrading themselves often have trouble enjoying their successes. Matina Horner's research indicates that college women's motives to achieve are distorted by conflicting motives to *avoid success*. [9] She reports that this avoidance is learned in early childhood along with other ideas of what it means to be feminine. She also found that women who do achieve often experience anxiety and guilt. Such success is not feminine.

DIFFERENT CULTURAL ATTITUDES ARE HELD TOWARD MEN AND WOMEN

To gain further insight into attitudes that we hold toward men and women, take a few minutes and work through the following exercise. [10] * You might find it more enjoyable if you do it with someone else.

---

* This is another exercise that has worked effectively with groups of men and women in affirmative action training.

Complete the sentence: Women are _____ .

Fill in the blanks below with at least ten adjectives or phrases about women that a little girl or a little boy might hear in a supermarket, in a home, in a department store, or at a social gathering. If you think of a phrase or a word that seems questionable, ask yourself, "Would little girls and boys commonly hear this?"

_____	_____
_____	_____
_____	_____
_____	_____
_____	_____

After you have finished the first part of the exercise, try the next part. Complete the sentence: Men are _____ .
Again, fill in the blanks with words or phrases commonly heard by boys or girls.

_____	_____
_____	_____
_____	_____
_____	_____
_____	_____

Now, look over what you wrote concerning women and ask yourself the following questions.

- How many of them would you consider as being negative traits and how many positive?
- How many would you consider would be attributed to a childlike person or to a full-grown adult person?
- In a generalized sense of being OK or not-OK, do women seem to come out sounding OK or not-OK?

Now do the same thing with the list you made for men. What patterns appear?
If these kinds of messages are sent to little boys and girls, how would they affect their scripts? How might they affect the achievement level in adult life of both men and women? How

might they affect how and where men and women function within organizations now?

It might be interesting for you to explore the possibility that many attitudes applied to women now reflect centuries of thinking.

Historically, fears about women, their childbirth functions, and the menstrual cycle resulted in a downgrading of women that has held over to modern times. For example, women of ancient Greece were not allowed to worship in the temples during their menstrual period. Many women today still think of themselves as sexually unclean. The $6 billion feminine-deodorant industry attests to this fact.

Many great men — philosophers, theologians, educators — have contributed important and valuable ideas in their special fields. However, many of these men professed attitudes that negated women and put them in an inferior or unclean position.

HAVE YOU HEARD WHAT THEY SAY ABOUT WOMEN?

Prominent people today and throughout history have frequently fostered negative attitudes about women and their proper place. Such attitudes both reflected and reinforced common cultural beliefs about women. As you read the quotations below, consider the cumulative power of these ideas over the centuries. Feel the bounds these messages have built around the potential of women. Also consider the bounds that such attitudes cause women to build around their own potentials.

Pythagoras (540-510 B.C.) taught:

There is a good principle which has created order, light and man and a bad principle which has created chaos, darkness and woman. [11]

Aristotle (384-322 B.C.) described women as:

Female by virtue of a certain incapacity. . .(They) are weaker and cooler by nature than. . .males and we must regard the female character as a kind of natural defectiveness. [12]

St. Thomas Aquinas (1223-1274) believed women to be:

...*defective and accidental.* ..*a male gone awry*. ..*the result of some weakness in the (father's) generative power*. ..*or of some external factor, like the south wind, which is damp.* [13]

Martin Luther (1483-1546) expressed his feelings towards women's function:

If a woman grows weary and at last dies from childbearing, it matters not. Let her only die from bearing, she is there to do it. [14]

Napoleon Bonaparte (1769-1821) purported that:

Nature intended women to be our slaves. ..*they are our property; we are not theirs. They belong to us, just as a tree that bears fruit belongs to a gardener. What a mad idea to demand equality for women!*. ..*Women are nothing but machines for producing children.* [15]

In a recent *Life* article Richard Gilman reported Freud's (1856-1939) teachings about women:

...*women's destiny was determined through beauty, charm and sweetness*. ..*Freud at the same time enunciated a scientific schema of feminine sexual and intellectual being that powerfully reinforced age-old prejudices. In the tradition of Aristotle and St. Thomas, he considered woman an insufficient or defective creature whose entire psychosexual life was shaped by her having been "deprived" of a penis, and whose mortal and social existence was marked by "envy," "insincerity," "secretiveness," an underdeveloped sense of justice and honor and an incapacity for the "higher human tasks."* [16]

Even in 1972, Spiro T. Agnew, who is only one of many influential contemporary men holding such attitudes toward women, speculated in a major speech:

I leave with you the words of an old Welsh proverb: "Three things are untamable: Fools, women, and the salt sea."

This is a great moment for civilization. ..*We stand at the threshold of taming the sea, taming fools and women may take a bit longer.* [17]

In the past, women's struggle for equal opportunity has frequently been a laughing matter. It still is to many people.

However, it has not only been men who have downgraded women. Often the same attitude is held by other women — even women in positions of great power.

Queen Victoria decried "the wicked folly of women's rights." [18]

Recently, a woman who had run for high political office in California was asked by a newsman when a woman might run for Vice President. Ironically, she was reported as answering "I don't know, but if they ever name one to be President, I'm going to leave." In today's working situation these same attitudes are passed on to another generation when women say, "Well, I certainly don't want to work for a woman!"

SOME WOMEN ACHIEVE ANYWAY

In spite of limiting script messages, some women choose to achieve great things. The following incident in the life of Elizabeth Cady Stanton (1815-1902) illustrates this point.

> Elizabeth Cady Stanton dedicated over 50 years of her life to leading the struggle for the vote for American women. Elizabeth Cady grew up one of five daughters in a family of six children. The only son was her father's pride and joy. When Elizabeth was eleven, her brother, Eleazor, was killed as a result of an accident. Elizabeth tried to console her father at her brother's death by telling him "we all miss him so deeply, but you know we love you too and we will strive all the more to be the kind of children you would like us to be." Her father, Judge Cady, sighed and answered, "Oh, my daughter, I wish you were a boy!" [19]

> Young Elizabeth decided that what boys could do that girls couldn't was ride horseback and study Greek. She determined to become skilled in both of these. In addition to becoming an accomplished horseback rider, she also won a coveted prize for Greek scholarship at Johnstown Academy. She brought the prized Greek testament home for her father's approval in hopes that he would accept her as much as a son. His devastating response was, "My daughter, it's a pity you were not a boy." [20]

As an adult, Elizabeth became the brilliant philosopher of the women's movement for the vote. Her work with her lifelong friend, Susan B. Anthony, focused the nation's attention on the political status of women. Yet they both died before the Nineteenth Amendment, which gave women the franchise, was ratified. Even though Elizabeth's sexuality and talents were negated by her father, her life was filled with the richness of human purpose.

Women such as Elizabeth Cady Stanton, Lucretia Mott, the Grimke sisters, Susan B. Anthony, Sojourner Truth, Carrie Chapman Catt, were giants in the annals of American history. Indeed, they were giants in the history of the political liberation of humankind. Yet, it is sad to report that they are likely to be unknown to the average American teenager.

Recently we asked a bright, 16-year-old woman, "What have you learned in history about Susan B. Anthony?" Her wide-eyed response was, "Susan who?" Such young women who are deprived of knowing their own history are eventually destined to relive the same struggles. The scripts of a culture that are not understood and evaluated are repeated over and over again.

CULTURES HAVE SCRIPTS

Like single bricks in a wall, the ideas of individual men and women build on each other to form a strong, almost inpenetrable wall — a cultural script. [21] Such scripts pervade every corner of community life — from patterns of humor to patterns of homicide. They form the community conscience.

A cultural script has many of the same elements as an individual script: themes, costumes, directions, and prescribed roles. It is the culturally prescribed roles for women that have helped produce many female teachers, nurses, social workers, and secretaries and few female truck drivers, principals, doctors, pilots, and presidents.

Women and men alike live out their lives under the pressures of their personal and cultural scripts. A cultural script, like an individual script, may make sense for today's living or may be out of step with contemporary needs.

Cultural scripts prescribe the expected and accepted *places for women to be* and *things for women to do*. Organizations reflect and institutionalize many elements of the cultural script.

WOMEN LEARN ORGANIZATIONAL SCRIPTS

Board room or clerical pool? Just where is woman's place in the organization? A woman working in an organization operates under the influence of expectations in much the same way as a little girl growing up in a family. These dramatic assumptions are part of the organizational script and often dictate for a woman who she is, what she is to do, and where her place is. [22]

Hundreds of subtle and not-so-subtle messages proclaim woman's prescribed place. The little girl at home and the woman at work both figure out where they should be. Each also figures out what gets approval from the people with power. The message may be "nice girls don't play football" or "of course you won't be interested in this job; it involves travel." The approval may be a smile from Daddy or a new carpet from the division manager, but the message is the same. "Here's what you do to get along around here." In other words, "Here's what you do to live out your script and fit into our script."

Just as individuals have themes to their scripts, so do organizations. Most organizations have specific script themes for women. Which of these themes sound familiar? Women are:

Only working until. . .   Not rocking the boat
Working for pin money   Not making a scene
Always there to help   Keeping their place
Decorating the office   Being satisfied
Always loyal   Letting someone else decide
Being good girls   Trapping the boss

Just as individual negative life themes limit the development of people, so do negative organizational themes. Organizational themes often discourage women from giving a fair return on the organization's investment in their talents.

Lorine Pruette writes:

". . .The woman worker may never have learned shorthand and she may type with one finger, but if she does not watch out, business will catch her and make her a stenographer at heart. One of the enlightened woman's agencies has been known to advise girls to conceal their knowledge of stenography, but this is not enough; they need to get a change of heart. Many an assistant chief and many a woman executive remains always in the stenographic *attitude toward some man in the organization, while he never quite ceases to expect her to remind him to wear his rubbers and to look after his cough."* [23]

Personal and Organizational Scripts Often Fit

Organizations and individual women have often held the same picture of the possibilities for women. Many women have had low expectations for themselves; and organizations, in turn, have had low expectations of women.

In some instances individual scripts of women have changed more rapidly than organizational scripts. This is true of one company that for 30 years had an all-male traveling sales force. A woman who recently applied for a sales job was turned down because "women aren't mobile."

In contrast, some organizations have changed their scripts more rapidly than individual women. One example of this lag occurred in a company that actively sought women for management training, and no women responded.

Why didn't any women apply? The reasons are, of course, complex. Little girls learn to negate their abilities. Prominent leaders throughout history have put down or limited women's potential. Organizations have expected little and have offered little opportunity. In addition, early job experiences have often squelched women's aspirations and locked them into low-level work. For example, in an 18-grade scale, women make up three-quarters of all Federal employees in the bottom three levels.

Early Work Experiences Shape Career Goals

Just as early life experiences form the future dramatic life plan of an individual, early work experiences often determine future career direction. Sterling Livingston found that college graduates often make long-lasting decisions about their personal abilities based on the experiences on their first jobs. [24] The most important "director" in this organizational scene is the manager.

Managers who give demanding, but reasonable, work assignments and have confidence in the new employee usually get a high level of accomplishment. In contrast, managers who hand out routine, unchallenging work assignments and doubt the new employee's ability usually get a correspondingly low level of accomplishment in return. First-time employees respond to managers' expectations. Such expectations are one of the most important influences in determining the employees' long-term self-concept and future on-the-job success.

New employees make job decisions that parallel individual life-script decisions. Since prophecies become self-fulfilling, script-reinforcing behavior emerges and perpetuates patterns of achievement or nonachievement. How such patterns develop is shown in the following diagram.

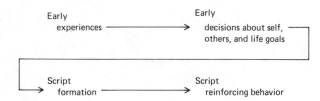

What are the Early Job Experiences of Women?

Think about the women you know. How did they start their working lives? It is very likely that they, like thousands of other working women, put in time at the typewriter keys. For many years the prescribed career paths for most women started with clerical jobs. The clerical starting point is so pervasive it is not unusual for a woman seeking a supervisory job to be asked, "How fast do you type?" One woman quipped an unexpected answer, "I'm better at dictating than typing!"

Women who enter the job market as secretaries often learn patterns that influence their future in organizations. For example, success in many management positions requires having a broad vision over detail, being aggressive rather than passive, focusing on tomorrow rather than on today, being proactive instead of reactive, and making decisions rather than following directions. Most women whose first work experiences are in clerical jobs gain rewards for paying attention to details, being passive, concentrating on today's problems, reacting and following directions. While these attributes in themselves are not negative, they do not prepare women with management potential for management jobs.

You can see how the organizational structure that encourages all women to work up through the clerical ranks may actually lower overall productivity. The same characteristics that made Sally the supersecretary may also make her the incompetent supervisor. The message "we want all of our people to work up from the bottom of the company" often produces controllers who are excellent bookkeepers but poor controllers, sales managers who are good salesmen but poor managers, research directors who know laboratories inside and out but can't direct, and third-level managers who wear themselves out keeping a finger in every pie in the organization, but make no major decisions.

Just as nonproductive and losing scripts limit the achievement of family members, nonproductive and losing organizational scripts limit the contributions employees and managers may make to the organization. Organizations that encourage women to live out nonproductive and losing scripts are paying a high price. They are paying a price in dollars and cents and lack of human fulfillment. They are paying a price in absenteeism, high turnover, and lack of motivation. These high costs are unnecessary. Motivated women, like motivated men, need less supervision, less control time, fewer pep talks, and fewer reprimands.

Thus we see one reason why women who are offered management training opportunities, even though they have the potential, do not apply. Their first manager's evaluation and reward system may very well have determined their future corporate life. This is similar to children who form their future life plan on the basis of the meager experiences of little people.

First job experiences often hit an individual with the impact of a massive tidal wave. They vividly scar or enhance a person's entire corporate life.

Repeated script messages wear with the eroding power of a constant trickle of water on stone, yet people may be completely unaware of their eventual long-lasting effects.

Organizational scripts can erode, maintain, or enhance women's potential. They can stretch, as well as squeeze, unique possibilities. As you read the following cases, which situations sound familiar? The winning, the getting nowhere, or the losing?

Some Organizations Have Scripts
that Encourage Women to Go Nowhere

Here are some messages that Nancy S. heard when she started to work at the Smith Company.

"We know you just wouldn't feel right in a man's job."

"Women always do better in these kinds of jobs."

"You know, that's good money for a woman."

"I know you have a degree, but all our girls start as secretaries."

"I know it's a never-ending, detailed, production job, but you know what they say, 'Women's work is never done.'"

Nancy was a loyal employee who worked many years for the Smith Company. She knew how the job was done and she was rewarded for always doing things *the right* way. People often referred to her as "Nancy, the dependable hard worker down in the production department." After 35 years of loyal, faithful service, most of it in the same job with the Smith Company, Nancy retired with a carnation corsage, a gold watch, and a $67-a-month pension.

And the people in Nancy's organization are still convinced that women are dependable and hardworking even if they lack initiative — just like good old Nancy.

Some Organizations Have Scripts that Encourage Women to be Losers

Loretta C. heard another set of messages when she joined the Roberts Company.

"Well, we know you'll just work until you get married."

"We know women don't want to take jobs away from breadwinners."

"We don't expect a lot from you since you probably won't be working very long."

"Isn't that just like a woman, wanting time off every month."

"And we know you're mainly interested in helping your husband."

"Our office always hires the cutest chicks; we don't want any of those bitchy bra-burners around here."

"The problem in this company is that all the girls just stand around the Xerox machine gossiping all day."

"The 'girls' around here don't want much."

"Just treat 'em nice and they'll be happy."

Loretta receives a lot of attention when she makes a mistake, but she gets very little attention on the occasions when she does her work well. Her supervisor frequently says, "Why should I tell people they're doing a good job when that's what they're paid to do? They should know that if they don't hear anything, it's OK. My job is to tell them when they are doing something wrong."

Loretta may end up quitting or being fired. Or she may end up being transferred to a dark closet in the organization where she can bumble away the next years without blocking productivity too much.

And the people in her organization are convinced that "Women are all alike. They just can't hold responsible jobs."

But a Few Organizations Have Scripts that Encourage Women to be Winners

Wanda J. heard still a different set of messages when she started working for the Miller Company.

"We have a job to get done and we're looking for people who can cut the mustard."

"Who's the best person to do the job?"

"We'll give everybody a chance to prove themselves."

"We need new ideas to keep ahead of the market."

"We're willing to pay for those new ideas no matter who they come from."

Wanda's experience on the job was quite different from the woman's in the first illustration. Wanda received recognition for getting the right things done rather than for making sure that everything was done the right way. She was encouraged to present new ideas, and these ideas were evaluated on the basis of their usefulness to the organization. Wanda progressed through several different jobs and new assignments. After ten years she was promoted to the home office. Her ideas did not leave, however. The staff she developed to take her place continued getting the job done and creating its own ideas.

The people in Wanda's organization are convinced that using the talents of women is good business.

These preceding examples show how organizations can provide a climate in which women may produce just enough to get by, produce more trouble than results, or produce at a high level and also develop their own talents.

The following checklist can help you spot script elements that may be limiting the contribution of women in your organization.

Organizational Scripts for Women Can be Analyzed

You may want to use these questions to check your organization's scripts about women. Which of the questions fit your situation?

Hiring

- Do recruiting brochures and advertisements carry pictures of women as well as men?
- Who makes recruiting visits?
- How are openings in your organization advertised?
- Do recruiters visit women's colleges as well as men's and coed colleges?
- Does your organization use "Help Wanted: Men" columns?
- How are the selections made?
- Who determines the criteria for selections?
- During job interviews are women asked questions about caring for children, plans for family, or husband's opinion of the job or of her working?
- What would commonly be said that women in your organization are good for?
- Why do most managers think women work?

Promoting

- How are promotions made?
- How do people find out about promotions?
- How are women treated who get promotions into management?
- What do people say about any high-level successful women in the organization?
- Does your organization have a "men only" club?
- Is business conducted in places usually frequented by men only?

Training and Development

- Are women involved in informal developmental assignments that often lead to management jobs?

- What training or upgrading activities are open to women?

- How are these opportunities publicized?

- Are women given choices about their careers rather than having choices made for them? For example, "Of course you won't be interested in this new job, it will involve a transfer to another city" instead of "Are you interested in a new job which would involve a transfer to another city?"

- What means are open to women to find out about general company activities?

- Are salary levels for women comparable to those for men in similar positions?

SCRIPTS CAN BE CHANGED

All scripts — personal, organizational, and cultural — are based on decisions and consequently can be changed by new decisions. The process looks like this:

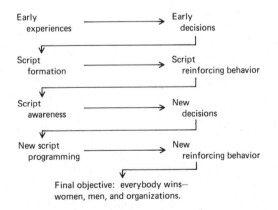

Final objective: everybody wins— women, men, and organizations.

The first step in change is becoming aware of unconscious programming that shapes individual, corporate, and cultural lives. People who are not aware they are sick will not go to a doctor for a cure. People who are not first aware they are living out old wasteful patterns will not look for a cure. Like individuals, it is difficult for organizations to change for the better without awareness of past faults.

The process of fulfilling new decisions and commitments may be painful and awkward. Old ways of doing things are at least predictable. Glacier-like momentum has perpetuated many practices long after their usefulness has died. This is similar to a child who grows up hating an abusive alcoholic parent yet later marries an alcoholic, lamenting, "Well, that's the way I knew it would be." Changing scripts means giving up the comfortable robe of predictability.

Script changes sometimes seem harder than they actually are. It is important to foresee that the first steps to change sometimes feel strange. This was the case of an accountant who rarely greeted other workers but decided to change. After his first attempts he complained, "That's not the real me. It feels phoney." Then he remembered that the "real him" was often a pain in the neck to others and he decided to go ahead with his new pattern, although it felt strange at the moment. Now he reaps the rewards of risking being human and warm with his organizational roommates. Each time the accountant says "Hello," each time anyone demonstrates new behavior, the new script is reinforced.

IN SUMMARY

- Everyone has a psychological script. Such scripts are the dramatic life plans decided on by children, based on their interaction with the outside environment and significant authority figures.

- Women frequently receive scripting messages which negate their intellectual abilities and unique talents. Such downgrading of women's full potentials lies deeply embedded in thousands of years of hostility, fear, and misunderstanding felt and expressed toward women.

- Even today many men negate women, and many women negate themselves and other women.

- Cultural scripts influence the expected life paths of a significant number of men and women.

- Organizations tend to reflect the conscience of the larger culture, and, in turn, perpetuate sex roles no matter how unrealistic they are for today's corporate life.
- Scripts which are compulsions from the past can be examined and changed.

We want this book to facilitate the process of change. We also hope that organizations who meet their moral and now legal obligations to the 51% of the population who are women will:

▲ enjoy more effective use of human resources,

▲ facilitate the sharing of corporate burdens by both men and women,

▲ come in closer touch with current reality, and

▲ move graciously from where they are in their scripts to where they could be.

This book's contributors have provided you with a list of questions to guide you in your reading. We suggest that you turn to the contents page and select those chapters which best help you to understand, develop, or improve your Affirmative Action Program for Women.

REFERENCES

1. Morton M. Hunt, *Her Infinite Variety* (New York: Harper & Row, 1962), p. 255. Reprinted by permission.
2. Muriel James and Dorothy Jongeward, *Born to Win: Transactional Analysis with Gestalt Experiments* (Reading, Massachusetts: Addison-Wesley, 1971), see Chapter 3.
3. Eric Berne, "Analysis of Scripts", *Transactional Analysis in Psychotherapy* (New York: Grove Press, 1961), pp. 116-127.
4. Eric Berne, *What Do You Say After You Say Hello?* (New York: Grove Press, 1972).
5. Paul McCormick, *Guide for Use of a Life-Script Questionnaire in Transactional Analysis* (Berkeley, California: Transactional Publications, 1971).
6. Eric Berne, *Sex in Human Loving* (New York: Simon and Schuster, 1971), p. 193.

7. Dorothy Jongeward and Muriel James, *Winning With People: Group Exercises in Transactional Analysis* (Reading, Massachusetts: Addison-Wesley, 1973), p. 7.

8. James and Jongeward, *Born to Win*, p. 75.

9. Matina Horner, "Woman's Will to Fail", *Psychology Today* 3 (No. 6, 1969): 36 ff.

10. Jongeward and James, *Winning With People*, p. 92.

11. Robin Morgan, ed., "Know Your Enemy: A Sampling of Sexist Quotes", *Sisterhood Is Powerful: An Anthology of Writings from the Woman's Liberation Movement* (New York: Vintage Books, 1970), pp. 31-32.

12. Richard Gilman, "Where Did It All Go Wrong", *Life Magazine* 71 (No. 7, August, 1971): 51.

13. *Ibid.*, p. 52.

14. Richard Gilman, "The Women Problem", *Life Magazine* 71 (No. 7, August, 1971): 45.

15. Robin Morgan, ed., "Know Your Enemy: A Sampling of Sexist Quotes," *Sisterhood Is Powerful*, p. 34.

16. Richard Gilman, "Where Did It All Go Wrong", *Life Magazine* 71 (No. 7, August, 1971): 51. (c) Time Inc. Reprinted by permission.

17. From a speech to American Management Association in New York, February 24, 1969; reprinted in John R. Coyne, Jr., *Impudent Snobs: Agnew vs. the Intellectual Establishment* (New Rochelle, New York: Arlington House, 1972), pp. 192-195.

18. A film: *Women on the March: The Struggle for Equal Rights*, Part I, National Film Board of Canada.

19. Mary Ann B. Oakley, "Elizabeth Cady Stanton," a brochure, (Long Island, New York: Feminist Press, 1972).

20. *Ibid.*

21. James and Jongeward, *Born to Win*, p. 66.

22. Dorothy Jongeward and contributors, *Everybody Wins: Transactional Analysis Applied to Organizations* (Reading, Massachusetts: Addison-Wesley, 1973), see Chapter 1.

23. Lorine Pruette, "Why Women Fail," from *Woman's Coming of Age* by Samuel D. Schmalhausen and V.F. Calverton (New York: Liveright Publishing Corp., Copyright (R) 1959), pp. 252-53. Reprinted by permission.

24. Sterling Livingston, "Pygmalion in Management", *Harvard Business Review* **69407** (July-August, 1969): 81-89.

3

LEGISLATION AND LITIGATION: IMPACT ON WORKING WOMEN

by Osta Underwood

When she urges young women to seek "the best education possible, not just to make a living, but to make a life," Osta Underwood speaks from experience.

Ms. Underwood, past national president (1971–72) of the National Federation of Business and Professional Women's Clubs, Inc., and of the Board of Trustees of the Business and Professional Women's Foundation, has a distinguished career and community record. Currently she is serving on the Research and Education Committee of the Business and Professional Women's Foundation.

A member of the Tennessee Bar, she is a graduate of Nashville Business College and has a Doctor of Jurisprudence degree from the YMCA Night Law School in Nashville, Tennessee.

In addition to her private law practice, she heads the advanced underwriting department in the fields of employee benefit plans and estate planning, and serves as legal counsel of Mutual Benefit Life Insurance Company in Nashville. Previously she had been chief clerk of the Farm Mortgage Division of Metropolitan Life Insurance Company, office manager of Pirtle–Woodard Realty, and then an agent for Mutual Benefit. In 1955 she received the coveted Chartered Life Underwriter designation, and since has earned advanced certificates in *Estate Planning* and in *Pensions and Profit Sharing Plans.*

Since joining BPW in 1943, she has served in a great many capacities with the organization, each duty increasing in scope and importance. She was vice president and president of the Nashville BPW club and legislation chairman, and third, second, and first vice president of the Tennessee Federation, which she also served as president in 1957–58 and 1958–59.

In 1973 she served as Chairperson of the Governor's Commission on the Status of Women in Tennessee.

When asked what working women's role is, Ms. Underwood replied, "Whatever needs doing is a woman's business in the community, just as it is a man's. That means leadership, sponsorship, and work." Exemplifying this philosophy, she has been extremely active in her community and has several professional affiliations.

Reviewing the past decade, Ms. Underwood feels working women's major accomplishment has been "the breakthrough in the changes in state and national law which has brought the beginning of a discernible change in the attitudes of the younger men from that of older men toward women at work."

Key Questions

1. How do new laws and government regulations affect employers and working women?

   Fair Labor Standards Act?

   Equal Pay Act of 1963?

   Title VII of the Civil Rights Act of 1964?

   Education Amendments of 1972?

   Executive Order 11246 as Amended?

   Department of Labor's Revised Order 4

2. What can employers do in response to these regulations?

3. What can working women do who feel discriminated against?

In recent years, many laws dealing with discrimination in employment have been enacted on both the federal and the state levels. In addition, executive orders and guidelines have been issued. Since a number of governmental agencies have the responsibility for handling complaints and for enforcing the laws and orders and since Congress has created overlapping responsibilities in these areas, it has become difficult for employers to remain up to date in their knowledge of what is required of them. It has been equally difficult for employees to know what rights they have and how they can secure the benefits of those rights. Frequently it is difficult for the governmental agencies themselves to be certain which portions of various laws they are responsible for enforcing.

Perhaps one of the best examples of the difficulties faced by employers and employees trying to keep abreast of the rapid change is illustrated by the difficulties federal agencies themselves experience.

A news release from the U.S. Department of Labor's Office of Information in Washington, dated June 23, 1972, stated that the Labor Department "will promptly issue legal interpretations of the Equal Pay Act as it applies to the newly covered occupations." However, a request of the department's Wage and Hour Division in a state capital city on September 7, 1972, disclosed that the office had not yet been furnished with any legal interpretations for its own use, none were available for distribution, and the office knew no more than what the release contained. When the Interpretative Bulletin was furnished to the local office it contained on the cover the provision: "This publication is based on the provisions of the Fair Labor Standards Act before its amendment by Public Law 92-318, effective July 1, 1972, which extends equal pay protection to executive, administrative, and professional employees and outside salesmen and brings pre-school facilities under coverage of the Act. Revision of the publication will be made to conform to the new amendments. Specific questions should be addressed to the nearest Wage-Hour Office." In April 1974 the same office was furnished a "Committee Print" titled "Fair Labor Standards Amendments of 1974 (P.L. 93-259) (Showing changes made in the Fair Labor Standards Act of 1938, as amended)."

This is not to be interpreted as criticism of the federal agencies charged with the responsibilities of disseminating information and handling complaints. Rather, it is to show that the rapid expansion of legislation in the field of civil rights has caused difficulties in all areas, especially in the field of employment open to women.

In the meantime, however, many complaints are being filed, and many are being well handled and settled by the field forces of the federal agencies responsible for enforcement. The main difficulty is that with the growing awareness of women, the field force of the federal agencies cannot keep up with the number of complaints being filed.

FAIR LABOR STANDARDS ACT

Perhaps the first of all the tools that became available to women (and to men) to give them a more tolerable return for their hours of work was the Fair Labor Standards Act of 1938.

There are many facets under this Act and it has seemed, at least at times in the past, that more business and industries were exempt from, than were covered by, its provisions. This was changed as a result of amendments in 1961, 1966, 1972, and 1974 which expanded the coverage of the Fair Labor Standards Act and made it an even more potent legal weapon for employed women.

The basic requirements of the Act were the minimum wage and overtime provisions. In 1961, minimum wage coverage was extended to an additional 3½ million employees, principally in the construction and retail industries (a large percentage of retail employees are women).

Approximately 11 million additional workers were brought under the Act's minimum wage coverage by the 1966 amendments, which revised the definition of "employer" and "enterprise engaged in commerce." The Act was extended for the first time to employees in state and local hospitals, schools and colleges, laundries (other than industrial) and dry-cleaning establishments, hotels and restaurants, and on certain farms, again a large number being women.

The Education Amendments of 1972 included provisions that extended the minimum wage and overtime protections of the Fair Labor Standards Act to a group of employees very likely to be predominantly women. These are the employees of nursery schools, public and private kindergartens, and other preschool enterprises. The 1972 amendments can be as beneficial to perhaps as large a group of wage-earning women as were the amendments of 1966.

The 1972 amendments provided that the minimum wage provisions would cover employees in industries engaged in interstate commerce, or in the production of goods for such commerce, if

a) the enterprise had an annual gross volume of sales made or business done, exclusive of certain excise taxes, of at least $250,000, or

b) the enterprise is engaged in the business of construction or reconstruction or both (regardless of dollar volume), or

c) the enterprise is engaged in laundering, cleaning, or repairing clothing or fabrics (regardless of the dollar volume), or

d) the enterprise is engaged in the operation of a hospital (except a federal government hospital), nursing home, or school (whether public or private, profit or nonprofit, and regardless of dollar volume).

An exception is that none of the above enterprises will include any establishment which has as its only regular employees the owner or the spouse, parents, children, or other members of the owner's family.

However, in 1974 other changes were made applying to a) above. Whereas retail establishments with less than $250,000 annual sales were formerly completely exempt from the Equal Pay Act's requirements, under the 1974 Amendments they are obligated to pay equal wages to male and female workers for equal work performed under similar circumstances, if the establishment is part of a "conglomerate" whose annual gross volume of sales made or business done exceeds $10 million. The designation "conglomerate" also applies to agricultural operations.

Prior to the 1974 law, employees of retail and service establishments grossing less than $250,000 annually were not subject to the Equal Pay Act. It did not matter whether the establishment was a small independent store or part of a large chain or "enterprise" earning millions of dollars. The 1974 Amendments phase out the exemption for these small stores of large chains over a three-year period, beginning January 1, 1975. On that date the dollar test for the retail exemption became $225,000 instead of $250,000. It drops to $200,000 a year later and is repealed altogether on January 1, 1977. A small store that is not a part of a $250,000 operation was exempt before the 1974 Amendments and will continue to be.

There is no way to estimate the power to improve women's earnings in the minimum wage and overtime benefits provisions of the Fair Labor Standards Act. The 1974 Amendments give women an even broader coverage by specifically covering the small store which is part of a large organization.

However, another provision of equal magnitude is the Equal Pay Act. In fact, this is the only provision in any law regarding discrimination in employment which is confined exclusively to sex-based discrimination.

EQUAL PAY ACT OF 1963

The Equal Pay Act of 1963 — effective in 1964 — amended the Fair Labor Standards Act to require that men and women performing equal work must receive equal pay. The Equal Pay amendment covered employees affected by the Fair Labor Standards Act but did not protect employees in executive, administrative, or professional capacities (including academic administrative personnel or teachers in elementary or secondary schools), or outside salesmen. Such employees were exempt from the minimum wage and overtime requirements of the basic Wage and Hour Law.

On June 23, 1972, a section of the Education Amendments of 1972 provided another breakthrough for the working woman. Section 906(b)(1) of the new law expanded coverage of the Equal Pay Act to include an estimated 15 million executive, administrative, and professional employees, and outside salespeople, an estimated four to five million of whom are women.

These amendments mean that the Equal Pay Act now covers all employees of all private and public educational institutions at all levels — preschool, elementary and secondary schools, and institutions of higher education — regardless of whether the institution receives federal funds.

The Equal Pay Act as extended can thus have a tremendous impact on business and industries where there are large number of women employees but where there have been, admitted or not, discriminatory pay scales based on sex.

In addition to the academic field, areas in which the latest amendments can have the greatest impact, so far as women employees are concerned, include retail stores (especially since the

1974 amendments), insurance companies, interior decorating and designing, personnel, public relations, and job analysis, to name but a few. Because these job categories had formerly been exempt from the FLSA and the Equal Pay Act, many women and their employers are still unaware that the 1972 Education Amendments have changed so drastically the classifications of employees covered by the Equal Pay Act. It is as important for employers as for employees to be aware of these changes, since most employers seem acutely conscious of the federal government's powers of regulation and its far-reaching powers of enforcement. In addition, it would appear that more and more employers of good will are becoming aware of discriminatory practices and are willing to make changes. Some of these employers, knowledgeable about the law and willing to comply, are victims of entrenched attitudes in lower and middle levels of management in some departments. Employers of good intent, as well as employees, still have considerable difficulty getting top-level decisions implemented through the lower levels of management.

If the equal pay provisions (in the past and especially now) are so important to employers of women and to the women employees themselves, what are the basic provisions of the Act?

The Equal Pay Act provides that no employer may discriminate between the sexes in the matter of pay where both men and women are engaged in equal work on jobs that require equal skill, equal effort, and equal responsibility, and that are performed under similar working conditions.

All four tests must be met in order for the equal pay standard to apply. But courts have ruled that jobs do not have to be identical, only "substantially equal," for an Equal Pay Act comparison to be made.

In the *Wheaton Glass* case, considered to be a landmark decision, Chief Judge Abraham L. Freedman said:

... Congress in prescribing "equal" work did not require that the jobs be identical, but only that they must be substantially equal. Any other interpretation would destroy the remedial purposes of the Act ...

The Act was intended as a broad charter of women's rights in the economic field. It sought to overcome the age-old belief in women's inferiority and to eliminate the depressing effects on living standards of reduced wages for female workers and the economic and social consequences which flow from it. [1]

The Department of Labor, in one of its publications, uses an example:

> In a machine shop, a male employee operates a particular type of punch press while a female employee operates a press which differs slightly in design. The operation of the two presses is the same in that the work is locked into place by the employee and the machine is activated by means of a lever. The two machines make different kinds of parts. The fact that the machines differ somewhat in design and that the parts turned out on them are different would not, in itself, result in a conclusion that unequal skill is involved in operating the two machines.

One of the more striking illustrations of this principle is the case of *Hodgson* v. *Daisy Manufacturing Company*, [2] decided by the Eighth Circuit Court of Appeals in 1970, which upheld the decision of District Judge Miller of the Western District of Arkansas. One aspect of the case involved a comparison of the respective duties of men and women punch press operators. Judge Miller concluded:

In summary, male and female press operators have the same primary job function and perform essentially the same duties. Male press operators engage in occasional materials handling and engage in greater physical effort in closing the larger shot tubes and barrels. Female press operators have substantially higher production quotas and exert greater mental effort when operating high-speed presses. The differences in job requirements between males and females are incidental and unsubstantial. [3]

Similarly, courts have ruled in cases involving hospitals that orderlies and nurses aides are performing substantially equal work even though, in some instances, orderlies perform additional or different tasks. Those tasks have been found not to involve significantly greater skill, effort, or responsibility than do the primary patient care duties performed by both sexes. [4]

A particularly interesting case involves a department store that paid salesmen in the men's clothing department more than it did saleswomen in the women's and children's clothing departments. In addition, a tailor altering men's suits was paid up to 52¢ an hour more than a seamstress altering women's clothes. The store claimed that wages were determined not by sex, but by the type of product sold and that selling and altering men's clothing required greater skill than selling and altering women's clothing. The court disagreed. It found no difference in the skill, effort, or responsibility of the two groups of salespeople, saying:

It is clear that both men and women salesmen in their respective departments are responsible for the successful presentation of their items to their customers ... There is no evidence to indicate that one of the groups has greater responsibility than the other for the maintenance and procurement of proper inventory. [5]

In comparing the tailor and seamstress jobs, the court said:

Defendant's argument that the fitting of a man's suit differs in kind from the fitting of a woman's pants or dress suit or coat is wholly unpersuasive and contrary to common sense .. the same tools are employed and the alterations are performed in essentially the same surroundings. [6]

It is only too true, however, that some courts are construing the evidence in the narrowest possible sense, making expensive appeals necessary to get redress. Fortunately, most courts are following the doctrine that "equal" does not mean identical.

It must, of course, be borne in mind that an employer has the full right to make distinctions in pay when it is done pursuant to a bona fide seniority system that treats men and women equally, or a merit system equally applied, or a piece-work system. In short, there can be wage differentials, but they must be based on bona fide factors other than sex.

Employers have tried to justify a wage differential based on training programs but, in many such instances, the training programs were open only to men and there were women outside the programs performing equal work at lower rates of pay.

In order to justify such a differential, training programs must (1) be open to both men and women, (2) have more or less fixed beginning points, (3) have specified courses of activity or regimens, including both study and on-the-job training, (4) have a reasonable progression from simple duties to complex duties, and (5) have an ascertainable termination point. As a result, employers have either abandoned training programs that were not justified in order to comply with the Equal Pay Act, or have opened bona fide programs to women, either voluntarily or when challenged.

Two significant court cases in this area are *Hodgson* v. *Fairmont Supply Co.* [7], which held that working one's way up through the ranks of a company performing a variety of clerical and stock duties is not a bona fide "training program" under the Equal Pay Act, and *Hodgson* v. *First Victoria National Bank* [8], which held the same with respect to bank tellers.

How can women employees find out whether they have a valid complaint under the Fair Labor Standards Act? If so, how can they complain?

Although there have been drawbacks in that the equal pay provisions apply only to employees working for employers covered by the Fair Labor Standards Act, enforcement under this law also offers distinct advantages.

The first advantage is that there is not so large a backlog of complaints under the Equal Pay Act as there are under Title VII of the Civil Rights Act, and therefore if the Equal Pay Act is applicable, remedy is much more likely to be accomplished quickly.

In addition, the Department of Labor need not wait for an employee to complain before it checks for compliance under either minimum wage or equal pay. Each year the Wage and Hour Division, which administers the Fair Labor Standards Act, reviews a certain number of businesses of all kinds. Under this review, compliance with *every* aspect of the Act, including minimum wage and equal pay, is investigated.

If, in the opinion of the compliance officer, there are violations of any portions of the law, there is an effort made toward conciliation through conference with the employer. No publicity is given during the time of these conciliation efforts. If there is a difference of opinion between the employer and the Wage and Hour Division, or if the employer willfully refuses to comply, the Department of Labor can institute a suit in the federal courts against the employer.

In addition, however, many complaints from employees are received by the Wage and Hour Division and each complaint is given careful consideration. In this respect, one of the greatest advantages of the Fair Labor Standards Act — to both employers and employees — is the complete anonymity afforded. The identity of the complainant is never revealed by the division without that person's knowledge and consent. Similarly, the identity of employers (and labor unions where involved) is not made known during the investigation and conciliation attempts, but only if and when court action is instituted. It is generally the Labor Department, not the individual, who files a suit (employees may file private suits, but most of them prefer to have the Labor Department act on their behalf).

When a complaint is made and an investigation follows, the investigation is not necessarily limited to the matter contained in the complaint. The entire establishment may be checked for compliance with one or more of the laws for which the Wage and Hour Division has the responsibility of enforcement.

As early as September 1972 over 400 Equal Pay Act suits had been filed in court; about 74 percent of those were decided or settled, most of them favorable to the Labor Department. It is indicative of the care of the investigations and the good will of a majority of employers that the Wage and Hour Division was able to obtain voluntary compliance in more than 95 percent of its investigations in which violations existed.

As knowledge of the laws and remedies have become more widespread, more and more complaints have been filed, and for the first time in its history, the Wage and Hour Division does have a backlog of cases for investigation.

Suppose discrimination is found. What are the remedies?

The first remedy is that the pay requirements must be met. If the minimum wage has not been paid, or if overtime due has not been granted, restitution must be made retroactively as well as for the future.

If the pay has not been equal for equal work, the pay rates must be brought into conformity. Pay rates *cannot* be equalized by reducing the wages of the sex receiving the higher pay. Instead, the wages of the lower-paid sex must be raised to the higher level. Thus, if men earning $2.10 an hour and women earning $2.00 an hour are found to be performing equal work, the women's rates must be raised.

In addition, back pay must be paid as required by the statute. Since the Equal Pay Act took effect in 1946, through fiscal 1972 when so many new laws became effective, nearly $48 million was found owing to 113,000 employees, nearly all of them women. The cases have continued to be filed since 1972, and many large awards have been made rather consistently.

Filing a complaint under the Fair Labor Standards Act is quite easy. No formal complaint form is required. A simple letter or a telephone call to the nearest Wage and Hour office will suffice. Offices are located throughout the United States, Puerto Rico, and the Virgin Islands. If there is none in your community, you can contact the nearest branch office or the Wage and Hour

Division, Employment Standards Administration, U.S. Department of Labor, Washington, D.C. 20210. Simply identify the locality, the employer, and the discrimination alleged.

In summary,

1. Minimum wage and overtime benefits have been extended in recent years to a number of industries never before covered, many of whom employ great numbers of women.

2. The Equal Pay Act has been broadened to include executive, administrative, and professional employees, and outside salespeople, and is applicable to almost every kind of business employing women.

3. If an employee feels discrimination in pay exists *because of sex*, a letter or telephone call to the Wage and Hour Division of the Department of Labor, either locally or in Washington, D.C., will bring investigation.

4. Neither complainant nor employer need be identified during investigation or conciliation efforts. Employers have an opportunity to state their positions. Trained compliance officers from the Wage and Hour Division have access to the employer's books and records. Facts of possible discrimination must be provable in court if conciliation is not reached.

5. If discrimination in pay on the basis of sex does, in fact, exist in the opinion of the investigator and no agreement with the employer is reached, suit can be instituted by the Department of Labor as part of the enforcement procedure.

TITLE VII OF THE CIVIL RIGHTS ACT OF 1964

The Equal Pay Act was the first of the legal tools women had and is still the only one which concerns itself solely with sex discrimination. Title VII of the Civil Rights Act of 1964, however, has perhaps even greater impact on working women since it applies to discrimination in all terms and conditions of employment.

As originally introduced into Congress, Title VII did not include "sex" in the list of bases for discrimination. At that time it was concerned only with discrimination in employment because of race, color, religion, and national origin.

In fact, opponents of the Act added "sex" because they felt it would jeopardize passage of the bill. Fortunately, some members of Congress, aware of the discrimination that existed because of sex, actively supported the addition. Thus, when Title VII was passed, women gained another device with which to fight discrimination.

As amended by the Equal Employment Opportunity Act of 1972 (Public Law 92-261), Title VII covers employers with 25 or more employees, public and private employment agencies, labor unions with 25 or more members, labor-management apprenticeship programs, state and local government agencies, and public and private educational institutions. Effective March 24, 1973, employers with 15 or more employees and labor unions with 15 or more members will come within the provisions of the law.

Title VII forbids an employer to discriminate between men and women with reference to hiring, discharge, and compensation, and to terms, conditions, or privileges of employment. Employees may not be segregated or classified in any way that would tend to deprive a woman (or a man) of employment opportunities because of sex. Employment agencies may not refuse to refer for employment or in any way classify referrals because of sex. And labor organizations may not exclude from membership or classify, segregate, or refuse to refer for employment any person because of sex.

Conditions of employment in which it is unlawful to discriminate include (but are not limited to) job assignment, layoff and recall, promotions, training, sick leave time and pay (including maternity leave), medical and insurance coverage, vacations, and overtime.

There is only one general exception to the ban on sex discrimination, and that is in instances where a different treatment of the sexes is based upon a bona fide occupational qualification (bfoq). A bfoq means that a sex-based characteristic is necessary for performance of the job. In the *Guidelines on Discrimination Because of Sex*, published by the Equal Employment Opportunity Commission (EEOC) which enforces Title VII, the commission makes clear that it "believes that the bona fide occupational qualification exception as to sex should be interpreted narrowly. Labels — 'men's jobs' and 'women's jobs' — tend to deny employment opportunities unnecessarily to one sex or the other."

As an indication of the kinds of situations which do not warrant bfoq exceptions, the guidelines include:

1. the refusal to hire a woman because of her sex based on assumptions of the comparative employment of women in

general (such as the assumption that the turnover rate among women is higher);

2. stereotyped characterizations of the sexes (for example, men are less capable of assembling intricate equipment; women are less capable of aggressive salesmanship); and

3. refusal to hire an individual because of the preference of co-workers, the employer, clients, or customers except for the purpose of authenticity or genuineness (such as an actor or actress).

"The principle of nondiscrimination," the guidelines point out, "requires that individuals be considered on the basis of individual capacities and not on the basis of any characteristics generally attributed to the group."

These guidelines, although lacking the force of law, have been adopted in principle and in substance by several courts. In *Weeks* v. *Southern Bell Telephone & Telegraph Company*, [9] the Fifth Circuit held that to establish sex as a bfoq, the employer must establish that all, or substantially all, women cannot perform the job. The Ninth [10] and the Seventh [11] Circuits have established an even tougher standard holding that each individual woman must be given an opportunity to demonstrate that she can perform the job.

Thus, the commission's narrow interpretation of the bfoq exception is the standard to be followed by employers. The guidelines were first issued in December 1965 and have been updated periodically, most recently in April 1972.

The employment opportunities of many women have been restricted by the so-called state "protective laws." Originally promulgated to protect women, these laws prohibit or limit employment of women in certain job categories, set limits on the amount of weight that women can lift, the number of hours they can work, etc. In the guidelines, the commission states it "has found that such laws and regulations do not take into account the capacities, preferences, and abilities of individual females and, therefore, discriminate on the basis of sex."

The courts have agreed and, in cases challenging particular state laws, have found those laws nullified by Title VII. Many states, however, retain or have failed to repeal "protective" labor laws. Nevertheless, employers may not rely upon such laws to establish a bfoq for discrimination.

The guidelines and the courts state that employer rules which forbid or restrict the employment of married women but not married men, or mothers but not fathers, are illegal. Separate lines of progression or separate seniority lists based on sex which would adversely affect either men or women are also prohibited.

Another area of the guidelines which can have a tremendous impact on women is that of fringe benefits. These include medical, hospital, accident, life insurance and retirement benefits, profit-sharing and bonus plans, leave, and other conditions of employment. Employers are forbidden to make available benefits for wives and/or families of male employees that are not made available for husbands and/or families of female employees. And employers cannot use the defense that the cost of such benefits is greater with respect to one sex than another.

Benefits available to employees and their spouses and families based on whether or not the employee is a "head of household" or "principal wage earner" are also unlawful. The guidelines explain:

Due to the fact that such conditioning discriminatorily affects the rights of women employees, and the "head of household" or "principal wage earner" status bears no relationship to job performance, benefits which are so conditioned will be found a prima facie *violation of the prohibitions against sex discrimination contained in the Act.*

The guidelines point out that it is unlawful for an employer to have a pension or retirement plan which establishes different optional or compulsory retirement ages based on sex, or which differentiates in benefits on the basis of sex. In just such a case, the Seventh Circuit Court of Appeals found that a retirement plan negotiated by a company and a union which required women to retire at age 62 and men at age 65 violated Title VII. The court said:

The plaintiff, by virtue of the plan, is forced to give up three years of work together with the money she would have earned during that period. Such a forced retirement is tantamount to a discharge. [12]

Newly added to the guidelines in 1972 is a section covering employment policies relating to pregnancy and childbirth. These state that written or unwritten employment policies or practices which exclude applicants or employees from employment because of pregnancy are *prima facie* violations of Title VII. Disabilities caused or contributed to by pregnancy, miscarriage, abortion, childbirth, and recovery therefrom, are to be treated under insurance policies or sick leave plans as temporary disabilities.

The thrust of these guidelines is that pregnancy is not in itself a disability, and should not be the cause of special treatment. Any disability which accompanies pregnancy should be treated like any other temporary disability. Similarly, employers are not required to provide special benefits for women who are not disabled, but who wish to take leave for other reasons (for example, care of the child).

The EEOC is nonpartisan in composition (not more than three of its five members shall be of the same party), with members appointed by the President with the advice and consent of the Senate. It is empowered to prevent any person from engaging in any unlawful employment practice, and is charged with the responsibility of receiving complaints, notifying employers thereof, and attempting to conciliate.

With the inclusion of the 1972 amendments, if conciliation cannot be reached, the EEOC is empowered to bring a civil action against any respondent which is not a government, governmental agency, or a political subdivision. In these latter instances, if the commission is unable to reach conciliation after investigation, it can take no further action, but refers the case to the attorney general, who may bring a civil action in the proper Federal district court.

Not only can a person feeling she has been discriminated against because of sex file a complaint with the EEOC, but an aggrieved person also has the right to intervene in a civil action brought by the commission or the attorney general. Further protection is given to a complainant in that, if a charge is dismissed after filing with the commission, or if within 120 days from the filing of the charge, the commission or the attorney general, depending on the situation, has not filed a civil action, the aggrieved person must be notified and may institute civil action personally.

The procedure for complaints under Title VII is somewhat complex because certain steps must be taken. The first step is to complain if you feel you are being discriminated against.

You must complain about the discrimination within 180 days after it occurs. The 180-day limit is strictly applied where a specific act has been alleged, such as failure to hire, discharge, failure to promote, etc. Sometimes an employee feels that over a period of time she has been, and still is being, discriminated against by a practice or policy of her employer, for example, maintenance of segregated departments. So long as the discrimination continues to exist, she can file, and the complaint will be "timely."

How does one complain? Write a letter to the nearest Equal Employment Opportunity Commission office. If you don't know whether there is one in your community, write to the EEOC, 1800 G Street N.W., Washington, D.C. 20506.

All that is necessary to file a complaint is a letter to EEOC specifying what unfair thing has been done. The charge will be transferred to a special form known as a "discrimination form," and must be notarized. If an EEOC office is nearby, it is often helpful to obtain the discrimination form before filing the charge.

Many employees are inclined to defer action if they have to complete a form, but they should not. This form is not formidable. Primarily you need to describe the discrimination as accurately as possible. Then take the form to a notary public and sign it, being sure the notary completes the portion of the form showing the statement has been sworn to or affirmed by you, as this is a requirement of the law. If a notary public is not available, the commission will provide one for you at the time you file, if filed in person, or later, if filed by mail.

The completed form must then be returned to the EEOC, and what happens next depends upon your own state laws. If your state has a law similar to the Federal law regarding the type of discrimination you are complaining about, the EEOC is required first to defer the charge for 60 days to the state agency charged with enforcement of the state law. The commission will assume jurisdiction over the charge after 60 days or at the termination of state proceedings, whichever is earlier.

If the state does not stop the discrimination, or if the state does not have a comparable law, the EEOC will notify your employer of your charge within 10 days. While your employer must know that you are making the charge, *it is unlawful for you to be discharged, demoted, or in any way discriminated against, either during the investigation or afterwards, because you have filed a complaint.* If necessary, the commission can obtain from the court a temporary restraining order prohibiting the employer from taking adverse action against you while the charge is before the commission.

In addition, the new law permits a charge to be filed on behalf of an aggrieved employee by a third person (or organization). This section was designed to protect the anonymity of employees who fear retaliatory action by the employer. If a charge has been filed on behalf of an employee, the commission will not reveal the name of the aggrieved employee when it serves the charge, nor will it do so, if at all, until absolutely necessary to the investigation of the charge.

The EEOC is authorized to send an investigator to talk with you and with your employer about the complaint, and to investigate your charges. If the EEOC believes you have good grounds for your complaint, it will try to have the discrimination stopped through persuasion. If the commission is unable to stop the discrimination through conciliation, you will be so notified, and either the EEOC or the attorney general, depending upon who your employer is, may bring a civil action.

It may be that the commission will dismiss your complaint because it does not believe there has been sex discrimination. As an individual, you still have the right to file suit in a Federal district court.

Regardless of who files suit, if the court finds that the employer has intentionally engaged in or is intentionally engaging in an unlawful employment practice charged in the complaint, it can order the practice stopped and require such affirmative action as may be appropriate. This may include, but is not limited to, reinstatement or hiring of employees, with or without back pay or such equitable relief as the court thinks proper. Equitable relief may include alteration of recruitment policies, merger of seniority lines, promotion, training programs, or anything else that may be necessary to eliminate the effects of the discriminatory practice.

While reference is made to "employer" in outlining the procedures to follow in filing a complaint, it must be remembered that it is against the law for an employment agency to discriminate in referring applicants for jobs and it is against the law for labor unions to discriminate in referring applicants or in offering labor-management apprenticeships. The procedures for relief against discrimination by employers are equally applicable for relief against employment agencies and unions.

For example, one section of the guidelines states that "it is a violation of Title VII for a help-wanted advertisement to indicate a preference, limitation, specification, or discrimination based on sex unless sex is a bona fide occupational qualification for the particular job involved. The placement of an advertisement in columns classified by publishers on the basis of sex, such as columns headed 'Male' or 'Female', will be considered an expression of a preference, limitation, specification, or discrimination based on sex."

Very interesting in view of this section is a case in which the EEOC notified a group of plaintiffs that they had grounds to sue a newspaper (this took place before the 1972 amendments). The plaintiffs sued, seeking a preliminary and permanent injunction against the newspaper prohibiting the listing of jobs under male and female headings where sex is not a bona fide occupational qualification. The EEOC entered the case as *amicus curiae*. The court ruled in favor of the newspaper publisher, but it said:

It seems appropriate to suggest, however, to the defendant, however gratuitously, that the position of the plaintiffs is an idea whose time has come and that serious consideration be given to a revision of the classification practices in employment advertising without reference to and free from the compulsion of jurisdiction of the court. [13]

Whether a newspaper or publisher can be directly sued under this section is being pursued with varying decisions in various courts. Probably only a decision by the Supreme Court will settle the issue.

There are before the courts constantly, in all areas of the country in all states of appeal, cases on discrimination filed under Title VII. Some cases are won, some are lost. The courts seem, generally, to be building a fairly strict interpretation of the provisions of Title VII, but enough decisions are accumulating so that employers are less inclined to discriminate and employees are more inclined to seek the legal recourses available.

To summarize:

1. Title VII of the Civil Rights Act of 1964, as amended, offers women an excellent avenue of recourse for discrimination based on sex. Unlike the Equal Pay Act, which is concerned solely with discrimination in pay because of sex, Title VII also

covers discrimination in hiring, discharge, compensation, promotion, fringe benefits, and other terms, conditions, or privileges of employment.

2. If an employee believes discrimination because of sex exists, a discrimination charge form should be requested from the nearest EEOC office or from the Equal Employment Opportunity Commission in Washington, D.C.

3. EEOC will investigate, either through the appropriate state agency (if applicable) or through one of its own investigators. The identity of the charging party will be made known to the employer charged, but recriminations against the complaining employee are expressly forbidden. If the charging party is someone other than the complaining employee, the employer will not be notified of the true complainant unless necessary to the investigation.

4. If EEOC feels discrimination exists, efforts will be made to conciliate. Employers have a complete right to state their positions, and these must be carefully noted in case conciliation fails and court action is sought. The commission is prohibited from revealing or using as evidence anything said or done during conciliation endeavors.

5. If conciliation fails, the EEOC or the attorney general, depending upon the employer, can file suit on the employee's behalf.

6. If EEOC dismisses the complaint, an employee can still sue in Federal court. Many communities have groups of women lawyers who help out at reduced or token fees in cases where there is overt discrimination. In addition, Title VII allows attorneys' fees to be obtained by the prevailing party. The courts tend to be generous in the provision of attorneys' fees, as an incentive to attorneys to handle these important cases.

7. If the court finds there has, indeed, been sex discrimination, it can order the discriminatory practices stopped and restitution made to the employees.

EDUCATION AMENDMENTS OF 1972

In many respects, 1972 was a landmark year for women in education. As was just mentioned, the Equal Employment Opportunity Act amended Title VII of the Civil Rights Act to forbid job discrimination on the basis of sex for employees of educational institutions. Reference has also been made to the Education Amendments of 1972 (Public Law 92-318) and the change this makes in the Fair Labor Standards Act by extending equal pay to executive, administrative, and professional employees (which, of course, includes faculty women).

But the provisions of the Education Amendments of 1972 are even more far-reaching in that they go beyond employment in education and have the effect of opening school doors to women seeking equality of education.

When business, industry, or the government are pressed to hire women for management, scientific, or engineering positions, or seek to place women in vacancies which heretofore were considered to be in men's fields, the argument is given that it is impossible to find any "qualified" women. The pool of available qualified women is not as large as it might be, and there are reasons for this.

First, those women who secured the necessary training in men's occupations found they had no place to go with it. Second, when young women saw this, they tended to stay within traditional fields where they could find employment. And third, women have found it extremely difficult, if not downright impossible, to enroll in many schools which would prepare them for careers traditionally occupied by men. This was especially true on the graduate level, but has also been the case to some extent on the undergraduate level and in the vocational areas.

Congressional hearing held by Representative Edith Green (D-Oregon) in 1970 documented a pattern of discrimination in admissions, particularly in graduate schools. In some instances, qualified women applicants were turned down because of quota systems, while in other cases women students were required to have higher grades than men students in order to enroll and remain in particular graduate schools.

Interestingly enough, this kind of discrimination against women is beginning to cause male students to worry. Male students who can enter graduate schools with normal grades find themselves competing against the very top women students. Now the young men are contending this is unfair competition for them. And it is!

Title IX, Section 901 of the Education Amendments of 1972 provides, in part:

No person in the United States shall, on the basis of sex, be excluded from participation in, be denied the benefits of, or be subjected to discrimination under any education program or activity receiving Federal financial assistance. . .

These provisions cover public and private preschools, elementary and secondary schools, and institutions of vocational, professional, and higher education. Exempt are certain institutions controlled by religious organizations and schools for training individuals for the merchant marine or the military service of the United States. This latter exemption is particularly interesting in 1972 when a woman for the first time became an admiral in the Navy, but women are not permitted to enroll in the U.S. Naval Academy. Perhaps someday training and employment in the military service or merchant marine will be open to women who would be willing and able to serve their country in these areas.

Regarding *admissions* in Section 901, the antidiscrimination provision applies only to institutions of vocational, professional, and graduate higher education and to *public* institutions of undergraduate higher education. Exempted from these provisions are private undergraduate institutions of higher education, public undergraduate institutions which traditionally have had a policy of admitting only students of one sex, elementary and secondary schools other than vocational schools, and schools in transition from single-sex to coeducation. It should be noted here that these exemptions apply to *admissions only*. These institutions are still subject to all antidiscrimination provisions of the Act other than admissions.

While the admissions provisions of Section 901 are not as comprehensive as many people would desire, the Act nevertheless provides another valuable tool for women. It will help them to enter occupations from which they have been barred because they could not enroll in schools offering the necessary training and because of the quota systems, admitted or denied, in law schools, medical schools, engineering schools, and schools in many other of the graduate disciplines.

Already referred to under the discussion of equal pay, but of extreme importance in Title IX of Public Law 92-318, are the provisions which extend the Equal Pay Act to executive, administrative, and professional employees and outside salespeople. Until very recently, there was nothing to prevent a college or university from paying male professors and female professors entirely different and unrelated wage rates. The female professor had no recourse.

Colleges and universities are finding that it costs money to equalize the pay scales so that men and women in comparable positions are paid comparable salaries. But this is money which should have been paid to women over many years. Now these colleges and universities have no choice — they must stop the discrimination.

In addition, Section 906 of the new law also amends Title IV (Desegregation of Public Education) of the Civil Rights Act of 1964 to include "sex". And Title IV of the Education Amendments prohibits lenders who use the Student Loan Marketing Association from discriminating.

Thus, Public Law 92-318 opens the doors of schools previously closed to women. It provides equal pay to women in academia and extends the provisions of minimum pay laws to preschool, nursery, and kindergarten employees. And it makes the funds of the Student Loan Marketing Association available on a nondiscriminatory basis.

If a woman feels she is being discriminated against by an educational institution receiving Federal financial assistance, how does she complain? The Office of Civil Rights of the Department of Health, Education, and Welfare in Washington, D.C., is responsible for enforcement of the new law. Once more, start with a letter, setting forth the facts as succinctly and accurately as possible.

Following the filing of the complaint, the Federal agency conducts an investigation. If, in the opinion of the investigators, there is a violation, once more settlement is attempted through conferences and conciliation efforts.

Where there are differences of opinion and the education institution feels it is not in violation or refuses to correct willful violations, formal hearings are conducted by the agency. If the charge of discrimination stands, the result will be the withholding or termination of Federal financial assistance.

Under certain circumstances, the attorney general may initiate a suit on behalf of individuals who allege they have been denied admission to or have not been permitted to continue in attendance at a publicly supported institution by reason of sex, or where the individual alleges a public institution is depriving her of the equal protection of the laws under the Fourteenth Amendment to the Constitution.

Title IX of the Civil Rights Act of 1964 is also amended to extend to cases of sex discrimination the attorney general's power to intervene, on behalf of the United States, in litigation already begun by others claiming denial of the equal protection of the laws under the Fourteenth Amendment.

Proposed Title IX regulations drew such attention that the usual six-month period for public comments was extended to nine months. Over 9,000 comments were analyzed, the regulations rewritten, and a final version was sent to President Ford for his signature. However, a storm of protest from colleges and universities has urged the President to veto the regulations. As of May 1975, there were no published regulations.

To receive information on the Title IX regulations (if and when they are signed), contact the local offices of HEW, OEO, or the Wage and Hour Division of the Department of Labor.

In the Education Amendments of 1972, it is significant that the prohibition against discrimination on account of sex is limited to Federally assisted *education* programs and activities, whereas the prohibitions against discrimination on the basis of race, color, and national origin under Title VI of the Civil Rights Act apply to *all* Federally assisted programs. However, Title VI specifically excludes employment from coverage except where the primary objective of the Federal aid is to provide employment. There is no exemption for employment in the sex discrimination provisions relating to the Federally assisted education programs.

In summary,

1. The 1972 Education Amendments prohibit sex discrimination in all education programs receiving Federal financial assistance and in admissions, with certain exceptions.

2. Lenders who use the Student Loan Marketing Association are prohibited from discriminating against students on the basis of sex.

3. Written complaints setting forth the facts of discrimination should be directed to the Office of Civil Rights of the Department of Health, Education, and Welfare.

4. Federal investigators will conduct a study of the complaint. If a violation is found, attempts at conciliation will be made. If these attempts fail, formal hearings are conducted by the agency.

5. If discrimination is found, the results will be either withholding or termination of Federal financial assistance from the educational institution. In some instances, court action

can be sought. The attorney general may intervene in certain cases.

EXECUTIVE ORDER 11246 AS AMENDED

Another important source of help to women experiencing job discrimination because of sex is not a law passed by Congress, but rather an executive order issued by the President of the United States. Executive Order 11246 forbidding discrimination against minorities in employment, signed by President Johnson in 1965, was amended by Executive Order 11375, effective in 1968, to include a ban on discrimination because of sex.

The order applies to *all* Federal contractors and subcontractors who hold a Federal contract or subcontract of $10,000 or more. It does not cover just the employer's facilities applicable to the contract, but extends to all facilities of the contractor, regardless of whether or not they are involved in the performance of the particular contract. For example, if a university has a Federal contract in one department, then all departments of that university must comply with Executive Order 11246 as amended.

Further, government contractors with more than 50 employees and contracts totalling $50,000 or more are required to develop an affirmative action plan which will correct any inequities in employment that may exist. In cases where the contract exceeds $1 million, there must be a compliance review before the contract is awarded. The order says that affirmative action

shall include, but not be limited to the following: employment, upgrading, demotion, or transfer; recruitment or recruitment advertising; layoff or termination; rates of pay or other forms of compensation; and selection for training, including apprenticeship.

The Labor Department's Office of Federal Contract Compliance (OFCC) is the agency charged with enforcement. OFCC monitors, evaluates, and directs the compliance branches of 15 major government agencies which are involved in certain Federal contracts. For example, the Department of Health, Education, and Welfare is the compliance agency responsible for the executive order in educational institutions, while the Interior Department handles compliance in contracts in petroleum refining and related industries.

In 1970, OFCC issued *Sex Discrimination Guidelines* which spell out forbidden employer practices. These state, among other things, that contractors may *not*

- advertise for workers in newspaper columns headed "male" or "female" unless sex is a bona fide occupation qualification;

- make any distinction between married and unmarried persons of one sex unless the same distinctions are made between married and unmarried persons of the opposite sex;

- penalize women in their conditions of employment because they require time away from work for childbearing;

- deny a female employee the right to any job that she is qualified to perform because of state "protective" laws; nor

- specify any differences for male and female employees on the basis of sex in either mandatory or optional retirement age.

DEPARTMENT OF LABOR'S REVISED ORDER 4

Order No. 4, which applies to nonconstruction contractors, was also issued by OFCC in 1970 to explain how affirmative action programs were to operate and what steps contractors were to take in order to be in compliance. It called for the setting of goals and timetables for the employment of minorities where they had been underutilized. A Revised Order No. 4, requiring goals and timetables for employment of women as well as minorities, was published in 1971, and contractors were given until April 2, 1972, to incorporate the requirements for women into their then existing affirmative action plans. It should be pointed out that the establishment of goals and timetables does *not* require quotas.

The penalty for noncompliance with Executive Order 11246 is the withholding or cancellation of the Federal contract. The employee benefits when the contractor, either on his own or through threat of contract loss, fulfills the requirements of the order.

Employees who need more information can ask the OFCC for copies of Executive Order 11246, the *Sex Discrimination Guidelines*, and Revised Order 4. OFCC will also tell you whether or not an employer is covered by the Executive Order.

Individuals and groups with grievances may file complaints alleging discrimination with OFCC, which will forward the complaint to the proper government agency. The letter outlining the alleged discrimination should be sent to the Office of Federal Contract Compliance, Department of Labor, Washington, D.C. 20210. It should ask for a full investigation by the compliance agency of the contractor's employment practices.

One area in which Executive Order 11246, as amended, has been used frequently is in cases of sex discrimination against colleges and universities. Complaints against more than 350 educational institutions have been filed to date. In virtually all instances, the threat of withholding or terminating funds has been sufficient to bring about compliance. For example, the withholding of a contract at Columbia University led to the development of an affirmative action plan.

In summary,

1. Executive Order 11246 as amended by Executive Order 11375 forbids discrimination on the basis of sex by employers doing business with the Federal government (this includes most large employers).

2. Contractors with more than 50 employees and contracts totalling $50,000 are required to develop affirmative action plans to correct inequities.

3. Complaints alleging discrimination can be sent to the Office of Federal Contract Compliance and an investigation will be undertaken.

4. The penalty against the contractor for noncompliance can be delay of new contracts, cancellation of existing contracts, or debarment from future contracts. The result for the employee is job equality.

There has been considerable dissatisfaction on the part of many women and many women's organizations with the lack of enforcement of the Executive Orders, as there has been with the enforcement of others of the laws. Women and women's groups are using the laws, and the inevitable must be that laws will be enforced, and that Congress will allocate and appropriate funds necessary for enforcement. Such funds and such enforcement will come about only as women continue to use the laws as the stand on the books, and not become discouraged nor deterred.

OTHER LEGAL REMEDIES

Just a few more legal protections against job discrimination might well be called to mind. Employees of the Federal government are covered by Executive Orders and other equal employment opportunity laws, rules, and regulations. If you feel you are being discriminated against because of sex, be sure to talk with your Equal Employment Opportunity counselor within 15 calendar days from the time of discrimination. If you do not know the person to contact, ask your personnel officer or the nearest Civil Service Commission office, or write to the Civil Service Commission in Washington, D.C.

If you belong to a union which does not, in your opinion, fairly represent you, write to the National Labor Relations Board and/or the Equal Employment Opportunity Commission, both in Washington. Set forth clearly, factually, and objectively your complaint. Unions are required by law to represent their members fairly and to bargain for the same working conditions for women as for men, including wages, hours, retirement, seniority, and promotions.

Often it is difficult for a mature woman to get a job if she has been terminated from her present employment or if she is reentering the labor market. The Age Discrimination Law in the Employment Act of 1967 is a law which does not apply specifically to women, but which may be of great help since women as a group have a greater longevity than men.

The Age Discrimination Law protects individuals between the ages of 40 and 65 from discrimination on the basis of age in hiring, promotion, or job retention. It applies to companies with 25 or more employees, employment agencies serving such employers, and labor organizations with 25 or more members. The Act is administered by the Wage and Hour Division of the Department of Labor, and complaints under it are handled similarly to those under the Equal Pay Act.

CONCLUSION

These are not all of the laws which might be tools for women, nor is this a comprehensive discussion of them. Over and over, various laws and executive orders have been referred to as tools. The reason is that there is no automatic protection under any law. A complaint must be filed before the provisions of the laws can be brought into play and corrections made.

Some employers are not aware of the need to change employment practices. Others are aware, but feel it would cause disharmony and labor trouble to change existing policies. Where employers are aware that changes need to be made but fear disharmony, they might not be at all unhappy if a complaint were filed so that an investigation would be made. This way they could do what they know is right and at the same time avoid trouble by blaming it all on the government!

Some employers do not know or, knowing, do not care about fair employment practices, regardless of whether they pertain to minorities or to women. It is because of these employers that enforcement powers are available and that harassment of complaining employees is illegal.

In many communities it is difficult to find the proper office to file a complaint. In one state capital with a population of over half a million, there is no HEW office where complaints about discrimination in education may be filed and no office handles complaints on contract compliance. At first glance, it was very discouraging for a woman with a grievance to know where to go. But the Wage and Hour office of the Department of Labor, although not the proper place to file the complaint, offered help and assistance. It identified the proper Federal agency where the complaint should be filed, explained what was necessary to file the complaint, located the nearest office of the proper agency, and assured the woman that an investigation would be made by a compliance officer from the nearest regional office.

Thus, if you feel you are discriminated against because you are a woman, the *tools* are available. The employees of the Federal government are there to help. If you don't know where to go, start with the Department of Labor, for it is concerned with the welfare of working persons of all levels.

Part of the difficulty lies in the different governmental agencies charged with the enforcement of various laws or parts of laws. It is as frustrating in many instances to the local government employees who are trying to be of assistance as it is to those seeking assistance. In some instances when you try one government agency and are referred to another, only to be referred to another, it is only natural to feel you are being given the "runaround." In the local offices, the opposite is true — they are doing their best to be of assistance, but the overlapping responsibilities of the various agencies make it difficult to be of the assistance they would like to be.

Other encouraging things are happening. On October 28, 1975, the Equal Credit Opportunity Act, which forbids discrimination by creditors on the basis of sex or marital status, will become effective. On March 19, 1975, the Supreme Court in *Weinberger, Secretary of Health, Education, and Welfare* v. *Wiesenfeld* issued an opinion that gave women's earnings and payments into Social Security equal status with men's in the area of death benefits.

During the depressed economic period women continued to fight for the affirmative action programs in spite of labor agreements, and ultimately this will have to be decided by the Supreme Court on the question of "Last hired-first fired."

WHAT EMPLOYERS CAN DO

Employers need not wait for complaints to be filed or for employee disharmony to erupt. They can take affirmative steps to see that their employees are not being discriminated against.

Employers should begin by finding out what laws apply to them and what these laws require. Employers not covered by any equal employment opportunity legislation might also want to change employment practices, either because they care or because they find themselves at a disadvantage when competing with employers covered by the law.

The Women's Bureau of the Department of Labor has publications which can give some guidance. One in particular, entitled "Suggested Steps in the Right Direction to Eliminate Sex Discrimination in Employment," contains 20 suggestions on how employers can offer true job equality to men and women.

To find out if any changes need to be made, the employer should first examine his employee records carefully. Are most women in lower-paying jobs? Do pay scales differ greatly between men and women? Why? Are certain lines of upward mobility closed to women? Do men and women employees receive the same fringe benefits? How about their spouses and other dependents? These are just a few of the questions that must be asked.

It is then up to the employer to develop a clear company policy on nondiscrimination and to make sure that all employees, including those in management, know and respond to this policy. The results will not only avoid legal action against the employer, but will go a long way toward producing a more efficient and harmonious workforce.

Laws are not perfect and their administration is not perfect. Employers are not perfect and neither are employees. It is to make possible a fair and equal chance for both employers and employees that laws, executive orders, and guidelines exist. Voluntary compliance with these measures can be advantageous to employers and employees alike.

Editors' Note

This chapter is an overview and is not intended to substitute for the advice of a labor-law attorney.

REFERENCES

1. Schultz v. Wheaton Glass Company, 421 F. 2d 259 (3rd Cir. 1970) *certiorari* denied, 398 U.S. 905 (1970).

2. Hodgson v. Daisy Manufacturing Co., 445 F. 2d 823.

3. 317 F. Supp. 538, quote at 544.

4. Hodgson v. Brookhaven General Hospital, 436 F. 2d 719 (5th Cir. 1970); Hodgson v. Lancaster Osteopathic Hospital Assn., Inc. 66 CCH Lab. Cas. 32, 543 (E.D. Pa. 1971); Hodgson v. Stastny 67 CCH Lab. Cas. 32, 654 (D. Ill., 1972).

5. Hodgson v. City Stores, Inc. dba Loveman's, 332 F. Supp. 942 (M.D. Ala. 1971).

6. *Ibid.*

7. Hodgson v. Fairmont Supply Co., 454 F. 2d 490 (4th Cir. 1972).

8. Hodgson v. First Victoria National Bank, 420 F. 2d 648 (5th Cir. 1969).

9. Weeks v. Southern Bell Tel. & Tel. Co., 408 F. 2d 228 (5th Cir. 1969).

10. Rosenfeld v. Southern Pacific Co., 444 F. 2d 1219 (9th Cir. 1971).

11. Bowe v. Colgate-Palmolive Co., 416 F. 2d 711 (7th Cir. 1969).

12. Bartmess v. Drewrys Limited U.S.A., Inc., 444 F. 2d 1186 (7th Cir. 1971), *certiorari* denied *sub nom* Drewrys Limited U.S.A., Inc. v. Bartmess, 404 U.S. 939.

13. Pat Greenfield et al. v. Field Enterprises, Inc., U.S.D.C.N. Ill., February 1972.

4

WOMEN IN GOVERNMENT AND AFFIRMATIVE ACTION

by Jayne B. Spain

Jayne Baker Spain became a member of the
United States Civil Service Commission on
June 14, 1971, after nomination by
President Nixon and confirmation by the
Senate. The sixth woman to serve as a Civil
Service Commissioner in the commission's
88-year history, she was designated vice
chairman of the commission by the President.

Appointed to the Board of Directors of
Litton Industries in 1970, Mrs. Spain headed
her own company for 20 years. In 1951 she
became president of the family business, the
Alvey-Ferguson Company, of Cincinnati, an
internationally known manufacturer of con-
veyor and unit-handling equipment which
employed about 450 people. She served as
its chief executive officer until 1966, when
it was merged with Litton Industries, and
continued to be president of the company as
a Litton division until her resignation in
March 1971.

Mrs. Spain is vice chairman of the
President's Committee on Employment of the
Handicapped, having been appointed to the
committee by President Johnson in 1966 and
reappointed by President Nixon in 1969. She

believes, and has demonstrated, that handicapped persons properly trained and properly
placed are not occupationally handicapped,
and if given an equal opportunity will prove
to be successful, and often superior,
employees.

A native of Cincinnati, Mrs. Spain was
educated at the University of California
(Berkeley) and the University of Cincinnati.

Key Questions

1. How does the Federal government rate as an employer of women?

2. How high can women go in the Federal service?

3. How can women get started?

4. How can women best prepare themselves?

WOMEN IN GOVERNMENT: WHERE THEY ARE TODAY

There are many aspects of government service in which women may be found today; there is Federal, state, and local government, and within each there are elective and appointive positions. Employment in governmental service may be *political* or *nonpolitical*. *Political* appointments are usually made by the President, a governor, or a mayor, often with partisan identification. *Nonpolitical* appointments are made through employment procedures commonly called civil service. This chapter will be concerned with women employed in the civil service of the Federal government.

The Federal government today is one of the most enlightened and progressive employers of women in the United States, and among large employers (it is the largest in the country), probably the *most* progressive.

Equal employment opportunity has been a principle of the Federal civil service since 1883, when the Civil Service Act replaced the corrupt spoils system with the modern system of competitive examinations for government positions — the "merit system." The translation of principle into practice, however, has been a long, slow process, which in fact is still going on.

Women have equal opportunity to compete in all civil service examinations and equal opportunity to be considered for job opportunities in the order of their examination scores. They receive equal pay for equal work. They have equal rights with respect to in-service training and advancement, fringe benefits, and lay-off rules. These are facts, and show the Federal civil service to be far ahead of employers in the private sector.

Unfortunately, Federal employment statistics do not seem fully in consonance with these facts.

Approximately one-third of Federal civil service employees are women. Even though women are a majority in the general population, this may be considered a fair proportion. There are far more women than men who choose to be out of the labor market. However, when we look at the different salary levels, we do not see a fair distribution of these women salary-wise.

There are 18 grades of positions in the General Schedule (GS), 15 regular and 3 supergrades. Each position is assigned to one of these grades on the basis of duties and responsibilities. The grade decides the salary level. If we divide the schedule into thirds, we find the following results.

- Nearly half of all employees in the lowest third, grades 1 to 6 ($5,294 to $9,473), are women, with by far the largest number in grades 4 and 5 ($7,596 to $8,500).
- One-fifth of the employees in the middle third, grades 7 to 12 ($10,520 to $18,463), are women.
- Women hold only one-twenty-fifth — 4% — of the positions in grades 13 to 18 ($21,816 to $36,000).

Thus it is that although equal pay for equal work is a fact (the job, not the person in it, is graded), there are far more women in the lower-paid jobs. The pay for women in government averages no more than 60% of that for men.

This is one aspect of the Federal employment which should look noticeably different by the end of this decade. Marked changes are going on. The government-wide Equal Employment Opportunity Program, which is administered by the Civil Service Commission with statutory authority for enforcement in all Federal departments and agencies, includes as one of its parts a Federal Women's Program. This program emphasizes upward mobility, with the objective of achieving an equitable distribution of women employees throughout the entire grade-and-salary structure.

Under the Federal Women's Program, the head of each Federal department or agency designates a coordinator, or a committee. The coordinator acts as contact point, source of information, and counselor on matters related to advancing the status of women in the agency. Among other things, the coordinator gives attention to opening up "closed" occupations to women;* altering organizational patterns to provide escape routes from dead-end jobs; counseling women about opportunities and encouraging them to plan ahead for a career, not just a job; and promoting continued education for employees.

The concept of upward mobility, which is being pushed at all levels, goes deeper than merely assuring the advancement of women to higher levels for which they are already qualified; it includes getting women trained for higher-level work. Training is

---

* There are no longer any occupations in the Federal civil service that can legally be limited to one sex or the other, except for certain institutional jobs (e.g., prison guard) or situations requiring use of common sleeping quarters. But old habits die hard, and constant effort is needed to see that personnel officers keep open the doors of formerly closed occupations.

the key to upward mobility, for the "token" placement of inadequately prepared women in upper-grade positions, just to make the statistics look better, is worse than useless. It is destructive both to the individual and to the program.

The latest enactment to enhance career opportunities for women is the Equal Employment Opportunity Act of 1972. For the first time prohibition of discrimination against any Federal government worker on the basis of race, color, religion, national origin, or sex is enforceable by statute. The Civil Service Commission has statutory authority to see that all personnel actions in the Federal government are not only free from discrimination, but also are actively oriented toward equality of opportunity. Agencies must provide action plans which include provisions for training and upward mobility. These plans *must* include women, as well as members of minority groups.

There is a very wide range of training offered in the Federal civil service, some in individual agencies, some across agency lines, and some conducted by the Civil Service Commission for all agencies, with participants selected by agency managers from among their respective employees. Courses in "office skills" and similar subjects are heavily populated with women employees. However, the presence of women in other types of training courses has been far below what it should be in terms of their numbers in the various grades. Until recently this has been particularly true of training designed to prepare employees for advancement to management and executive levels.

This is one of the major fields in which significant changes are taking place during the 1970's. Results will be seen in increased numbers of women both in higher grades and in jobs formerly considered exclusively men's.

In spite of its negative aspects — which have at last been admitted and are now being actively attacked — the Federal civil service offers outstanding career opportunities for women. In addition to the absolute impartiality of the competitive examining system, the Federal service provides a unique range of occupations. It covers almost every kind of work that is to be found in private employment, and several kinds that are found only in government. Qualified women must now be accepted in all these occupations on the same terms as men, and paid at exactly the same rates. Advancement depends primarily upon performance and potential, plus the ever-present factor of "a little bit of luck" — being in the right place at the right time.

A number of cases of actual women in the Federal civil service have been selected to illustrate this chapter. These are certainly not "average" cases; they could not even be called "typical"; they are, in fact, examples of the successful careers that can be achieved in government by women of more than ordinary ability and determination. They don't prove that "any woman can do the same"; but they do show that there are no arbitrary barriers of sex in the career civil service of the Federal government, and that opportunities exist in many fields.

There are, in fact, many thousands of women in successful and satisfying government employment who provide us with indications of what has been possible for many in the past and of what will be possible for many more in the future.

Of course at this point women still predominate in the traditional "women's occupations."

Illustration

E.B., a high-level secretary, was born in a small midwestern town of parents who had come from central Europe. She had just completed a year of business college when she got her first appointment through a traveling government recruiter. She came to Washington, where she was assigned to a stenographic pool in a military department. After two years, attracted by overseas assignments being made by another department, she applied for a transfer and was sent to Japan for two years. From that time on her career progressed (on her own initiative) through a half-dozen agencies and as many countries, with tours of duty in Europe, Washington, Korea, and back to Washington; she was always moving up and finding opportunities for a broad and varied learning experience wherever she went. At local colleges she has pursued academic learning as well, taking after-hours courses in languages and other subjects. At present she is again in a headquarters office, as private secretary to a top official (deputy head of an agency, appointed by the President) who describes her as of "absolutely immeasurable value." In addition to such qualities as competence, resourcefulness, and judgment, she provides the background of government experience which is one of the chief assets of career secretaries to Presidential appointees. Of particular interest is the fact that for the first time in her career as a private secretary she is working for a woman, and is very pleased about it; her answer to the inevitable questions about a comparison is "I don't really think of her that way particularly — I think of her as a fine executive."

Illustration

E.M. was born in a small town in the South, one of five children, all of whom completed their education in professional fields. E.M. earned her Bachelor's degree in psychology and her Master's in social work. She applied for and received an appointment as a social worker in a Veterans Administration hospital. The force of her determination and concern for others was soon felt, as one after another of her original ideas became standard practice. She encouraged the development of community foster homes for improved psychiatric patients instead of continuous institutionalization, special attention to the social and emotional problems of families caring for paralyzed and other severely disabled patients, and so on. "I was never allowed, and so never learned," she says, "to make excuses for lack of achievement on the basis of being a woman or of being black. I would accept no limits imposed from outside." She went to the V.A. hospital to stay one year, having been warned that government formality and rigidity would stifle creative expression and block the natural flow of innovation; "but no one held me back." Over a period of 16 years, during which she also married and had two children, she was promoted successively from case worker to case supervisor, to assistant chief, and then to chief of the social work service at that hospital. Finally, she was transferred to headquarters as chief of social work programs in the department of medicine and surgery for the entire agency — and the promotions continue to come.

Even though Federal personnel officers were formerly permitted to specify "men only" in filling professional jobs, not all of them were limited by the common man's-world attitudes and habits.

Illustration

About 15 years ago, the U.S. Naval Ordnance Laboratory employed K.S. as a research chemist. Inasmuch as she came with excellent qualifications, including a Ph.D. degree, college teaching experience, and a research fellowship at Oxford, there was nothing remarkable about her application or the acceptance of it — except that she had then been no less than 25 years away from her chosen profession! Fully aware of the rapid advances in physical science that had taken place over that quarter-century, K.S. — now a widow with four grown children and five grandchildren — modestly applied for an assistant's position; but her remarkable talent was soon recognized. Given freedom to do fundamental research, her inventive genius produced, among other things, a new high explosive of great stability, resistant to unprecedented extremes of temperature and altitude. It was this explosive which made the Apollo moon landings possible, for it could be relied upon (as it was) to lift the landing module *off* the moon, enabling the astronauts to return to their spacecraft. Though research can be frustrating and discouraging, she says, the peaks of achievement are higher than the depths of failures.

HOW DOES THE FEDERAL GOVERNMENT RATE AS AN EMPLOYER OF WOMEN?

The Federal government is the largest single employer in the United States, employing 2,850,000 people, in thousands of different occupations, and in every state, city, and crossroads town in the country. Only about 12% of its employees are in headquarters offices in the nation's capital; an approximately equal number are in the state of California.

As an employer of women, the government is unquestionably among the best in the nation. All of its many occupations are open to competition by women on equal terms with men, and uniform pay within each grade of work is guaranteed. Discrimination in any aspect of employment on the basis of sex (or of race, religion, national origin, or physical handicap) is specifically prohibited by law.

Under the Civil Rights Act of 1964, as amended in the Equal Employment Opportunity Act of 1972, discrimination against any Federal government employee on the basis of race, color, religion, national origin, or sex is prohibited. The Civil Service Commission has statutory authority to see that all personnel actions in the Federal government are not only free from discrimination but also are actively oriented toward equality of opportunity. The law requires all Federal agencies to submit annual action plans for the commission's review and approval; these plans must include provisions for training and upward mobility. These plans must include women as well as members of minority groups. In addition, the commission must review and evaluate all agencies' equal employment opportunity programs in operation, and report on them twice a year.

The Civil Service Commission carries on a continuous personnel management evaluation program with periodic inspection of agency activities, through which it can discover any patterns of discrimination in agencies and order them corrected. It also provides a discrimination complaint procedure by which individual cases can be brought to its attention.

But laws and rules are not the whole story. Through the Federal Women's Program and other activities, the commission works constantly to break down, or wear away, the outdated but still deeply ingrained mental attitudes that for countless years have kept women in an inferior status. As a result, the position of women in the Federal civil service is constantly being strengthened, and the Civil Service Commission is determined that the government shall maintain its standing as the most progressive employer of women.

WOMEN IN GOVERNMENT: THE PAST

The Federal civil service was the first employer to offer true equal employment opportunity to women when the Civil Service Act of 1883 created the Civil Service Commission and established the system of employment by practical examinations open to all citizens. In their first annual report to the president, in 1884, the

Civil Service Commissioners noted the benefits of the merit system to women, pointing out that "the need for political influence or for importunate solicitation, especially disagreeable to women, for securing appointments in the classified service exists no longer."

Illustration

In the early summer of 1883 Mary Francis Hoyt, a bright and adventurous girl recently graduated from Vassar College, came to Washington from her home in Connecticut and was among those who assembled for the first time to compete for government positions through practical tests of ability. She made the highest mark on that first civil service examination, and was placed at the head of the list. Unfortunately, Mary left town for a little while and was not available when the first appointment was made from that list, so it went to the second-place eligible, a man named Ovington Weller. We regret that we can't say "the first competitive civil service appointment in the United States was won by a woman," but we *can* say, proudly, "a woman made the *highest mark* on the first civil service examination, and received the *second* appointment!" Mary Francis Hoyt was appointed (seven days after Mr. Weller) to a clerkship in the Treasury Department at the going rate of $900 a year. In 1888 she married Brice J. Moses, another Treasury employee, and resigned from the service — as was the custom in those days.

In its second annual report the Civil Service Commission said: "It is now generally recognized that women can successfully perform the duties of many of the subordinate places under the government. In many cases they have shown eminent fitness for the places they have held and high qualities in their work. There is simple justice in allowing them to compete for the public service, and to receive appointments when, in fair competition, they have shown superior merit."

It is regrettably true, however, that for many years equal employment opportunity remained more of an ideal than a reality, for agency heads and appointing officers (who of course were all men) made a practice of requesting *men only* from the civil service lists for almost all but routine clerical positions.

It should be explained that for each position to be filled, the Civil Service Commission certifies to the appointing agency (that is, sends the papers of) the three persons standing highest on the list of successful competitors for the particular occupation. The appointing officer is at liberty to select any one of the three, and the other two are returned to the commission's list to be considered for the next vacancy. Until quite recently, however, appointing officers were allowed to request certification of men only (or women only) on the basis of nothing more than personal preference. Thus many well-qualified women who passed the civil service examinations with high marks were never even known to exist so far as agency appointing officers were concerned.

The proponents of civil service reform recognized that the practice was not wholly in keeping with the merit-system principle, but it was generally believed that appointing officers had a legal right to make appointments on the basis of sex.

One of the most forceful and effective civil service reformers was Theodore Roosevelt, who served as a Civil Service Commissioner from 1889 to 1895 and may justly be credited with getting the fledgling civil service system firmly on its feet. In a letter written during this period, answering a query from Wellesley College, Commissioner Roosevelt said: "No distinction is made in the examinations, or in any proceedings under the commission, between men and women. They compete on precisely the same basis. The sole discretion whether men or women shall be appointed rests with the appointing officer . . . ." But he added, "Most appointing officers seem to prefer men . . . ."

(This option was thought to be sanctioned by an ambiguously worded law which had been enacted 13 years prior to the Civil Service Act, presumably for the purpose of authorizing government agencies to appoint women to the "higher clerkships and pay them the same salaries as men," *at their discretion.* Appointments of women had previously been limited to the lower-grade clerkships, and women's salaries had been limited to half those for men — $600 and $1200 a year, respectively.)

It is ironic that women always advance occupationally during wartime. Except for a few isolated instances in earlier years, the employment of women in the Federal government actually began during the period of the Civil War, when the Treasury Department — flying in the face of propriety and all sorts of social and economic taboos — courageously hired a number of "lady clerks" to work in the office of the Treasurer of the United States.

The entrance of the United States into World War I brought an immediate increase of about 100,000 positions in the government, in addition to many vacancies left by the men who went into military service. The Civil Service Commission reported in 1918: "The most notable change in government personnel brought about by the war is in the employment of women. They are everywhere . . . ."

Illustration

N.J. came to Washington in 1917 to take an accounting job with the War Department, one of 40,000 women who were appointed to the departmental service in Washington during the two-year period of the war. She was assigned to a large, crowded work space in a jerry-built temporary building on the Mall, and housed in another jerry-built temporary building — one of the "government hotels for women" which filled all the open space of the great plaza between the Capitol and the Union Station. A competent and energetic worker, N.J. was advanced to a supervisory position in a matter of weeks and began to have hopes of a real professional career in government. But by Christmas of 1918 she was back at her home in Chicago, having been in the first wave of dismissals. Her superior officer expressed great regret at having to let her go, and made matters no better by adding: "Now if you were in a clerical job we might be able to keep you, but a supervisory professional position — well, you know, that's a *man's* job."

Women's permanent gains were, indeed, largely limited to the clerical field, but their temporary service in the many professional and technical positions had at least served one good purpose: it had demonstrated that such occupations were not beyond the capacity of women.

In 1923, 40 years after the Civil Service Act, equal opportunity took another giant step forward with passage of the Classification Act. It was this law that established for the Federal service the principle of equal pay for equal work as a requirement rather than a matter of administrative discretion, setting pay rates according to the duties and responsibilities of each job without regard to the person in the job. This action put the government far ahead of anything comparable in private employment — and in many cases it is still far ahead.

The departments had actually made comparatively little use of the permissive power granted in 1870 to pay equal wages to women; they knew a bargain when they saw one. But the Classification Act of 1923 included this specific statement: "In determining the rate of compensation which an employee shall receive, the principle of equal compensation for equal work, irrespective of sex, shall be followed."

Thus the philosophy dating from the Civil War, that women were valuable chiefly for their low wage scale, was abandoned once and for all. Thereafter, women advanced in the Federal service by reason of their abilities and not because they were a cheaper labor commodity than men.

Just as wars increase women's employment opportunities, periods of widespread unemployment tend to limit them severely. Nevertheless, many women entered the Federal civil service during the Depression, mostly at very low grades and often as the sole support of a family, intending to stay only until the male breadwinner could find employment. But a very large proportion of them did not leave, even when times got better; they found government work to their liking and government careers attractive and fulfilling.

Illustration

M.F. was one of those who were glad to get a job with the government in 1933. Hardly any other employers were doing any hiring at all, and Grade 1 in a New Deal agency was $1,260 per year more than nothing. Starting thus at the very bottom, M.F. decided before long that there were possibilities in this great organization too good to abandon, and that it was not in her nature to ignore the challenge that all those ascending steps in the career ladder presented. From typist to payroll clerk to budget technician to financial analyst to budget officer was the path she followed, each assignment a step up from the last. Learning and growing with each new experience, she was never afraid to leave a familiar office or agency to take on a new and more challenging opportunity in strange surroundings, and she never failed to put something new into the job. Thus she progressed through the entire civil service structure, raising two sons and completing a course in business administration along the way. Now at the very top, as comptroller of the great research operation of a major government department and architect of its financial management system, she has helped to destroy forever the barriers of sex of the kind that cut short the budding career of N.J. in 1918. She describes her work with such words as "exciting" and "fascinating" — in spite of "inexorable deadlines."

Following the usual pattern, women made tremendous gains in government employment during World War II. From June 1941 to June 1943 the number of women in government increased more than three-and-a-half times, and by 1945 their total was over one million. This time, however, the outcome was different; although their number was reduced by half after the war, and although most of the "Rosie, the Riveter" types left the industrial plants, women retained the foothold they had gained in many professional and managerial positions. Since that time, women's position in the higher levels of the Federal civil service has been continually expanded and strengthened.

WOMEN IN GOVERNMENT: THE FUTURE

Equal employment opportunity for women in the Federal civil service is now on a clear course of advancement. It is on a firm foundation of law and executive orders prohibiting discrimination in any aspect of employment.

The Federal civil service of the present and the future offers more career scope, more diversity, more breadth of occupation and profession, and more room to grow, than any other employer. And it gives women a better break — not as good as it should be, in comparison with men, and not as good as it is going to be, as we continue to improve, but still better than almost any other employer.

Among the advances still to come — such as more equitable management training and executive development opportunities —

one of the most significant is the development of new patterns for part-time employment. Through the Federal Women's Program, agencies are being urged to broaden their concepts of what kinds of work can be handled on that basis and to encourage more women to make use of such arrangements. Part-time employment, in the middle of the day when small children are in school, can enable many young women to keep up their skills — anything from shorthand to nuclear physics — while providing needed service to agencies. They will thus be ready for full-time employment when their children are older, without the need for refresher education or retraining at either their own or the agency's expense.

This is an example of the future of women in government from the institutional viewpoint. What can be seen from the viewpoint of women *now* interested in the possibilities of government careers?

Illustration

The sky is the limit. R.T. joined the Civil Aeronautics Administration (later the Federal Aviation Agency) during World War II, right out of high school, and literally grew up with air traffic control. After three years of experience in the Midwest, she went to Alaska at the age of 20, and over the next 20 years progressed steadily upward in one of the most physically and emotionally demanding fields of work in the whole range of government occupations. She obtained a private pilot's license in order to gain a better understanding of the needs and feelings of the pilots she directs. Now Assistant Chief of the Air Route Traffic Control Center at Anchorage, she has not only served with great distinction, but has also opened yet another door to women.

Illustration

The bottom of the sea is the limit. J.K. is a psychologist whose special field is vision research. She directs a research branch of the Navy's Submarine Medical Center, and has become an authority on problems of night vision, the effect of submarine service on vision, improving visibility for divers, and many other fields of visual research. She is recognized as the top expert in the United States on underwater vision. Wanting to learn first-hand the problems encountered by divers, she became an accomplished scuba diver herself and regularly participates in ocean studies, leading investigations of underwater problems.

Illustration

The most basic secrets of the human organism may be the limit — if there is any limit. J.A., a young research biochemist with the Agricultural Research Service, played a vital role in determining the first known molecular structure of a ribonucleic acid (RNA). This was termed a scientific breakthrough of the highest magnitude, as RNA's help determine how living cells make and utilize proteins. An understanding of the process by which this is done brings us much closer to the control of genetic defects and certain diseases, including cancer.

HOW HIGH CAN WOMEN GO IN THE FEDERAL SERVICE?

For the future, women can go as high in the Federal civil service as it is possible for anyone to go, given the necessary qualifications. There are always limits, of course; limits of program, of money, of organization, and so on. But these will, increasingly, be limits for *people*, not for *women*. The only limits that still survive from the past are those of mental attitudes that cling to the idea of "woman's place," but they are rapidly diminishing.

The only limitations that will be significant in the future will be self-imposed limitations, such as lack of vision, lack of effort, lack of preparation.

HOW CAN WOMEN GET STARTED?

If you want a career in government you should start early, for preparation is of fundamental importance. Young women should begin in high school to identify their best talents and interests and to pursue them with determination. Do not permit anyone, at any stage in your education, to talk you out of preparing for an "unfeminine" occupation or a "man's" profession on the grounds that a woman can't succeed in such fields. If this was true once, it is not true now; the scarcity of women in many occupational areas is not due to women's innate inability, but to their having accepted that kind of discouragement for countless years.

There are many professions, from medicine to management, in which there are severe manpower shortages today, but for which very few women are trained or are training. This gives the opposition (and let's face it, there is still an opposition) a ready-made alibi: "There aren't any qualified women available."

HOW CAN WOMEN BEST PREPARE THEMSELVES?

When you know what you want to do, and have enough training to begin — whether it be in automobile mechanics, electronic engineering, landscape architecture, sign painting, veterinary medicine, stenography, or anything else — then go to a Federal Job Information Center and ask questions. There are over 100 such centers in principal cities throughout the United States, and they are listed in the local telephone directories. If you don't find one in your city, write to the Civil Service Commission, Washington, D.C. 20415, for the address of the center nearest you.

It must be understood that not all occupations are available at all times. Sometimes the government needs additional cartographers, for instance, and sometimes it doesn't. The Federal Job Information Center can tell you about the current employment situation, both local and nationwide, and in general what the prospects may be in various kinds of work.

If it looks favorable, apply for the examination in your field of interest. You may have to take a written test, along with other applicants, or you may have to submit a detailed statement of your training and experience from which your qualifications will be determined. You will be notified of the results of the examination; if you are eligible, and high enough on the list, the next move will be a communication from an employing agency. At this point, however, patience is necessary, for sometimes the lists move slowly.

Do not be afraid to start out on a modest level, but do not be content to stop short of your ultimate goal just becasue you are a woman. Remember that you have the same rights as men to try to reach your particular star; to fail, if you must, because you reached a little too far, but not because you weren't allowed to try; and to try again if you want to.

But remember also that you have the same obligations as men, and that if you are going to compete with men on a basis of equality, you must be equally willing to accept responsibility. Most men are success oriented from childhood, and grow up in the assumption that they will work toward some kind of occupational goal. Most women, at the present time, have not had that kind of conditioning, and consequently may be inclined to give up too easily and too soon.

A "better" job is usually not an easier job but a harder job. Expect, and be willing, to work harder as you progress, to get additional training if you need it, and to believe in yourself.

To be sure, not everyone wants to work up to the very top. For every woman and every man there is an optimum level of employment, a place at which work is agreeable and one's potential is realized but not exceeded. No one should be obliged to press on beyond that point; the most truly successful people are probably those who knowingly stop just short of their "level of incompetence" and thereafter have excellence of production in that place, rather than unlimited advancement, as their goal.

The goal of the equal employment opportunity program in the Federal civil service, as focused on women through the Federal Women's Program, is to make that kind of achievement possible for everyone — to make sure that the career of every person in government employment will be determined by that person's individual ability, effort, and accomplishment. "Woman's place" in government will be whatever she can make it.

REFERENCE

1. Patricia Marshall, "Women at Work," *Manpower*, U.S. Department of Labor, June, 1972.

5

WOMEN IN ORGANIZED RELIGION

by Dr. Cynthia C. Wedel

Dr. Cynthia C. Wedel, the associate director of the Center for a Voluntary Society, Washington, D.C. is a native of Dearborn, Michigan. She holds B.A. and M.A. degrees from Northwestern University, and a Ph.D. in psychology from George Washington University.

Ms. Wedel has held executive positions in church organizations and has taught at the National Cathedral School for Girls and at American University. Her major interest, however, has always been in voluntary organizations and working with volunteers. She has been a consultant to the National Office of Volunteers of the American Red Cross; a member of the National Board of the Girl Scouts; chairman of the Committee on Volunteers of the National Assembly for Social Policy and Development; a member of the President's Commission on the Status of Women, 1961-63, and of the subsequent Citizens Advisory Committee on the Status of Women. In Washington, D.C. she was active as a volunteer on the Health and Welfare Council, United Givers' Fund, and Advisory Committee on Public Welfare.

Dr. Wedel completed a three-year term as the
first woman president of the National Council of
Churches in 1972. Her present major volunteer
activity is as National Chairman of Volunteers for
the American Red Cross. She is a member of the
American Psychological Association and of the
International Association of Applied Social
Scientists.

Key Questions

1. What part has religion played in the oppression or liberation of women?

2. What changes are taking place in organized religion today?

3. How do these changes affect the role of women?

4. What will need to be done — by men, by women, by the institutions of religion — if women are to have a more significant role?

5. In what ways could transactional analysis be a useful tool in and for organized religion?

RELIGION AND THE OPPRESSION OR LIBERATION OF WOMEN

Because there is so little common experience or agreement as to what "religion" or "organized religion" means, it is necessary to set the stage by looking into human experience in the past. Religion in some form has been a significant part of human experience from earliest times. Archeology and anthropology tell us that the most primitive people had a sense of forces outside themselves and beyond their control that affected their lives for good or evil. The beginnings of organized religion can be seen in rituals, sacrifices, and festivals devised to appease or praise these powers. Since the forces of nature — rain, wind, lightning, animals — so deeply influenced the lives of nomadic and later agricultural peoples, much of early religion was a form of nature worship. The sun, moon, wind, and water were often personified as gods. Altars were built to these gods, offerings were made, and sacrifices were performed. Such ceremonies were passed from one generation to another and often became entirely separated from their original purposes. They became the traditions of a tribe or nation.

In much the same way, as Simone de Beauvoir points out in the early classic of women's liberation, *The Second Sex*, a division of labor between the sexes was developed in very primitive society. While there were a few exceptional matriarchal societies, biological and physical differences generally resulted in the larger, more muscular males roaming abroad to kill animals for food and hides, and the females staying near the cave or shelter tending the precious fire and the helpless infants. There probably were few absolute reasons for this division of labor, except for the brief time immediately before and after the birth of a baby. But the pattern was fairly general and soon became fixed. Since "religion" was related to field and forest, many of the rituals became male inspired and dominated. Since the males were free to move around, they had wider experience and knew more about "the world" than the home-bound females. Different roles, a difference in status, and male superiority all became invested with tradition and a mystical or religious significance. During the thousands of years while humankind was emerging into history, the plots and rules of early, and almost universal, "games" were developed.

Sex Differences in Role and Status

The earliest historical records show clear patterns of sex differences in role and status. And because religion was so pervasive a part of life, these distinctions became a part of the religious structure. *It is fair to say that primitive religious practice played a significant part in the subordination of the female.* As religions became more highly developed in ancient civilizations, they had many variations. Goddesses shared worship with gods. But the dominant figure was always a god. With very few — always short-lived — exceptions, ancient societies were thoroughly patriarchal.

As monotheism developed in the Judaic world, the symbols surrounding God became exclusively male. Judaism and Christianity not only worshipped a male God, but they also fought hard against the fertility cults, priestesses, and religious prostitution which marked many of the other religions of early civilization. Nor, as they arose, did the other great religious movements — Islam, Buddhism, Hinduism — accord to women any significant place in the scheme of things. *A pretty good case can be made by those who claim that organized religion is one of the major forces which has kept women in subjection through most of history.* Not only have women been excluded from most of the life of organized religion, but also religious doctrines and traditions have rationalized and "explained" the subordination of women. The usual interpretations of the stories of creation in the Bible are a clear example of this.

In view of these circumstances, it is surprising that Judaism and Christianity — which are the two forms of organized religion which are most significant in the Western World — have within them certain contrary elements which need to be noted. Although the Jewish religious life was entirely male dominated, and the Jewish man thanked God daily that he had not been made a woman, the Old Testament records many women who played important roles in the history of their people — often heroic and quite "unfeminine" roles. All women were accorded more respect and treated with more dignity in Jewish culture than in other nations at that time, but their place was clearly subordinate to man.

Jesus and Early Christianity

Christianity grew from Judaism and carried into its life not only the Jewish scriptures, but many religious attitudes and customs. Jesus, as the center of Christian belief, was a notable exception. In all the records of his meeting, talking, dealing with women, he seems to have had *no feeling of their being inferior*. He took women seriously, asked for and gave help to them, and carried on many serious conversations with them which are recorded in the scriptures. While there were no women in the small group of twelve with whom he traveled and worked, there are clear records of a number of women in the somewhat larger group of those who considered themselves his disciples. At the beginning of the early Christian Church, the records are clear that women were very much a part of the Church. They are referred to by name, and it is obvious that they played a significant role as Christianity spread across the ancient world.

Within a century or two, however, the young Christian Church had yielded to the prevailing customs of the secular society, and women slipped back into subordinate positions. A totally male-dominated church, in which only men were trained and educated, developed practices and teachings which justified the inferior place of women.

The Old Testament story of Adam and Eve was used to prove that women are essentially dangerous and evil and will tempt men to sin. Portions of letters to the early churches that referred to some specific problem were universalized to say that women must not be allowed to speak in church, must be obedient to their husbands, and must ask men to interpret God's word to them. Such ideas, reiterated over almost 2000 years, and personified in a male hierarchy, have resulted in the churches being one of the strong forces against the liberation of women.

Effective Women in the Christian Church

But, as in most things, there is another side. From very early times there have been strong, effective women in the Christian Church. When it was impossible to crack the male hierarchy, these women founded convents and orders of religious women. While hardly a model of liberation for women, during centuries when even queens were usually illiterate and little more than chattels, nuns were often brilliantly educated and managed great institutions. The latent capacities of these black-robed females are beginning to be seen as they now carry on a fight for their proper place in the Church.

Some Protestant groups, for at least the past three centuries, have treated women as people. The Quakers have always given women equal status with men. A woman was the respected and revered founder of Christian Science. For more than 50 years, several Protestant denominations have ordained women to the ministry. Orders of Deaconesses and powerful women's organizations have developed in many churches over the past century.

It is easy to prove that in spite of these positive signs, the position of women in most churches — even when they were allowed to be ordained — was distinctly subordinate to men. But in 1948, when the World Council of Churches was formed, there were enough capable, angry women to hold a meeting and demand that the question of the status of women be considered. They won, and a department was established in the World Council of Churches to study the role of women in the Church. It soon expanded to look at the place of women in society. Almost 20 years before "women's liberation" became a common phrase, some church people had been doing solid research and writing on the subject.

On balance, organized religion has probably been the tool and helper in the oppression of women, by giving religious sanction to the dominance of the male. But there are some little gleams of light in the dark picture which are today being used very effectively by women (and many men) in all religious bodies, to bring women back to a role of equality, and to develop theological justification for this.

THE CHANGES TAKING PLACE IN ORGANIZED RELIGION TODAY

Like all institutions in our society, organized religion is today reeling under the impact of rapid change. People who are increasingly well educated, well informed, and ready and eager to share in making the decisions which affect their lives are questioning all hierarchical structures. Church structures, most of which took shape centuries ago, are rooted in the assumption that most people will not question authority and are incapable of making right moral choices. As has been said more than once, most religious institutions are well equipped to answer questions which people are no longer asking. The very fundamental truths about human life and human nature which are contained in the Judeo-Christian faiths have become so entangled in obsolete thought forms that they are all but incomprehensible to skeptical modern man. Astronomy and space exploration have undercut the traditional religious cosmology. The agricultural and pastoral imagery of the Bible and hymns are almost meaningless to dwellers in an urban, technological world. Mobility, and changing patterns of work and leisure, are making Sabbath and Sunday observances inconvenient, if not actually dysfunctional.

Theological education — the backbone of the ministry and religious institutions — is being sharply criticized today. It is seen as overintellectual and quite out of touch with the world in which the minister must function. The truth of such criticism can be seen in the growing gap between clergy and laity, and in the number of ordained men giving up their ministry in despair.

Lay Liberation Movement

There is an almost unidentified, yet very strong, lay liberation movement working in most religious bodies. Sometimes it takes the form of vigorous efforts to change the structure, or liturgy, or teachings of the Church. More often it is seen in lay people simply "opting out," sometimes dropping all religious ties, other times moving into far-out, advanced, or "underground" churches or into fundamentalist bodies. In a few places, where the leadership is skillful, the laity and ministry find new and truly creative ways of working. Since bad news spreads more rapidly than good news, there may be more of these successful experiments than anyone realizes.

Another change which is either needed or taking place in most units of organized religion is an increasing role for groups formerly excluded from positions of leadership — women, young people, and members of racial or economic minorities. Again, when skillfully handled, this can result in new vitality and effectiveness. But when such moves are resisted or forbidden by the authorities, tension and disruption can wreck the institution.

Changes in Church Structure

While there are still religious groups which are local, independent congregations, the general pattern of American church life is organized in national and regional denominational structures. Until fairly recently, most of these structures were strong and seemingly necessary to support the local congregation. They provided programs, structures, and channels for giving to missionary programs. Today, people in local groups are less and less interested in programs, however good, drawn up in a remote national office, or in giving money to be spent by someone else. As national leadership has moved out into new areas of social concern, regional, cultural, and economic differences among local congregations have created great dissension. One result has been the withholding of funds from national bodies, either as a protest or because of what seemed to be more pressing needs in a locality.

The financial pinch is being felt by almost all national religious bodies. While painful, it is forcing a healthy reassessment of programs and priorities. It seems obvious to many leaders that the role of the national denomination must change radically — from making all the decisions and handing them down, to becoming responsive resources to help local congregations do what seems good to them. Many of the major religious bodies are in the process of reexamining and changing their structures. In this process, attempts are usually included to give more freedom and autonomy to regional and local groups, and to include more lay people — including women — in decision-making bodies.

Changes in Theology

In addition to organizational change, there are dramatic changes taking place in the theological world. Process theology, situational ethics, ecumenical dialogue are all part of these changes. They grow out of many influences: new and better biblical scholarship, new discoveries in the physical and social sciences, and events in the world which have smashed old ideas of "progress" and raised fundamental questions about the nature of humanity and its relation to the universe.

The result of this ferment has been to shake all kinds of old certainties, and to raise questions about much of the traditional teaching of religion. Changes in values and morals are a noticeable evidence of this. While to many traditionalists morals and values are declining (see almost any popular poll on the subject), a very good case can be made that while they are changing, many of the changes are for the better. Certainly there is, in much religious teaching and writing today, a new emphasis on the worth of the individual, on freedom and justice.

From a religious point of view, it is very possible to see divine guidance in the breaking up of many old hierarchies and thought patterns in order that new and more humane ones may emerge. The fact that so much of organized religion is disheartened, discouraged, and fearful may simply be evidence of a lack of prophetic insight. At any rate, for the poor, the oppressed, and those who have been the victims of old patterns (including women), the changes in religious institutions may be the greatest sign of hope.

HOW DO THESE CHANGES AFFECT THE ROLE OF WOMEN?

The roles played by women in organized religion vary from one type of church to another. Typically, however, religious institutions maintain a fairly sharp distinction between masculine and feminine roles. Men predominate on official decision-making assemblies, boards, and committees. Men take the leadership roles in public worship. Women often have a great deal to do, but it is in "supporting" services. They teach, raise money, serve meals, often prepare what is used in the services of worship. Increasingly, women meet in study groups or prayer groups. If a local congregation engages in community service, it is often the women who perform the service.

Almost without exception, women are in the majority in the membership of religious bodies, and in attendance at worship and most other functions. Many of these women are deeply involved in and extremely well informed about all aspects of the life and work of the church or synagogue. This may be one reason why there *are* more women members. People tend to join and stay with voluntary associations with which they feel a real involvement. This may say something, too, about the lesser participation of lay men because the number of real leadership positions is limited.

Women's Earlier Involvement in the Church

During the centuries when the place of women was sharply delimited in all of society, there was no occasion to raise questions about their place in the Church. Since the late nineteenth century, women in most American churches have gathered together in missionary societies, women's guilds, and other forms of organizations. In many a local congregation, the women's society became the largest, most active, and often most affluent group in the church. More than one church building has been paid for almost entirely by money earned or given by the women. While these women's organizations were indispensible to the local congregation, and offered excellent opportunities to many women for leadership training and experience, they also presented a real or imagined threat to the clergy and to the official boards — all male.

When effective and powerful local women's societies began to band together at regional and national levels, they again did two things. They offered even wider and more stimulating opportunities to many women and helped them to know more and more about the national and worldwide work of their religious bodies. At the same time they became more essential to the work of the whole organization and more of a threat to a male hierarchy. In a number of the larger Protestant denominations, women's groups provide millions of dollars each year for the work of the denomination.

Women's Later Involvement

Since World War II, when many women entered the labor force for the first time and began to break out of the "church, children, and kitchen" ghetto, women's religious organizations have been changing. Increasingly well-educated women, experienced in working with men in offices and factories, found the traditional "women's work" of the church less interesting. A few began to agitate for a place in the total life and work of the institution. A larger number simply turned to other pursuits. Many continued to work after the war, until today close to half of the adult women in the United States are employed. Others entered with enthusiasm into voluntary organizations where they could use all their talents, and rise in the structure if they were able and willing.

The women's societies didn't yield without a valiant struggle. They tried changing their forms of organization and times of meetings. They organized Business and Professional Women's Groups. They added welfare, social betterment, and other programs and projects. In some instances they were successful. But there is little question that the great day of the woman's society in organized religion is past. While this change will bring some losses to women and to the institutions they served so well, the results need not be all negative.

The basic problem, which none of the efforts to improve women's work faced, was that the second-class citizenship of women in religious institutions was becoming increasingly apparent. As the status of women in the whole society began to be widely discussed, and more and more women were accepted in political life, community activity, and business and industry, the very religious institutions which preached the equality of all human beings in the sight of God began to be seen as one of the last bastions of male supremacy. Legislation (up to and including the Equal Rights Amendment) could force employers and government to give women the same opportunities as men. But religious and other voluntary groups were not subject to such laws.

Role of Women in Organized Religion

When, about 1950, the World Council of Churches took leadership in study and action related to the place of women in the Church, it set out to work on three fronts. One was the place of women in decision-making bodies. Another was women in staff roles in religious organizations. The third was the ordination of women.

In Decision-Making Bodies

When we speak of women in the decision-making bodies of religious organizations, we refer to those groups which make decisions for the whole Church. These would include the board of the local congregation (vestry, session, trustees); major regional and national boards (other than those of women's organizations); and the governing body of the denomination — convention, assembly, general conference, or whatever it is called. Every organized religious group has some such "ultimate authority," with the exception of the Roman Catholic Church and possibly some of the small sects.

In the Roman Catholic Church there is considerable agitation for a National Pastoral Council to include bishops, priests, and religious and lay men and women, which would have such legislative authority as can be exercised by a national church within the Roman Catholic system.

While some Protestant denominations have always included women in their legislative structures, many have not. In the Presbyterian system, the lay people who attend the General Assembly must be elders. Women became eligible to be elders only recently. The Episcopal Church finally admitted women to its General Convention in 1970. Even when women are permitted to serve in these posts, they tend to be in a very small minority. One argument against admitting women has often been that "there are so few things for lay men to do. We shouldn't take this away from them."

Since, as has been suggested, the lack of sufficient involvement of lay men in the total work of a religious body may account for men having a lesser commitment to religion; and since the total number of openings in top decision-making bodies is too small to help solve *this* problem; this argument for keeping major boards entirely male is not persuasive.

It would seem far wiser to work at eliminating sex stereotypes and to provide a variety of service opportunities for men as well as for women. A hundred years ago, when the majority of men worked twelve hours a day, six days a week, it *was* hard for men to enter into many activities. But this is no longer true. The trouble is that many religious bodies are still living back in the nineteenth century and replaying old scripts which may have been valid once, but are no more.

Occasionally the argument used against women in religious boards and assemblies is that these groups deal largely with problems of property, business, and finance, to which women could make little or no contribution. This is ridiculous on two counts. First, women have always had to deal with such questions even when their sphere was limited to the home. Today, millions of women are employed specifically because of their business and professional skills. But more importantly, such an attitude assumes that all the distinctive work of religion — worship, education, missions, evangelism, social action, fellowship — is the province of the professional or ordained leadership.

The implication is that lay people – the 99% of any religious institution – have no interest or competence in these fields. If this were true, it would negate some of the most basic theological concepts of organized religion. There simply are no valid arguments against women sharing in decision making, and there are many important reasons why they should.

Staff Roles

When women are adequately represented in decision-making bodies, it should be easier to open more professional opportunities to women in the work of religious institutions. National and regional offices, church-related agencies, and larger congregations usually have both professional and clerical staff positions. When it is pointed out that – like most institutions of our society – the important and well-paid posts tend to go to men and the less remunerative jobs to women, there are a variety of interesting defensive reactions. Some are the usual, now disproved, notions that women don't stay on a job, that they are less reliable and are absent more often. One can point to numerous modern studies which show that these ideas are entirely unfounded.

Sometimes it is suggested that theological training is really a prerequisite for church positions. Actually, this has proved in many instances to be very unwise. Theological training, and perhaps successful experience as leader of a congregation, is frequently the worst possible preparation for becoming the executive of a large, complex institution with all the attendant personnel, financial, and management problems. Many positions in organized religious bodies could be far more effectively filled by competent, experienced lay men and women from business, industry, or professional backgrounds.

Probably quite unconsciously the ordained leaders of religious groups, who for centuries *were* among the best-educated people in a world where few had any education, have formed a close-knit guild. They know one another. They went to school together, or to similar kinds of schools. They talk the same language (full of technical jargon), and they share the same incompetencies. When a good job is open, they think of their friends and co-workers. These seldom include lay men, and almost never include lay women.

When the statistics regarding the employment of women by religious organizations are made public, [1] there is some concern expressed. The usual reaction is that there are no qualified women. The truth is that no one has really looked for them. Women on the boards of religious institutions can keep this issue alive, press for the employment and upgrading of women, and find women who are qualified for professional and management posts.

The Church Executive Development Board was created in 1965 to provide the kind of management training needed by executives in religious organizations. Well over 1000 people in top-level church jobs have attended the courses. But in spite of strenuous efforts to recruit women, only about 25 women have had the training. This reflects, in part, the scarcity of women in real management roles. But it also reflects a downgrading of women. The courses are expensive and the top management is unwilling to make that kind of investment in the training of a woman. Sometimes one suspects a fear of women becoming *too* competent. And it is only fair to say that some of the women themselves are the problem. They hesitate to ask for something for themselves; they are overly budget conscious; or they feel so indispensable that they cannot take the time required. It is sad to have to say that in its employment practices, organized religion is not only no better than business, government, or education, but also that it lags far behind the leaders in these other fields.

Ordination of Women

The real heart of the problem regarding the role of women in organized religion, however, lies in the area of ordination of women as rabbis, priests, or ministers. While, as noted earlier, a few religious bodies have admitted women to their ministry for a long time, the vast majority have not.

Limiting the chief leadership role in religion to men was clearly an accommodation to a patriarchal society in which women were considered, by nature, inferior. But through the centuries this socially determined practice has become encrusted with many different biblical and theological justifications, which are widely accepted by both men and women.

Although most intelligent modern people know that it is impossible — and indeed wrong — to "personify" God, to make him in *our* image, most of us still do it. We accept, almost unconsciously, the use of "he" and "him" and the father analogy. We fail to comprehend the biblical verse about the creation: "God

created man in his own image; male and female created he them."
(Genesis 1:27) Even that ancient, primitive myth understood that
the "image of God" is both male and female.

For Christians, the fact that Jesus was male is often cited as a
reason for a male ministry. But this seems rather strained. If God
chose — as Christian faith asserts — to come into the world in
human form, he had to be either male or female. To suggest that
the choice of a male for that particular role must be universalized
seems unjustified. Then it is pointed out that Jesus chose only
men for his twelve disciples. But again, this could readily be for
practical reasons in that place and time. He chose only Jews,
too — yet it has never occurred to Gentiles to universalize *that*
fact!

*A careful study of the teachings and actions of Jesus indicates
that he did not conform to the customs of his people or his time
in his attitude toward and treatment of women.* There is no
evidence that he considered them inferior or unimportant. He
talked with them as freely as with men, discussed religious
questions with them, and responded to their requests for his help.
There were many women among his followers, and women are
specifically named among his friends. In the story of Mary and
Martha, recorded in Luke 10:38-42, he seemed to specifically
reject the traditional feminine role of housekeeping as the "best"
one for women.

In the same way, the reports of the early church name many
women as playing significant roles of leadership. While there are a
few isolated verses which lay down restrictions as to what women
may or may not do in the church (see for example, I Corinthians
14: 34, 35, or I Timothy 2:9-12), these obviously relate to specific
problems, and are no more universal in their meaning than verses
which prescribe how to treat slaves.

Most arguments against the ordination of women go back to
these specific references, conveniently overlooking the place
accorded women in the early church. Other arguments stress the
centuries of tradition of a male ministry, overlooking the fact that
most of the same centuries saw discrimination against women in
every other area of life. If other discriminations are rapidly
disappearing in a changed world, it is hard to argue that religion
alone cannot change. Interwoven with arguments from the Bible
and from tradition are a number of arguments based on outmoded

sociology and psychology. It is suggested that the life of a minister would not be compatible with being a mother and homemaker, disregarding the number of women who manage, very successfully, to combine home and a demanding career. Some arguments clearly stem from ancient ideas of "uncleanness" of women.

One intriguing argument was that men are simply unable to look at a woman without having sexual impulses aroused. Therefore, obviously, it would be highly improper to have a woman up in front, leading worship, with men looking at her! One wonders if the originator of this argument has ever wondered why male-led churches are so filled with women!

As women have gradually merged into the rest of society, organized religion has slowly begun to change. At the moment, most Protestant churches ordain women, although the numbers are very small and few women ministers hold posts as the senior minister in a large congregation. Most of them serve in team ministries headed by a man — which can be a very rewarding assignment. Others serve in specialized ministries as chaplains in colleges, hospitals, jails, and other institutions. A few are now teaching in theological seminaries, and quite a few hold executive posts in regional and national offices of their denominations, or of interchurch agencies.

The churches of the "Catholic" tradition — Roman Catholic, Eastern Orthodox, and Anglican — do not as yet grant full ordination to women. There is little evidence of any pressure for this in the great churches of the East, although we know little about the details of life in their home-lands since many are in Eastern Europe. There is growing agitation for it, though, by women in the Roman Catholic Church in the United States and in parts of Western Europe. A few outspoken male theologians have advocated ordination for women, but a major difficulty lies in the fact that major decision making in that church still lies entirely in the hands of men.

In the Anglican churches around the world there is considerable ferment and movement. A number of study commissions, made up of reputable theologians, have reported that there is no biblical or theological reason why women should not be ordained. Some have gone on to recommend that it be done. More have tended to suggest that "the time is not ripe" for a variety of reasons. One of these reasons is that it would make unity with

Roman Catholics and Eastern Orthodox more difficult. Another is that it would create tension among the autonomous churches of the Anglican Communion around the world if some ordained women and others did not.

Within the past few years, it has been generally agreed that if the Anglican Church in a particular area of the world decided to ordain women, it could do so. Under that permission, the Bishop of Hong Kong ordained two women as priests in 1971. This has created a great deal of discussion and debate, but no real problems as yet.

Anglican churches, like many Protestant bodies, have long had an order of deaconesses, women especially trained and commissioned for various tasks in the Church. In 1970, the Episcopal Church in the United States voted that henceforth deaconesses would be ordained in the same manner as deacons, and have all of the same authority. Deacons are men, usually entering the first step toward the priesthood. While a motion at the same meeting to admit women to the priesthood and eventually the Episcopate was narrowly defeated, full ordination as deaconesses has led an increased number of women to seek this first step; and there is growing pressure for their admission to the priesthood.

It is, of course, the "sacramental" and traditional nature of the ministry in the Catholic churches which leads them to feel that they have special problems in ordaining women. A careful study of their arguments, however, and of the ministry of the Protestant churches, would indicate that there is by no means as much difference in either functions or expectations of their ministries as many suppose, and it is extremely difficult to find any of these which actually could not be performed by a woman. The real barriers are tradition and strong resistance to change on the part of a male hierarchy and of many lay people — both men and women. As a Christian, I do not know the specific problems and trends in the Jewish faith. However, a young woman has been ordained as a rabbi, and others are now studying for this post. Presumably the same forces operate in Judaism as in the Christian churches.

In conclusion, the place of women in organized religion other than in a segregated women's society, is beginning to change in the three areas of decision-making bodies, professional employment, and the ordained ministry. The changes are slow and vary between churches. But the pace of change is accelerating and it is safe to predict new breakthroughs and more rapid change in the years ahead.

WHAT NEEDS TO BE DONE?

If women are to have a more adequate role in organized religion, there needs to be a great deal of action by many different groups in many different areas. As in race relations, or any other human discord, there is the basic strategy question as to whether you try to educate and change attitudes first, or work to change the laws and rules.

Since there is no clear-cut answer to this dilemma, it is probably best to mount action on all fronts at the same time. Women, and the increasing number of men in leadership positions in organized religion who believe in the liberation of women, should be assessing the situation wherever they are in the structure, and should begin to work at getting women into decision-making bodies, into staff positions, and into the ordained ministry.

In any local congregation, Christian or Jewish, steps can be taken to press for women in decision-making bodies. If there have always been one or two "token" women, a discussion centering on the numbers of women and men members of the congregation may soon reveal the unfairness of this. Whether to press at once for a fully representative system, or to approach it gradually, will have to be decided locally. This can best be done in the context of a congregation-wide study of the roles and place of the lay people in the total life of the body. What things could lay people be doing that they do not now do? If there have been many activities traditionally done by women, could men be included in some or all of these? Are there other activities – adult education, social action, community contacts, or enrichment of devotional life – which would strengthen and expand the work of the congregation if lay people would assume some leadership? If more opportunities for lay decision-making and participation are developed, it will be much easier for women to be included at all levels more nearly according to their numerical strength.

Change the Rules

If participation of women in the major governing bodies of the congregation is prohibited by rules established at regional or national levels, it will be necessary to discover the legislative path for changing these rules. Most Protestant churches have a representative form of government in which, eventually, even the concerns of a single congregation can be considered at the national level. Roman Catholics will have to work on their own bishops first. In most Roman Catholic parishes today there is the possibility of a parish council, including both men and women.

Education and Attitude Change

At the congregational level, as everywhere else, those who seek to improve the status of women need to plan a campaign of education and attitude change. It may be best to begin with the women, because a demand for greater representation of women can be seriously undercut if the opponents can prove that many women don't want it.

Using all the existing groupings of women in the congregation — guilds, teachers, choir singers, and study and prayer groups — efforts should be made to offer speakers and study materials on the changing role of women in the Church. Protestant churches will often find such resources through their own denominational channels. Church Women United, in which Protestant, Orthodox, and Roman Catholic women participate, offers many resources for local groups. Jewish women will find that their national organizations, such as Temple Sisterhoods, the National Council of Jewish Women, and others, are good sources of help. A community interchurch or interfaith group on the place of women in organized religion might be advisable. Nearby theological seminaries can often provide open-minded theologians who would be very helpful, and many seminaries have young women students who have strong motivation to help other church women understand their hopes. A good many women in religious orders have been giving serious thought and study to this question.

As the women in a local congregation begin to see the need for the larger participation of women, strategies can be planned to involve the men. It will help, of course, if the rabbi, priest, or minister is positive in his attitude, but even he is human and can be changed! An opportunity for a presentation and discussion of the subject at a congregational meeting, a sermon or address on the role of women (by a woman if possible) at a service of worship, adult education programs on new understandings of sexuality and sex stereotyping, and "consciousness raising" groups among women, based on the concepts of transactional analysis, are some of the ways to raise the issue on a congregation-wide level.

Employment of Professionally Trained Workers

From a concern for the adequate representation of women in decision-making bodies, it is a fairly easy step to a consideration of the employment of women in religious organizations. If a local congregation is large enough for a multiple staff, what functions might well be served by professionally trained lay people — men or women? Business management, education, counseling, social welfare, community relations, youth work, or work with the aging are among the areas in which theological training and ordination are not essential. Well-trained laymen or laywomen as a part of a real team ministry could be very effective.

In an increasing number of communities, small congregations of various denominations — recognizing the value of various specialized ministries — are forming clusters, or coalitions, in which they pool their resources to provide one or more well-trained professionals to serve all of them in needed areas. A lay person — man or woman — can often be the best choice, since he or she presents less of a threat to the ministers of the separate congregations.

On a larger scale, congregations in a town or city frequently form an ecumenical agency through which they can work together on community or larger problems. There is no real reason why the executives of such agencies must be ordained. Most of them are, because everyone thinks first of a clergyman to head a religious organization. Yet this is a post which requires chiefly managerial, human relations, and possibly fund-raising ability. A good executive can recruit the theological and other talent needed for committees and programs. A woman could fill such a post very well.

Communication and Support of Women

Women in local congregations who become concerned about professional opportunities for women at the regional and national levels of their religious organizations can stimulate change by writing to regional and national offices requesting information on the number of women employed, their rank and salary ranges. Just the fact that someone asks these questions often initiates improvements. Armed with facts, letters, or articles sent to denominational journals, or resolutions directed to legislative bodies can be a further step. This is a kind of "sisterly" support very much needed by women in responsible positions today.

When the subject of the ordination of women comes up, once again women in local units can have an important influence. Since most of them have never thought of being ordained, and perhaps have never known a woman who wanted to be, some basic education may be necessary. If yours is a religious body which ordains women, it would be interesting to know when it began to do so and why. Then you need to learn how it has worked out — in history and at the present time — how many women have been ordained, and what has been their experience. The opportunity to meet, listen to, and talk with an ordained woman or a seminary student seeking ordination can be an eye-opening experience. When you learn what the situation is in your own religious group, what the problems are, and where things need to change, you will probably see various ways in which you can take action to improve things. You will almost certainly find men — both lay and ordained — who favor the ordination of women. And you will find women who do not. Feelings and attitudes are very important in as controversial an area as this. They need to be brought out into the open and discussed. The ultimate test question is: "How would you feel if you knew that the new minister, priest, or rabbi of your congregation was to be a woman?"

In those religious bodies which do not ordain women, the problem is different, but no less important. A little research will probably discover whether there are any groups in your denomination which are giving consideration to this question, or any studies which have been made. It may or may not help to have an ordained woman from another denomination talk with members of your group. For some, it is too easy to assume that yours is a totally different structure, theology, and tradition. But in almost every religious group today there are women pressing for ordination — for themselves or for other women. To discuss the issue with such a person can be very useful.

A basic problem is to awaken both men and women to the fact that the ordination of women is becoming a live issue in almost every religious group. The first reaction is often disbelief and a firm rejection of the idea. However, repeated exposure, a fresh look at the place of women in the Bible, and serious consideration of the particular gifts which women might bring to the ministry can often help to open people's minds. Such activities should not be limited to women's groups. Men's minds will have to be changed also.

Interest at Each Level — Local to National

Stress has been placed on the things which can be done in local congregations. This is very deliberate. In much of organized religion, regional and national bodies have seen new visions, inaugurated changes, and begun new programs only to find that their efforts were wasted because nothing changed at the local level. The tendency is to blame people in local congregations for being stupid or disinterested. The fact is that ideas and materials are often sent to them which have taken a long time to germinate, but local people are expected to accept them full-blown. Change doesn't happen that way, especially change which challenges fundamental presuppositions about "the way things are supposed to be."

Nevertheless, along with essential activity at the local level, the role and status of women needs to be tackled at regional, national, and — for some religious groups — world levels. In national or regional offices, where program materials are often prepared, conferences planned, and field workers trained, the issues of the place of women in the life of the organization need to be raised. Discussion of the issues can be done at these levels; the lack of women in decision-making bodies and the low status of women employees should be easy to document, and plans can be made to overcome these problems. If a woman's organization has staff members at regional and national levels, they can often be the ones to press for consideration of women's concerns.

Political Action

In addition to providing suggestions and materials for use in local congregations, and checking practices in regional and local offices, some political action may need to be initiated. If there are rules or laws which inhibit the full participation of women, steps need to be taken to change them. This may mean careful drafting of amendments to constitutions, by-laws, and rules of order. Plans should then be worked out to get such amendments introduced, to win supporters who will speak for them, and to persuade people to vote for them. Uncongenial as overt political activity may seem to many religious women, it is a legitimate and necessary road.

Improved Relationships Between Levels

The relationship between local, regional, and national structures ought, in all instances, to be more reciprocal — more of a two-way street — than it is in most religious organizations. Far too often all communication is from the top down. This is a serious weakness in almost all large religious bodies. If the discussion of the changing role of women could be consciously developed as a fully reciprocal activity, it would be of benefit to the entire structure, not just to women. This can happen if local congregations begin to press their regional and national bodies for information and ultimately for change. It can be strengthened as national and regional bodies both initiate study and action and support and serve those doing things at the local level.

The question of the ordination of women in most religious groups is one which must ultimately be settled at the national or world level. It is unlikely to receive any serious consideration until there is a reasonable representation of women in the highest legislative bodies. This is the reason for putting stress first on women in decision-making roles. This is an area where the women of various religious traditions can be extremely helpful to one another. Those who want to raise the issue can learn a great deal from those who have dealt with it for a long time. Within each religious tradition there are writings and studies which would be helpful to others. Some of those who are deeply concerned about this might well set up an informal network for the exchange of materials, experiences, and strategies.

Women Can Add New Dimension to Organized Religion

An important thing for women to keep in mind as they work on women's place in organized religion is that it is not primarily a "women's rights" undertaking. That women, as at least half of creation and an inseparable part of the "image of God," have rights which have long been denied is a fact. But far more important is the fact that women with a commitment to religion want the religious body to which they belong to be as effective

and good as possible. All of organized religion has been impoverished by the loss of the talents, the faith, and the enthusiasm
of women in every area of its life. A whole new force can be
brought to bear on organized religion as women are allowed and
encouraged to be full partners. It is this concern for the health and
wholeness of religious bodies which is the basic motivation behind
raising the status of women.

THE RELATION BETWEEN RELIGION AND TRANSACTIONAL ANALYSIS

One of the unnecessary tensions in modern life is the one between
religion and the psychological sciences. To a large extent it stems
from mutual ignorance. The majority of "religious" people know
relatively little about psychology or psychiatry. Most of what they
know is gained from popular articles which stress the sensational.
While many of them have never read Freud, or gained any real
understanding of his theories and his work, they know he talked a
great deal about sex. Since this was a taboo subject in most
religious circles until recently, Freud was known to be a dangerous
and evil influence. And few religious people could name any figure
in the field of psychology except Freud! Therefore, psychology
was dangerous and obviously antireligious.

While one may laugh at the ignorance of religious people,
psychologists and psychiatrists often exhibit similar ignorance
about religion. Many of them, like the great majority of
Americans, formed ideas about religion in their childhood,
depending upon personal and family experiences. For some these
were pleasant impressions, often carried into adulthood in an
uncritical sentimentality. For others, impressions of religion were
negative — being forced to go to Sunday School, having religious
sanctions invoked against things they wanted to do, and developing feelings of guilt or fear in relation to God. Since many
people take little active part in religious activity after reaching
adolescence, they go through life judging religion by the impressions of their childhood. Some look upon religious belief and
practice as a harmless and pleasant activity for children or
immature adults, but of no concern to a busy, mature man or
woman. Others see it as a dangerous influence, burdening people

with unnecessary guilt, or giving them excuses not to work for a better life on earth. Many psychologists and psychiatrists can be found in these two groups.

Yet as increasing numbers in both fields are discovering, there is a close bond and great mutual interest between religion and psychology. Both are concerned primarily with people, and in helping people live constructive, satisfying, and worthwhile lives. There is growing rapport between many psychiatrists and clergymen as they learn to supplement one another's efforts to help individuals. Social, counseling, and educational psychology are making great contributions to religious bodies, and theological seminaries are welcoming psychiatrists as both students and teachers.

Perhaps because of this growing openness, but more likely because of its congruence with much in religious experience, transactional analysis* has caught the imagination of many clergymen and other religious leaders. Most religionists would probably agree that the formative factors in human life are relationships — a person's relation to himself, to his neighbor, and to God. While TA may not concern itself with the relationship to God, it throws a great deal of light on interpersonal relationships. [2]

Women's Attitudes Must Change

It is becoming increasingly clear as the women's liberation movement grows and develops, that women themselves are frequently the worst enemies of liberation. Most women have been taught, almost from birth, that they are inferior, incapable, and "born to lose." These are "feelings" growing out of early actions and reactions of other people, rather than conscious conclusions. TA helps to uncover the origin of these feelings in the child's early transactions with parents and other significant adults, and with other children. The qualities which make for "success" as it is usually understood in our culture — aggressiveness, self-assertion,

---

* Transactional analysis (TA) is a method of understanding human behavior developed by Dr. Eric Berne and publicized in his best seller, *Games People Play*. Popular books on TA include *I'm OK — You're OK* by Thomas Harris and *Born to Win: Transactional Analysis with Gestalt Experiments* by James and Jongeward.

self-confidence, daring — are in the scripts which boys are encouraged to follow, but not in the scripts for girls.

Women's liberation, as a movement to make life more satisfying for women and more constructive for the whole society, will be limited in its success until these basic feelings can be brought out, understood, and handled. There is little value in fighting for equal employment opportunities for women who are afraid of the world of work. And training women for leadership is difficult if they don't want to be leaders!

Traditions Hamper Growth

Because the world of religion deals with feelings, emotions, and long-held "beliefs," it is difficult to initiate change based on rational and objective arguments. This can be seen in many areas other than the role of women. As profound changes have come in the field of education, many religious groups cling to outmoded educational practices whose effectiveness has been clearly disproved. When research reveals that many people do not understand, and are turned away from, religion by incomprehensible forms of liturgy and worship, religious people strongly resist any change because of the emotional pull of the traditional forms. It may be possible to bring real change in the status of women in government, business, and education by passing laws and providing objective evidence regarding discrimination and regarding the abilities of women. But in the field of religion, change can come only when people are helped to understand the origins of their presuppositions and prejudices.

Transactional Analysis Helpful in Group Change

Deep-seated feelings and reactions have their origin in early childhood. Psychoanalysis can often help an individual slowly uncover the sources of his or her own irrational feelings and behavior. But psychoanalysis is too lengthy and too costly a process for the widespread change necessary if the social behavior of a whole system is to be altered. Transactional analysis offers a tool which can be readily understood by any intelligent adult. It lends itself to group study, and to group or individual application. Many religious organizations are beginning to use the concepts of TA in their educational programs and organizational life.

It becomes easy, for instance, to identify the danger of members of a congregation pressuring the priest, minister, or rabbi to play the constant Parent role. [3] And he is quite likely to yield to this pressure readily, since his training has pointed to this. Some psychologists suspect that a tendency to play the Parent may be a characteristic of persons who choose the ministry as a vocation. Similarly, every religious body is plagued by those with an undue need to play the Child. This can show itself in unwillingness to take responsibility, in overstress on one's own sin, guilt, or unworthiness, and constant need for reassurance. It can be seen in the people who leave a church or synagogue because they do not receive enough "stroking" in terms of a warm welcome and expressions of appreciation. It may, indeed, be that the very traditionalism and person-orientation of organized religion tends to foster exaggerated Parent and Child reactions, and to militate against the encouragement of Adult development.

If this is true, religious groups especially need the help of TA as they seek to minister to the needs of modern people. If a group of concerned women, or a clergyman, could introduce a study of transactional analysis as one tool for helping women better understand themselves and their role in the religious institution, the entire structure could benefit. The insights gained would inevitably spread to others, and more constructive ways of relating to men, youth, minority groups, and people of other faiths could be discovered. One minister uses *I'm OK – You're OK* [4] as a textbook for his confirmation class, preparing people for membership. He feels that one task of religion is to help a person become a responsible adult. Increasing numbers of adult study classes are turning to the Harris book or a book like *Born to Win* [5] as texts for reading and discussion.

Those who are seeking a more adequate place for women in organized religion are doing so not primarily for the sake of the women, but because religious institutions cannot be fully effective when half of their members are denied full adult status. In overcoming outmoded traditions, and the irrational fears and emotions which support them, religion may, in reality, begin to enable all people "to have life, and have it more abundantly."

REFERENCES

1. Church Women United, Room 812, 475 Riverside Drive, New York, New York 10027, did a study on this subject in 1969.

2. See Chapter 12 of Thomas A. Harris, *I'm OK — You're OK* (New York: Harper & Row, 1969).

3. See Muriel James and Dorothy Jongeward, *Born to Win* (Reading, Massachusetts: Addison-Wesley, 1971), Chapter 9.

4. Thomas A. Harris, *I'm OK — You're OK.*

5. See footnote 3.

BIBLIOGRAPHY

Berne, Eric. *Transactional Analysis in Psychotherapy* (New York: Grove Press, 1961).

Bird, Caroline. *Born Female* (New York: Simon and Schuster, 1964).

Bliss, Kathleen. *The Service and Status of Women in the Churches* (London: SCM Press, 1952).

Buber, Martin. *Between Man and Man* (New York: MacMillan, 1968).

Concerning the Ordination of Women (Geneva, World Council of Churches, 1964).

Culver, Elsie T. *Women in the World of Religion* (Garden City, New York: Doubleday, 1967).

Cunneen, Sally. *Sex: Female; Religion: Catholic* (New York: Holt, Rinehart and Winston, 1968).

Daly, Mary. *The Church and the Second Sex* (New York: Harper and Row, 1968).

Doely, Sara B., ed. *Women's Liberation and the Church* (New York: Association Press, 1970).

Gibson, Elsie. *When the Minister is a Woman* (New York: Holt, Rinehart and Winston, 1970).

Harris, Thomas A. *I'm OK — You're OK* (New York: Harper & Row, 1969).

James, Muriel and Dorothy Jongeward. *Born to Win* (Reading Massachusetts: Addison-Wesley, 1971).

Jourard, Sidney. *The Transparent Self* (Princeton, New Jersey: D. Van Nostrand, 1964).

Mead, Margaret and Frances Kaplan, eds. *American Women* (New York: Charles Scribner's Sons, 1965).

Stendahl, Krister. *The Bible and the Role of Women* (Philadelphia: Fortress Press, 1966).

6

WORKING BLACK WOMEN

by Sharon Tolbert-Stroud

Sharon Tolbert-Stroud is a Ph.D. candidate
in administration and organizational studies
at Stanford University (School of Education).
She received her A.B. from Canisius College
and her M.A. from State Teachers College,
Buffalo N.Y. Currently on leave from HEW, she
is an instructor at Golden Gate University,
teaching courses in sociology and woman's
studies. She has been a project director of a
multiculture Headstart program of 240 children; a counselor for a teen group at the
YWCA; and a teacher in grades Kg-8. She
developed the Upward Bound Program for
Canisius College.

Ms. Stroud received the Canisius College
Alpha Da Gamma award in 1973 (for significant community contributions) and a
Commissioners Citation (1973) for her work
with the Upward Mobility College and the
women's program while with HEW. She has
written numerous federal proposals and
studies and currently has several articles
dealing with women, and with the area of
upward mobility and career development, in
press.

Key Questions

1. How does the history of American black women differ from that of white women?

2. Where are black women working?

3. What are the myths that hamper black women?

4. Is it true that the black community is a matriarchy?

5. What are the special affirmative action needs of black women?

INTRODUCTION

Historically and traditionally, black women have occupied a role as a distinctive social force in American society. A factor affecting and shaping this role has been the black woman's contact with the white world, a contact which differed from that of the black man in scope and contact. This chapter will analyze social trends that have shaped black women's lives and have affected their profile in the labor force. Additionally, the focus will be on stereotypes, or myths, resulting from these social trends. Lastly, there will be suggested areas of affirmative action peculiar to the needs of black women.

BLACK WOMEN IN THE PAST

During the time of slavery, black women did not just work in the "field" as most black men did. Black women worked in the slave master's house as cook or maid, often assumed the role of "nanny" in the rearing of the master's wife's children, and frequently served as the master's concubine. The life and lot of even the female field slave differed from that of the male slave in the financial value put upon slave children and in the rewards given to successful motherhood in cash and kind.

Within the slave family the black woman was independent of the black male for support, because, imposed by the master's rule, she assumed a type of leadership in her family not found in the patriarchal family.

In the plantation domestic establishment, the woman's role was more important than that of her husband. The cabin was hers and the rations of corn and salt pork were issued to her. She cooked the meals, tended the vegetable patch, and often raised chickens to supplement the rations. If there was a surplus to sell, the money was hers. She made the clothes and reared the children. If the family received any special favors it was generally through her efforts. [1]

The black slave woman frequently fought tenaciously, though often unsuccessfully, against the master's rule and illicit relationship which not only exploited her, but as a whole, weakened the black family by not allowing the black male to support and protect his wife and children.

In spite of these historical forces, American slavery produced such sturdy black women as Lucy Terry, America's first black poet; Elleanor Eldridge, an amateur lawyer, Sojourner Truth, a great abolitionist lecturer; and, Harriet Tubman, the great "conductor" of the Underground Railroad.*

Traditionally, black women have had a distinctive social role in relation to white society. Because they were women, white society has considered them more docile and less of a threat than black men. White society has rewarded black women by allowing — or forcing — them into service in the white family. Black women, ever since slavery, have nursed and raised white children, attended white people in sickness, and kept white homes running smoothly. In fact, even today black women account for the majority of domestic workers. Even though it was only domestic or unskilled labor, the black woman (for the reasons mentioned) found it easier than the black man to obtain jobs with white employers. Consequently, not only has it been necessary, but under many circumstances and in many ways, the black woman has acted out the traditional roles of both female and male in the socioeconomic arena.

---

*   The first black in America to find expression in poetry was a slave girl named Lucy Terry (born around 1726). A few years later another slave girl, Phillis Wheatley, published a book of poems (1797) which received international recognition.

It is noteworthy that Elleanor Eldridge (1785-1845) actually sued her white creditor who had confiscated her house due to a $240 note (which her creditor raised to $2,500). Elleanor raised $2,500 and paid the "new" price of the note, and then extensively published this social wrong-doing.

Black women became lecturing agents for the anti-slavery societies and spoke at women's right's conventions as well. Many went south after the war to address the newly freed negroes about "things connected with the welfare of the race." The lectures of women like Sojourner Truth and Francis Watkins Harper were pitched to the same key of sound morality, although the one, an ex-slave, and the other, a free black woman, came from vastly different backgrounds.

Harriet Tubman (1821-1913) had the goal of bringing hundreds out of slavery; beyond this she was head of the Intelligence Service in the Department of the South throughout the Civil War. She is the only American woman to lead both black and white troops on the field of battle, as she did in the Department of the South. She was with John Brown in his plans for his raid on Harper's Ferry. She was a compelling and stirring orator in the councils of the Abolitionists. In the underground-railroad period, she was ever in motion, guiding her charges along the escape routes from the South, or ministering to the needs of escaped slaves, or "conspiring" with Abolitionists of every political hue.

As a result of this dual role, we have seen in recent years (but well before the onstart of the Women's Liberation Movement) the names of daring black women leap from the front pages of our daily newspapers. Autherine Lucy, Rosa Parks, Daisy Bates, Vivian Malone and Gloria Richardson are but a few of many who have at various times become the focus of heated controversy. In most instances, their claim to front-page coverage followed their defiance of some aspect of institutionalized discrimination or segregation in areas where these practices were accorded the status of "divine law."

Another index depicting the black woman's role as a distinct social force in America is seen in her status relationship. "When the black female is viewed as 'Blacks among Blacks' she has higher status within the racial group than do white women in white society." [2] This paradox exists because white society has economically pitted black women against black men; yet it has also reserved the lowest status and lowest paid jobs in white society for black women.

Thus historical and traditional forces have tended to make the black female different from women of other races in America. Her history is particularly different from that of the prototypical white woman, and her present day behavioral patterns have evolved out of her historical experiences. Consequently she is described as more aggressive, independent, and nonconforming than white women. The most immediate effects of her independence and unusual resiliency are reflected in her stance and numbers in the labor force.

BLACK WOMEN IN THE LABOR FORCE

Most labor force analyses compare the economic status and educational attainments of black women with those of black men. A more useful comparison in understanding the black woman's social-force role is to analyze her labor-force participation in relation to that of the prototypical American woman, the white woman.

The United States Department of Commerce census reported there were more than seven million black women 18 years of age and over in this country in 1970. Of these, 56% were working compared to 49% of white women of the same age group. Among women in the age group 25 to 34 years, black women represented 58% compared with 43% of white women in the labor force. While black women accounted for less than 11% of all women 16 years of age and over in the population, they represented nearly 14% of all woman workers. [3]

It is somewhat of a paradox that black women experienced severe unemployment in 1970. The rate for those 16 years and over was 9.3%; for white women in the same age category it was 5.4%. Black teenage girls, particularly, experienced severe unemployment. Their rate was 34.4%, compared to white teenage girls whose rate of unemployment was 13.3%.

As for black working mothers in the labor force, 62% of them had children 6 to 17 years of age, and 47% had children under 6 years of age. Among white mothers, the comparable figures were 50% and 30%. Moreover, more than 28% of black families were headed by women compared to less than 10% of white families.

Among the families headed by a woman who worked full time the year around, the incidence of poverty was six times greater for blacks than for white families. The labor force participation rate for black married mothers and those of other marital status (widowed, divorced, and spouse absent) were roughly comparable. On the other hand, white mothers with husbands present had a much lower labor force participation rate than those of other marital status. [4]

In 1970 the median yearly earnings of black women was less than 79% of that of white women.

Table 1. Median Earnings 1970

White men	White women	Black men	Black women
$7,859	$3,640	$5,237	$2,684

Not only are black women as a group the lowest paid of all workers in the nation, but a greater percentage of black women than white women work after they are married and after they have children. Black women work more years of their lives than white women and, lastly, their unemployment rate is greater. In fact, on all levels that can be statistically counted — wages, income, health, life expectancy, and upward mobility — black women rank lowest in society. [5]

Usually there is a direct relationship between the educational attainment of women and their labor force participation. This does not appear to be true for black women. The absence of opportunities for black women in the middle-range jobs has made it necessary for black families to develop different employment expectations and educational goals from those of white families. Black families that could do so have often educated their daughters rather than sons, since it could be expected that girls would have to work most or all of their lives. [6] Hence, until recently, 60% of the college degrees awarded American blacks were received by black women. [7]* As stated, there were few semiskilled or middle-range jobs available to black women; therefore the only hope for a black woman to escape the unskilled and domestic service job trap was in getting an education.

Despite this, black women today are found in greatest numbers in the unskilled and semiskilled occupations. In 1966, 76% of all black women workers were employed in service jobs, domestic work, and farm and factory work (for white women the figure was 37%). Only 8% of all black women were in professional occupations (14% for white women) and 12% were in middle-range or saleswomen jobs (34% for white women). [8] Thus contrary to popular belief, black women actually need more education than white women to get the middle-range jobs, and they usually get paid less for the same work.

Both groups, white women and black women, were denied access to equal educational opportunities in professional education and advancement. But, professional education was denied longer to black women than to white women, and, as a result, black and white women moved into the professions at different paces. In fact, it was only through the Civil Rights Movement of the 1950's that greater educational opportunities became available for blacks, both male and female.

The results are seen in the 1960 census. This report shows there were 487 black female physicians, representing 9.7% of all

---

*   Through the steady improvement in educational level attained for the entire black population, the educational gap between black men and black women is fast closing.

black physicians, while the 14,031 white female physicians represented only 6.4% of all white physicians. The 222 black women lawyers and judges were 9.1% of all blacks in the profession, as against the 6,898 white women lawyers and judges representing 3.3% of white in the profession. There were 94,606 black women teachers. Among these, female elementary school teachers were 84.5% of all blacks in the profession (86% among whites) and the secondary school teachers were 54.5% (46.6% among whites). Black women make up 62.6% of all black social workers.

These figures indicate that the greater "visibility" of females among black professionals may relate to the fact that black women, whether married or not, are of necessity more likely to work than are white women. Black families raise their daughters to accept work or a career as a natural part of their lives; work to them, then, is not a liberating goal but rather an imposed lifelong necessity. The reality of this training may actually make black women better equipped for the demands of a professional career than are most white women in whom career demands often set up role conflict and uncertainty as to their femininity.

In summary, the black woman's historical and traditional contact with the white world has been a significant social trend in shaping her role. Additionally, this contact made her the interpreter and intermediary of the white culture in the black home. The effect of this social trend can be measured by her number and stance in the labor force — black women struggling in partnership with their men to keep the black family together and to allow the black community to survive. This dual and often conflicting role has imposed great tensions on black women and has given them unusual strength.

Paradoxically, this strength is described in the social and traditional description of black women: independent, liberated, free-thinking, goal-oriented, aggressive; yet, in reality, black women are the most powerless group in our society. In fact, in no area of life has the black woman ever been allowed to attain higher levels or even equal levels of status with white women. Indeed, the black woman has played a distinct, though ambiguous, social role in America. Perhaps because this role *is* ambiguous, she is often hampered through myths and stereotypes.

THE MYTH OF A BLACK AND WHITE ALLIANCE IN WOMEN'S LIBERATION

Women's liberation is a common
alliance for black women and
white women alike as they
resist a common oppressor.

To understand this myth, we need to look at black women in a different way. True, black and white women are oppressed, but the nature of the oppression is extremely different for each group. The historical interdependence of black and white women was nowhere more clearly evident than in the complex relationship of a white woman and her black slave. In fact, the very existence of the family style of the white woman was founded on the economic and physical exploitation of the slaves. The white woman's oppression was shaped by traditions and customs in a system that had a definite "place for women" (white women), while the oppression of the slave woman was more direct, more brutal, and without redeeming features. The black woman was exploited as a worker, as a breeder of slaves, and as a sex object for white men.

Despite the formal end of slavery, many features of the oppression of black women have remained unchanged.

No black woman could remain unaffected by the difference between *her* status as a woman and that of the white woman as a woman. Carolyn Rodgers, writer and professor at Washington State University expresses the sentiments of many black women:

The feminist movement is one of middle-class white women. Of course these are women whose humanity has been destroyed by their husbands, their fathers, their sons. White women who are housewives have been allowed to remain girls, while the black "girl" taking care of the house was indeed the woman. White women have been do-nothing dolls and one gathers now that they want to be white men or something else. White women with their private schools and summer camps and nursemaids for their children, and mechanical kitchens, want some satisfaction in being a woman. Black women are affected by some of the stereotypes that white women experience but these are minor irritations when we compare them with our greatest problem — that of being one of American apartheid. [9]

Black women have been nearly unanimous in their insistence that their own emancipation cannot be separated from the emancipation of their men. Their liberation depends on the liberation of the race and the improvement of the life of the black community. Black women have shown the pride and strength of a people who have endured and survived great oppression. This has given them a sense of their own function in life and a strong confidence in their own worth. Indeed, black women lose nothing by their greater tenacity — and that tenacity historically has been a source of strength in the black community, particularly to the black man. As one woman put it, "the black woman must take her place not behind or in front of the black man but beside, and together they must strive for the freedom of the black race." In other words, there can be no liberation of black women until black men — all black people — are free.

Thus if sisterhood between black and white women is ever to be attained, it must be based on an understanding of and a recognition of the differences in experiences, expectations, and self-definition of the two groups. Above all, it must be based on understanding and eradicating the persistent prevalence of racism as it victimizes black women and, despite the best efforts of individuals, benefits white women. [10]

THE MYTH OF THE BLACK MATRIARCHY

The black woman is responsible
for the black community being
organized along matriarchal lines.

The concept of a black matriarchy was strengthened by the Moynihan Report released in 1965. [11] Moynihan's central thesis proposed that:

1. The black family is crumbling and that the blame lies with the black matriarchy extant in the black community.

2. The black matriarchy is responsible for the low educational achievement of black males.

3. Twenty-five percent of all black families' households in the black communities have a female head which is an index of a matriarchal society.

If we examine this myth, we see that Moynihan's contentions do not hold up under scrutiny. Moynihan's first contention is based on studies that document the higher educational level of black females (quoted earlier in the chapter) in comparsion to black males. He overlooks the fact that many black males were forced to terminate their formal education early in order to help support their families. Also, since black males could not get jobs, why should they pursue higher education?

Proof that we were dealing with functional adaptation to discrimination patterns in the mainstream culture rather than the "matriarchy myth" can be found in the changing educational level of black males. As employment opportunities opened, the educational gap between black males and black females practically closed. The 1967 labor force statistics show that black men now stay in school as long as black women.

Moynihan's second issue fails totally to consider the effects on the black male of a white educational system with its often racist teachers. That black females were socialized differently from black males in regard to white culture and society, and thus did not experience the same degree of educational failure as the black male, supports the argument that the system (white educational system) must bear responsibility for the failure of black males to reach acceptable educational levels by white standards.

In his third proof of the matriarchal family, Moynihan fails to consider a basic and central point. Whom do these black female household heads (25%) have control over? Since his reference is to fatherless black homes, these black female heads cannot be controlling black men. Nor does Moynihan speak to the real problem or effect in this issue, which is, while there is nothing inherently wrong with a woman heading a family, the problem arises when she tries to compete in a society which promotes, expects, and rewards male leadership. Consequently, the woman is unable to bring to her family the share of economic and social rewards received by father-headed households. Combine this issue with the social and inherent problem of racial discrimination, and we readily account for the labor force statistics about black families that are headed by women: the incidence of poverty is six times greater for black than for white families.

Moreover, although the unemployment rate of black males is higher than that of white males, only a minority of black families with both parents present are dependent on the mother for their maintenance. Thus we question the report's logic to assume that black females who in 1960 earned an annual wage of $2,372 a year (white women earned $3,410), as compared to black males who earned $3,789, had an economic advantage over any group in this society. [12]

A fact of enormous importance to the discussion of the black woman as a matriarch is the whole discussion of black population as it effects marriage and family life. The 1960 census figure showed an excess of 648,000 black women over black men. More than a half million of these were 14 years and over. Consider specifically the marriage and family life years of 25 to 44 which has a ratio of 88 black men per 100 black women. These statistics indicate that black women have a difficult time finding a black mate for marriage. Many a black male's shortcomings must be tolerated for the choice of marriage and companionship. Thus this low sex ratio hardly allows black women to exercise any meaningful control over black men.

Lastly, referring to black women as matriarchs is in contradiction to the reality of their status and is also replete with historical and semantic inaccuracies. J.J. Bachofen in his study first uses the term "matriarchy." [13] His understanding, coupled with Margaret Mead's definition, is that a matriarchy is a society in which some, if not all, of the legal powers relating to the ordering and governing of the family over property, inheritance, and marriage are lodged in women rather than men. [14] If we accept and predicate on this definition, then the consensus of most historians is that "men reign dominant in all societies; no matriarchy (society ruled by women) is known to exist." [15] Thus the myth of a black matriarchy is unfounded and does not hold up under scrutiny.

THE MYTH OF THE BLACK WOMAN'S JOB ADVANTAGE

*Black women have an advantage
over black men in securing
employment.*

One often hears the comment "black women have had their share" — meaning, of course, that black women have an "advantage" over black men because they supposedly can secure employment more readily.

Unemployment statistics disprove this commonly held belief. The unemployment rates for 1966 and 1969 were as follows:

	1966	1969
Black men	6.6%	3.7%
Black women	8.8%	6.0%

Unemployment among black women increased sharply from 1969 to 1970. The rate for all those 16 and over rose to 9.3%. Black teenage girls experienced especially severe unemployment in 1970; their rate of 34.4% was nearly 1 1/2 times that of black teenage boys.

However one interprets the causal factors, one thing is clear: unemployment is more severe among black women than among any other group in the population.

AFFIRMATIVE ACTION AND THE NEEDS OF BLACK WOMEN

The establishment of an affirmative action program in an organization or company usually has two phases. The first phase is the need to demonstrate to the organization or company that a pattern of discrimination exists. The second phase translates stated goals into a plan of action and implementation.

The focus has been mainly (though indirectly) on the first phase of an affirmative action program in the discussion of the American societal pattern of discrimination to which the black woman is subjected; that is, she is economically exploited, politically invisible, unfairly maligned as a matriarch, etc.

This section, focusing on the second phase of affirmative action programs, will suggest areas of consideration that meet the special needs of black women. I propose that these needs are a result of historical and traditional social forces.

In the translation of affirmative action goals into a plan of action and implementation, consider the following:

1. *Don't bank on the old myth "black women have had their share (of jobs)!"*

   Look at your organization and see if it doesn't follow the pattern of most other American organizations, companies, and government agencies in regard to the employment of black women. Black women are usually concentrated in low-grade, low-status, or clerical jobs. There may be an "only" (or very few) at mid-level or mid-range positions. Look again and count the number of white women having higher-status and higher-paying jobs than black women. Take the next step and eliminate cultural or racial bias so more black women (with experience and education comparable to the white women in higher-paying jobs) may reach higher-status, higher-paying, and executive-level positions.

2. *Do be sure black female employees are aware and schooled in how to play the* informal *as well as* formal *rule game!*

Many organizations, companies, and government agencies evaluate and promote employees on peculiar informal rules. Because the "informal-rule game" often has subtle dominant cultural overtones, the black female employee may not even understand or interpret its significance in promotion practices.

3. *Do provide low-cost day-care programs or a financial subsidy for child care.*

Black women would benefit particularly from day care because of the number of black women concentrated in low-paying jobs. Additionally, 28% of all black homes are headed by a mother, and the majority of these household heads are in the labor force at low-status, low-paying jobs.

4. *Do be objective in performance evaluations.*

Take into account, though, the historical and traditional differences in the black woman and the prototypical white woman. The black woman may be more aggressive, active, nonconforming, and liberated. And, it is somewhat unrealistic to want her to match the image of the passive, white, middle-class "lady" who knows her place.

5. *Do be aware that the black labor force was never fully employed and that black women represent the highest percentage of unemployed in the American economy.*

Presently the black labor force, and particularly the female portion, may be driven into greater unemployment as white women converge at every level on an already dwindling job market. Additionally, in the struggle for jobs black women not only experience sexual discrimination, but also experience racial discrimination and are severely exploited as the lowest-paid workers and the highest rate of unemployed workers.

6. *Don't support "Miss Company," "Miss Beauty," or "Miss Whatever" contest in which the selection standards that prevail are those built around the culture of the white, feminine American woman.*

One of the most invidious ways in which racism and sexism functions together is in the idealization of white female beauty. Not only does this rob black women of their natural dignity, but it makes them victims of a special form of oppression that has several dimensions. First, the black woman must bear the burden of black skin in a white system. Second, she is female in a culture oriented to male dominance. Furthermore, black women may experience a very special mental brutalization because they are "black women" instead of "white women" in a white European-American culture that as a matter of course designates females as the "fair sex" with such associations as fair sex implies: light, white, clean, beautiful, smooth, gracious, honest. Where does this leave the black woman when a company, organization, or government agency supports such programs or contests?

7. *Do be aware that the black woman can be a bridging and untapped resource for organizations, companies, and government agencies that through affirmative action remedy their sex and race employment problems.*

Not only is this a positive affirmative action measure but this suggestion touches the severe economic problem of black women — they have the highest rate of unemployment, they are concentrated in low-status (90% of all domestics are black women) and low-paying jobs, and they are the majority of women in the work force.

Lastly, these "do's and don'ts" effectively packaged in an affirmative action plan of an organization (company or government agency) can begin to make a significant and positive difference in the black woman's role in America.

Editors' Note

Referring back to Chapters 1 and 2, you can see much of the scripting that is unique to black women in America. While white women and other minority women tend to learn to feel not-OK because they are women, this is not so with black women. Historically, a black woman's sex gave her what little power and status she had. The cultural scripting for black women teaches them to feel not-OK because they are black, not because they are women. The larger culture, however, has judged them as not-OK both because they are black and because they are women. As a result of this, they often suffer a degrading double bind.

Also we would like to suggest that you think over the possibility that it is indeed true that overcoming the oppression of black men is essential if black women are to take their rightful place in society as well as in organizations. However, in a sense, this is also true of white men — not necessarily in the economic arena but all too frequently in terms of emotional development, creativity, and mental and physical health. Unless white men are able to liberate themselves from fixed roles, especially in their stance with women, it will be difficult for white women to be able to shed the bonds of unrealistic servitude to archaic attitudes.

An unrealistic bondage to past assumptions inhibits the growth and the expression of full potential of any individual or group. And so the liberation of all women does hinge on the liberation of men.

REFERENCES

1. Maurine Davie, *Negroes In American Society* (New York: McGraw-Hill, 1949) p. 207. Reprinted by permission.

2. Gerda Lerner, ed. *Black Women in White America* (New York: Pantheon Books, Random House, 1972) p. 15. Reprinted by permission.

3. U.S. Department of Labor, Employment Standards Administration, and Women's Bureau, "Facts on Woman Workers of Minority Races," 1970.

4. *Ibid.* All figures in the preceding section are based on this report.

5. Linda J.M. LaRue, "Black Liberation and Women's Lib," *Transaction* **8** (November/December, 1970): 59.

6. Whitney Young, *To Be Equal* (New York: McGraw-Hill, 1964) p. 25.

7. Jean Noble, *The Negro Woman College Graduate* (New York: Columbia University Press, 1956) p. 64.

8. U.S. Department of Labor, Bureau of Labor Statistics, 1966.

9. Helen H. King, "The Black Woman and Women's Liberation," *Ebony* **26**, No. 5 (March 1971): 75. Reprinted by permission of *Ebony* Magazine, copyright 1971 by Johnson Publishing Company, Inc.

10. Gerda Lerner, "Black Liberation — Woman's Liberation: A Study in Ambivalence and Tension." (Unpublished paper presented at the 55th annual meeting of the American Council of Education, Miami Beach, Florida, October 6, 1972.)

11. Daniel Patrick Moynihan, *The Negro Family: The Case for National Action* (United States Department of Labor, 1965).

12. United States Census of Population Report, 1960.

13. J.J. Bachofen, *Das Mutterrecht Stuttgart*, 1861.

14. Margaret Mead, *Male and Female* (New York: William Morrow, 1949) p. 301.

15. William J. Goode, *The Family* (New Jersey: Prentice-Hall, 1964) p. 14.

7

A STRATEGY FOR CHANGE

by Pat King

Patricia King received her A.B. degree at the
College of St. Elizabeth, New Jersey. She has
worked in the business world for nine years.
While head of personnel research at a large
New York City bank, she identified the need for
an affirmative action program for women. With
several women in the company giving her their
advice and support, she established a successful
program much like the one she describes in this
chapter. She has since left the bank and is
working as a consultant and free-lance writer.
She lives in New York City.

Key Questions:

1. Where do I start to change things?

2. What are the facts you need to know about women in your organization?

3. Why set goals? And how?

4. How can you gain top level support for the program?

5. What steps will implement the program from top down?

6. How do you measure progress?

We now discuss how, by working on the inside, one gets an organization to respond in meaningful ways to women's (and government's) demands. We are dealing with the mechanics of an affirmative action program, not with the necessary (and more complicated) awareness issues. I'm going to describe the steps in "how to" terms with the hope that others will get some ideas or inspiration from what I write. Following these steps in order may not necessarily work. I have covered the process, but I have worked much of it out as I went along, and my action was not always logical and measured.

STEP 1.   GETTING INTO POSITION

To work with an organization meaningfully and profitably, you need to know the organization well, especially the key people in it. You need to be able to substantiate your arguments so that they will appeal to the person you're trying to convince. You also need to know the laws — Federal, state, and city — on equal opportunity for women. The Equal Employment Opportunity Commission (EEOC) publishes guidelines on the subject, and you should make sure you have the latest ones. The commission revises the guidelines from time to time when court decisions are made that effect interpretation of the law.

The information about your company that you need in order to argue your case for a program to upgrade women into higher-level jobs is usually available in the personnel department. Depending on the company, it may be easy or difficult to compile. (In some places you can use a computer to help you in working with personnel files and salary records.) If you are already in the personnel department or a related area, you can probably compile enough data on your own to support your argument for in-depth research into the subject.

Depending on your situation, you have either lots of data available to you (in which case go to step 2), or you have a little data available to you that you put together as best you can. If the latter, find (using government requirements) what troubles (law suits, etc.) have occurred in other industries. With this information and the data you have about your company, you may be able to convince the personnel director or industrial relations manager that the situation within the company should be more thoroughly researched. You will probably get permission if you keep your questions on a research basis.

Once you get access to the data, you have to know what to look for.

STEP 2. WHAT TO RESEARCH

Nearly every large company is required to file an EEO-1 report with the Federal government each year. These reports provide the basic data which will give you the following:

1. Percentage of women in the company,

2. Percentage of management (or professional or technical) jobs held by women, and

3. Percentage of women in the company who are managers compared with the percentage of men who are managers.

This will give you a picture of the company as it now stands. In making a case for a program to effect change, it is a good idea to get some trend data, using the past EEO reports and projecting for the future. A chart of a trend may look something like this:

Trends in Employment of Women at Y, Inc.*

	Actual					Projected		
	1968	1969	1970	1971	1972	1973	1974	1975
% women employees	28%	30%	31%	32%	32%	33%	34%	36%
% women managers	1%	1%	2%	2%	3%	3%	4%	5%
% women technicians or professionals	8%	10%	11%	11%	12%	13%	14%	15%

*Fictitious data

I call this kind of analysis (depending on the figures) "30 years to nondiscrimination." This means that if the same rate continues for 30 years, there will be no discrimination.

Salary information — even if it gives general, average salaries — usually has an impact. When comparing salary figures (or any figures), it is best to use the data on women as a base. For instance, if the average salary for men is $200 per week and the average salary for women is $150, one can say that either women on the average make 25% less than men or men make 33 1/3% more than women. For our purposes, the latter statement is clearly superior. (It is not cheating to do it this way. Always using male data as the basis is another manifestation of the male orientation of society.)

In looking at salary information, it is important to look also at length of service. Considering some of the myths about how long women remain on the job, you may have to show the salary discrepancies by pointing out the usually lower pay of women with longer service compared with the pay of men in the same job.

Myths

To counteract myths, you will want to collect data to use, not as part of a formal report or presentation, but in answer to probable questions. (There are arguments — such as the EEOC guidelines on sex-discrimination — against using these myths as excuses not to hire, train, or place women in responsible jobs, but what I am talking about here are ways to *use data* to counterargue the points. In my experience the manager who needs convincing responds better to data and statistics than to philosophy or government requirements.) The following are the myths I have heard most often.

The turnover rate for women is higher than it is for men.

This may or may not be true. If it is a small difference, you should do a test of significance to make sure there is a *real* difference. Even statistically significant differences, however, can be deceptive. In one study, it was found that although the overall rate of turnover was ten percentage points higher for women than for men, it really depended on job level, not on sex. In this situation, the higher-level jobs, which had very low turnover rates, were filled predominantly by men. The lower-level jobs, which had very high turnover rates, were filled predominantly by women. There was no significant difference within each level between the rates for men and the rates for women. (This might not be the case in another company, but it is an example of how one can explode old myths by delving more deeply into the data.)

Women only get pregnant and leave.

There are a couple of ways to counterargue the business risk here.

1. The overall percentage of women who resign because they are pregnant may be so low that simply stating it may show how negligible a factor it really is.

2. There are comparisons which can be made with military service, or with the combination of women who leave to go to other jobs and those who leave to have children (which is another job, really, even though society attaches more status to "productive" jobs in the economy) compared to the number of men who leave to seek other jobs.

Things are getting so much better for women here without a special program that we don't really need one.

The trend data described above may show that this is not the case. The trend may show some improvement, but it will probably not be in all areas where improvement is necessary.

The data that has been described in Step 2 is aimed at convincing management that a program is necessary. Even if management doesn't need convincing, it may be a good idea to compile this data anyway. You may want to have it in working with individual managers in the company. In any case, you will need some of it for Step 3 — setting goals.

STEP 3. SETTING GOALS

There are many pros and cons about goal setting and whether or not goals become quotas or lead to reverse discrimination, but in any business situation, specific goals are usually a way of getting things moving and are a yardstick against which to measure progress. And, of course, Revised Order No. 4 requires that goals be set. In setting goals, Revised Order No. 4 says an employer should consider the following five factors.

1. The size of the female unemployment force in the labor area surrounding the facility

2. The percentage of the female workforce compared with the total workforce in the immediate area

3. The general availability of women having requisite skills in the immediate area

4. The availability of women with requisite skills in the area among whom the contractor can reasonably recruit

5. The availability of women seeking employment in the labor or recruitment area of the contractor

There are also some internal factors to consider. If you are talking about placing women in jobs that are usually filled by hiring people from outside the company, you need to know how many such jobs will open up (through turnover or expansion) in, say, the next three years. (If you set three- or five-year goals, you should set "milestones" in between. If you don't have specific targets for each year in between, a five-year goal can mean four more years of discrimination.)

Once you know the number of jobs that will become available and the percentage of women in the labor pool available for that job, it is easy to estimate a goal. If there is no discrimination, people will be hired in the same proportion in which they are represented in the labor pool. An example follows.

Of the present sales force of 1000, a certain insurance company employs only eight women. The company usually hires liberal arts college graduates for these jobs right after graduation. Graduates of the local colleges who are seeking employment in business are 40% women. The annual rate of turnover in this job is 10%. Over the next three years the company expects to expand the force by 90 people, or 30 people each year. In that three-year period, therefore, 390 jobs will open up. If 40% of these go to women, there will be 156 additional, or a total of 164 women in this sales force. The number 164 would be a reasonable goal for this job over the next three years. In setting milestones for the intervening years, one would have to consider training time. Progress toward the goal may be slow the first year, but may pick up after that.

This is a very simplified example, of course. Usually, it is more difficult to calculate, particularly in figuring out the representation of women in the labor pool.

In setting goals for jobs into which present employees are promoted, as is the case with most supervisory and management jobs, things are a little more complicated. Again, nondiscrimination would mean that people would be promoted in the same proportions in which they are found in the next lowest-level job. If no women are getting the management jobs, there are two possible reasons. One, they progress up the career ladder to the job one step below manager, but never make that final step or two; they never get hired into the managerial "pipeline." If the former is the case, goals can be set as in the example above, using the proportion of men and women in the job just below manager and the number of managerial jobs you expect to fill in the defined time period. If the second situation exists, there are other steps to take. First, of course, is to start bringing women into the career ladder at the entry level. Goals should be set for that. Second, bring women with experience into the company or transfer them from other areas into the higher-level jobs on the career ladder.

In my experience, business people have set these kinds of goals with a great deal of trepidation, wondering how government compliance officers will view them. Government officials have not published any hard and fast rules for goal setting, but the officials I have talked to seem to have been looking for a logical approach that would lead to real change. One wants movement in the right direction, but if the goals are too easy, there will be too little movement. If the goals are unattainable, they will be ignored. The best goals are those that are attainable but have to be reached for.

STEP 4. GETTING SUPPORT FOR THE PROGRAM

We now consider how to persuade a bureaucratic organization to move on affirmative-action goals by using the bureaucratic structure. There are ways to gain support for such a program by using techniques of management awareness that have been developed in recent years. The first step, however, is to have the goals accepted as part of the corporate objective — not just have them written into an affirmative-action document (which is easy since the law requires that they be there.) We have seen that, depending on the corporation, having goals in the affirmative-action program does not necessarily mean that effort will be expanded to achieve them. (If support is not gained at a high level, it is best to work toward having the goals written into the affirmative-action program and getting as many managers as will listen to work with you. Progress under those circumstances is slower and more sporadic, but it is better than nothing.)

The best way to achieve goals, given the bureaucratic nature of most organizations, is to get top management to adopt them as corporate policy and fold them into the corporate planning process in the same way that earnings and sales goals are. Managers will be appraised on how well they achieve these goals in the way they are appraised on how well they achieve profit goals. Of course, to get as much power behind the goals as possible would be to have them accepted by the chairman or president of the company. In true "chain of command" style, you can work your way up, beginning with your boss, then going to your boss's boss, etc. At each step you need to gear your presentation to the person you are talking to, and more or less refer to the following topics.

1. The waste of resources (by not fully utilizing the talents and knowledge of women on the staff)

2. Missed opportunities (by not hiring women — "In looking for all the talent we need, why are we looking in only half the population?")

3. The government's requirements

4. The risk of loss due to law suits

5. The risk of bad publicity or consumer boycott

These topics should be backed up by the data described previously, followed by a list of goals and a statement of what you think the next step should be. At each step, of course, you ask for permission to go to the next level.

In organizations where there is already a high level of concern over this problem, the process should be easy. The lower the level of concern, the more difficult and time consuming the process. When you get to the chief executive, describe your implementation plans and ask for the authority to carry them out.

STEP 5. STARTING DOWN THE CHAIN OF COMMAND

Volumes have been written on how to motivate people to achieve goals. The most productive ones seem to me to be those which say that people are more interested in achieving goals when they help set them. Everyone can make suggestions, and when the goals are decided at the top, they can be carried down the organization and managers at each level can be given a chance to accept them and work out the details themselves. In carrying the goals down, it is best to make sure that managers realize that these are corporate goals, that they are not personal goals nor the personnel or labor relations expert's idea of what would be "nice."

One way to work toward goals is to use team meetings. A team is a group composed of the boss and the people who report directly to him or her.* Once the chairman or president has accepted the corporate goals, ask him to call a meeting of all managers who report directly to him. At the meeting, he can present the goals. It is essential that the chief executive positively state that the authority of his office is behind the goals.

Next, each of the second-level managers should call a meeting with his subordinates and present the goals. Continue the meetings step by step down through the organization (be prepared to spend a lot of time and energy) to the first-level supervisor. By the first-level supervisor, I mean the lowest organizational level with authority to make decisions about hiring, firing, promotions, and raises. You will work with these supervisors in planning and organizing the details of the program. They will know more about the way to implement action in their areas than anyone else, and your role with them should be that of consultant. Be sure, though, that whatever the methods of implementation are, you have a fairly easy way to measure progress.

STEP 6. KEEPING TRACK OF WHAT'S HAPPENING

Periodically, you will want to check and see what progress is being made. This should be done at least once a calendar quarter. General signs to watch would include the number of women in

---

*   The masculine pronoun will be used to mean both men and women in the rest of the article.

training programs and job-rotation programs. How you mark progress more specifically will depend on how goals are divided across the company. There are two ways of doing this.

1. *Mathematically proportioned goals.* Where your goal is to place or promote women into jobs that cross divisional lines, and where all divisions are starting from the same point with about the same circumstances (geography, growth, avail-ability, etc.), you may want to proportion your goals. For example, if the group-life division of the insurance company we used as an example earlier employs 5% of the sales force of 1000, they would be expected to account for 5% of the goal.

   Monitoring progress here is relatively easy and can probably be done by following the numbers of people in various job categories, using a computer printout.

2. *Progress according to potential.* What is meant by "progress according to potential" is that the current situation and potential for promoting women into more responsible jobs differs substantially from division to division.

   I suspect this will be the case in many firms, particularly where they are geographically dispersed. In this instance, you may want to begin by setting divisional goals with managers, and adding these together to make the corporate goals. Or, once the corporate goals are set and meetings with managers held, ask managers to set their own goals and add them together. If their goals don't meet the corporate goals, go back to the managers who seem to be in a position to do more, and renegotiate their goals.

With either of these choices, the individual managers become more involved in the process, which is good. It does, however, require more time and effort coordinating the process. If you proportion goals according to potential, you will want to monitor the progress of each division toward its goal. You should also be aware of women who have limited opportunities in one area, who would have a better chance of advancement if they transferred to another division.

MINORITY WOMEN

In all that you do in working for affirmative action for women, you must be aware of the special problems of minority women. The discrimination that a minority woman suffers is twofold — she is in a minority and she is a woman. There has been much discussion about how to handle this particular problem. My own feeling is that the status of minority women should be researched separately in the same way as that described for all women. Such a step would give you an idea of the dimensions of the problem. If it is acute, as it is in many companies, you might want to set separate goals for minority women.

FINAL THOUGHTS

For some people, expecially men whose concept of their own masculinity is closely tied up with success in business, and women who have forfeited being "feminine" to "make it in a man's world," the issue is emotionally charged. It is important to avoid polarization with such people.

You will find the reactions of some people to be out of proportion to the event or task at hand. If the only women to be promoted to management levels in the past have been far superior to their male counterparts, equality of opportunity for women will be assessed in a narrow way. Women may say the standards are lowered because new women managers don't have the high qualifications that previously promoted women showed. Men may say it is reverse discrimination.

Be prepared to handle these accusations calmly, understanding the threat that is felt by those who make them. After all, the eventual goal is for men and women to be able to work together.

8

OH! THE OBSTACLE TO WOMEN IN MANAGEMENT

by Saundra Daddio

Ms. Saundra L. Daddio, a graduate of Purdue University, is currently a senior training representative in the Manpower Planning and Development Division of the Consolidated Edison Company of New York. She began her business career as an executive trainee with Gimbel Brothers, Inc. in Pittsburgh, Pennsylvania. During her association with Gimbels, Ms. Daddio served as a training supervisor, research assistant, and director of Training and Development. She also served as the manager of Support Services for the National Alliance of Businessmen, and as such was the first female executive to be "loaned" to N.A.B. from the business community.

In the course of her professional career, Ms. Daddio has developed management programs for Dun-Donnelly Publications, a subsidiary of Dun and Bradstreet; taught management courses at the University of Pittsburgh, Robert Morris College, and Allegheny Community College; and conducted programs for various business, industrial, and professional associations concerning the role of women within organizational settings.

In recognition of her outstanding contribution to the Pittsburgh community through training,

Ms. Daddio received the 1971 Individual Achievement Award in the area of public service from the American Society for Training and Development.

Ms. Daddio is a member of the American Management Association, the American Society for Training and Development, the Purdue Alumni Association, and the W.I.L.L. Institute of New York.

Key Questions

1. Organizational homogeneity (OH), what does it mean to organizations and women?

2. How do the following patterns hold women back?

   The visibility system?

   The property-value system?

   The sponsor-protégé system?

   The legal system?

3. How can people identify, confront, and adjust to these systems?

Like creatures in the animal world, organizations have a drive for self-preservation. In the business world this drive is realized through a phenomenon called "Organizational Homogeneity." [1] Cutting through its textbook sound, OH simply says: Certain people, because of race, sex, age, or some other non-job-related characteristic *must* be excluded from executive positions. Such people are seen as unacceptable and it is not considered "good business" to allow them to hold various leadership positions within the company. In some instances, it is not even "good business" to employ them in *any* capacity.

Naturally, management has devised elaborate rationalizations to justify these exclusions. And once the theory of organizational homogeneity takes hold at top managerial levels, it covertly and sometimes unconsciously filters down until its impact is felt at all managerial levels. For example, we see that women traditionally have played an essential role in the operation of business and industry. Through womanpower letters are typed, mailed, opened, answered, and filed; clients are met; phones are answered; books are kept; appointments are noted; and, of course, coffee is brewed. Women are indeed essential to everything in the operation — everything but the decision-making process. Witness that 98% of all top-level executive positions in this country are held by men. Witness that women managers earn 54% of what their male counterparts earn. Witness that women need a college degree to earn just a little more than men with an eighth-grade education.

For years, the myth has been that these situations occur and will continue to occur because of some inherent deficiency or weakness within the female work force. Today, however, the evidence suggests that the "inherent deficiency" and "weakness" lie not within the female work force, but rather within the organizational homogeneity of business and industry.

This organizational homogeneity perpetuates itself via numerous behavioral systems and subsystems. The systems which seem to generate the most pervasive negative pressures on an aspiring female manager are

1. The visibility system,

2. The property-value system,

3. The sponsor-protégé system, and

4. The legal system.

An individual member of an organization who does not share the values being perpetuated has a difficult time dealing with his or her unwritten corporate policy. As the following cases illustrate, however, unless today's career-oriented woman is prepared to identify and confront these systems as obstacles to her upward mobility within an organization, she will be forced to withdraw, or to withstand the strain imposed by their negative pressure.

THE VISIBILITY SYSTEM

One of the primary elements of upward mobility within any organization is visibility. One must be seen before one can be recognized. And while female executives in male-oriented organizations are definitely seen, their visibility is often based upon sex, not achievement. Visibility based upon sex is a perceptual focus which perpetuates organizational homogeneity. It manifests itself by creating communicative distortions which either (1) "erase" the value of what a female executive says or does, or (2) encourage misunderstandings of what is being said to the female executive.

The Visibility System: Case Study A

As a child, Alice R. wanted to follow in her father's footsteps and become a partner in an accounting firm. Her natural aptitude for mathematics, encouragement from her family and friends, and a brilliant academic record all led her to believe that partnership was indeed a realistic aspiration. Following graduation from college, Alice was the first woman hired by the P & L accounting firm. Her promotional path followed that of her male counterparts — she was hired as a trainee, promoted to staff assistant after one year, and promoted to junior accountant after two years. The next step was senior accountant, and then partner. Alice sat for her C.P.A. exam and received the highest score. During each of her yearly progress reports she was told that her technical skills were excellent and her client relationship, although limited, was more than satisfactory. After several colleagues had been promoted to the rank of senior accountant, Alice asked her supervisor when she might expect a promotion.

"Oh," George replied, "I'm sure one is imminent. We've never had a female senior. You're going to have to give the partners a little time to get used to seeing a skirt in the office. Heh, heh. Don't worry, honey, you're on your way."

And so Alice did not worry — for two years she did not worry. However, as she began her fifth year with the company, and as she saw men with less seniority and men considerably less qualified than she was being promoted, she began to worry. Again she spoke to George, her supervisor. After a rather heated conversation, he, too, began to worry and promised to recommend her for promotion at the next staff meeting.

The meeting came and went. George said nothing to Alice. In fact, he said nothing about anything to her for more than a month. When she initiated a conversation, he would abruptly curtail it. Not only was George acting coolly toward her, but the other accountants were also keeping their distance. Finally the freeze was more than she could take. She asked a co-worker, who was a personal friend of George's, what exactly happened at the staff meeting.

"What happened! I'll tell you what happened," he roared. "Your damn pushiness almost cost George his job. He went into that meeting talking about this 'great accountant' with these 'fantastic credentials' who should be made a senior. The partners were thrilled. 'Who is this guy?,' they asked. 'He's Alice,' George replied. Well, that about blew their minds. After they stopped laughing, they realized that poor George was serious. So they got serious, too. They tore him up one side the room and down the other. 'What was wrong with his judgment? What did he have going for him on the side? When his wife finds out, is he going to bring his domestic problems to work? What will the clients think? How many will we lose the first week?' On and on they went. And I'm only telling you the polite things they said."

Alice was furious. "Now wait a minute. You and everyone else around here know damn well I'm qualified to be a senior. They shouldn't have done that to George, but what am I supposed to do?"

"Maybe they shouldn't have done that to George — but they did. With or without *your* credentials, *he's* in trouble. The best thing you can do for him is stop bugging him. The best thing you can do for yourself is go home."

Poor George. He didn't realize that he was upsetting the natural balance of homogeneity — that he was advocating hetero-geneity. The partners' fierce negative reaction to George's candi-date indicates that they, consciously or subconsciously, did realize the implication of his suggestion. Silently but certainly, they had told Alice, "You must look the part before you get the part." Alice did not "look the part." As the organizational decision-makers, the partners responded appropriately. They had main-tained organizational homogeneity.

Confrontation

Alice requested and received a two-month leave of absence. Having never been confronted with a blatantly discriminatory situation before, she was totally unprepared to deal with the overwhelming negative pressure. She needed time to recover from her shock, hurt, and bewilderment.

Alice was punished for not playing by the rules — rules she was unaware of. Alice committed a foul, and she served her time in the penalty box without realizing that she had been playing with a loaded puck. Her case is an extreme, but factual, example of an organization's "visibility system" at work. Alice had "visibility" within her organization. However, it was based upon her sex — the wrong sex for this job — which, in and of itself, created enough of a detraction to completely "erase" the value of her achievements.

The Visibility System: Case Study B

Cathy D. was an extremely attractive assistant buyer working in a high-fashion department of a major department store. Every day the chief executive would comment about some aspect of her appearance — her hair, her dress, her shoes, even her nail polish. He would often point to her manner of dress as the model to be emulated. It was obvious that he considered her the epitome of today's young fashion assistant. When Cathy's buyer quit she naturally assumed she would get the job. However, another buyer, new to the store and with less experience than Cathy, was hired.

Confrontation

Cathy immediately went to the chief executive, bypassing three supervisory levels, and demanded to know why she was passed over. The surprised executive replied, "Cathy, you should be well aware of the fact that promotional decisions are made by an individual's immediate supervisor in conjunction with the personnel department's recommendation. Although I hold the ultimate veto power, I usually act only in an advisory position."

"Well, why, then, did you lead me to believe that I was doing such a great job?"

"You inferred this, Cathy. I am in no position to evaluate your performance. I can only evaluate that which I see and I see you as a very knowledgeable and fashion-conscious young woman. This I approve of, as I have said on numerous occasions."

Giving this chief executive the benefit of the doubt, it is probable that Cathy "misread" his compliments. Given our cultural orientation, it's very easy for a woman to define herself in terms of her ability to "be attractive" and to consider acceptance of the way she looks as acceptance of the work she performs.

Adjustment

The primary task for both women is to identify the visibility system under which they are working. In both instances, their visibility was based upon sex. Rather than confronting the system, however, they confronted men who didn't know what they were talking about!

Adjustment for Alice can come only with the realization that the P & L company visibility system is based upon sex alone. As long as this system perpetuates itself, Alice's achievements will be irrelevant and her mobility limited. She must decide if she can work under such an "invisible ceiling."

Adjustment for Cathy is a bit more positive. Fortunately, visibility based upon sex does not have to preclude visibility based upon achievement.

Since men control most of the top executive positions, it is quite difficult to find a successful woman who has not used her initial sex visibility to her advantage. At best, however, it is an entrée which rapidly must be followed by tangible proof of achievement. Cathy has her entrée. If she hopes for upward mobility, she must follow through until her visibility is based upon achievement.

THE PROPERTY-VALUE SYSTEM

Within organizations, women are routed into jobs which reflect the tasks and status assigned them by our society. At home, a woman's job is nutritive, supportive, placating, and passive; thus, at work she represents 90% of all nurses, dietitians, baby sitters, receptionists, airline flight attendants, and clericals.

In her book *Born Female*, Carolyn Bird draws a "sex map of occupations" which illustrates how outmoded home-roles limit women at work. She concludes by stating that "women are least accepted in work involving machinery, negotiations, travel, risk, profit, and substantial sums of money." [2]

This school of thought manifests itself in the business community when, in personnel departments, a man hires executives while a woman hires entry-level employees. In banks, he is the loan officer, while she is the complaint adjuster. In sales, he is the "outside" salesman (with commissions), while she sells over-the-counter or over the telephone (without commissions). In employee relations a man handles union contracts while a woman handles compensations and benefits. A woman may balance the checkbook (as a bookkeeper or statistician), but a man makes the final financial decisions (as a comptroller or budget director). She may purchase the necessities (as a buyer or marketing specialist), but he sets the limits (as general merchandise manager or purchasing agent). If a woman is a supervisor, she supervises other women — in the use of women's tools (typewriters and telephones). If a woman works in male areas, it is within a female specialty (as a research analyst, not a portfolio manager; covering the woman's angle, not the world news).

The concept that work which a woman performs in the office should be similar to the work she performs in the home is the first premise upon which the property-value system is based.

The second premise is that work which a woman performs should be of less dollar value than work which a man performs. We know that every job carries with it its own price tag. The price or value of a job fluctuates in relation to the number and type of people available to fill it. When large numbers of women are available to fill a certain job, that job is labeled "a woman's job," one with a low property value.

The following case studies illustrate the property-value system at work, perpetuating organizational homogeneity through the differential placement and payment of women.

Property-Value System: Case Study A

Mabel R. worked as an employment office clerk in a small midwestern store. As time went on, the store grew and Mabel's duties increased to include interviewing, hiring, orienting, and training all new employees. When the work load became unbearable, the store president decided the time had come to formally organize a personnel department. Bob G. was hired as personnel director and Mabel remained the employment office clerk.

Property-Value System: Case Study B

Sarah S. was in charge of the accounts payable department until it was automated. With a great deal of fanfare, Ernest M. assumed the title of director of computerized services. Sarah is still in charge of the accounts payable department, only now she reports to Mr. M.

In a review of the evolution of jobs, a pattern becomes quite clear. When money and prestige come in, women go out. When the job becomes routine and supportive, men go out.

Property-Value System: Case Study C

Several years ago a new kidney unit was introduced into Western Hospital. Since no one knew much about it, the "junior" nurse on the staff was assigned to work with it. Sally spent many long hours, both on duty and off, mastering the old techniques and perfecting some new ones of her own. Western Hospital now has one of the most respected renal dialysis centers in the country. It is headed by Dr. Richard R., with nurse Sally assisting.

A prestigious job requires a man with prestigious credentials. The nonverbal cue a woman receives is that work which she performs is intrinsically of less value than a man's work.

Property-Value System: Case Study D

Margaret had been a communication specialist at a large service organization for the past seven years. In this capacity she was responsible for the monthly in-house journal, the orientation brochures, all press releases, and general public relations information. When Margaret left to take a position with another company, she was replaced by a man who, although responsible for the same activities, is called the director of communications and receives $2,500 a year more.

It is evident that paying a woman less than a man for the same work is a very common and profitable arrangement. Companies are not *creating* attitudes by putting a dollar value on them. They are simply *exploiting* them. The thought process of the property-value system as indicated in the above case study is: If a woman is promoted into a man's job, what will happen to its property value? As more women move in, salaries will go down and before long no self-respecting man will take the job.

Confrontation

Mabel and Sarah (case studies A and B) had not identified this property-value system. Consequently, they had no basis for confrontation; they had only a vague sense of injustice.

Sally (case study C), on the other hand, did identify the system. Her confrontation arose when she realized that the rigidity inherent within the medical community would never permit a non-M.D. to head a department. Rather than fight the organizational homogeneity of *both* her hospital and the American Medical Association, she searched for alternative methods of adjustment.

Margaret (case study D) also identified the system which was causing her negative pressure. She confronted it by becoming a "rate-buster," a woman who will accept low pay and little prestige in exchange for the experience of doing specific kinds of work.

Adjustment

Mabel and Sarah have come to accept the reality of their positions — they have even been convinced that since this is the way it *usually* is, this is the way it's *supposed* to be.

Sally adjusted to her situation by requesting and obtaining permission to lecture and write about the use of the artificial kidney machines, an area in which she is now a recognized and highly paid authority.

Margaret adjusted to her situation by quitting — but not before she acquired a wide range of experience and a degree of expertise in the field of communications. As the public relations director of a large manufacturing company, she has tripled her salary. Among other things, she has illustrated that "rate busters" can live to be "rate exploders."

THE SPONSOR-PROTÉGÉ SYSTEM

In one way or another, promotions to all top-level executive positions in all corporations are based upon the recommendations of the men in power. The top executives are looking for a way to assure continuity of leadership and to provide a source of informal training. This has led to the "sponsor-protégé system" — a system which has proven detrimental to female managers because it tends to inhibit their advancement. Under this system, the sponsor is usually a man, and although he might not object to having a female assistant, he often has mixed feelings about identifying *her* as the person who may eventually hold *his* job.

He feels his position is justified because of his sincere concern — concern about her commitment to the company and concern about the demands multiple wife-mother-worker roles impose upon her. Since he usually believes that his own personal risk of failure is higher if he recommends a woman rather than her male counterpart, he is also concerned for himself.

The Sponsor-Protégé System: Case Study

One morning last June, Robert R. called an "important" staff meeting to announce his resignation as director of personnel. His staff was sad about his leaving, but they were nonetheless pleased about his promotion. Naturally, a great deal of speculation arose concerning his replacement. The logical choice was Janice L., his assistant for the past five years.

He was asked by the company president to complete a final performance review on his staff. He felt it only fair that each evaluation be discussed with each staff member. During his meeting with Janice, he explained that he not only recommended a salary increase for her, but also that she be considered interim director until a replacement was appointed. After having praised Janice's leadership, organization, and planning abilities in glowing terms, he paused, obviously waiting for a flood of appreciative words. None came.

Confrontation

Instead, Jan coolly asked, "Robert, if I've been doing such a fantastic job, if I'm qualified to be the interim director, why am I not qualified to be the all-the-time director?"

"Gee, Jan. It never occurred to me that you'd want this job permanently."

"Robert, why do you suppose I've stayed here for five years?"

"Well, I thought you liked it," he replied, with more than a little hurt in his voice. "We've all been a close group. I can't understand why you're acting the way you are. I thought you'd be pleased with this review."

In actuality, Robert could not envision a woman (in this case, Jan) taking a "man's" (in this case, his) job. The position's status would have been lessened and Robert's image would have been demeaned within the organization. Here, the visibility system and the property-value system overlap in such a way as to define the operant limits of promotability within the sponsor-protégé system when the protégé is a woman. In effect, Robert was telling Jan that he could not take the "risk" — he would not be her sponsor.

Adjustment

Several days after Robert had left the company, Jan requested an interview with the vice president of industrial relations. During the interview she outlined her qualifications for the position of director. In effect, she was asking him to be her sponsor. Jan knew that a sponsor must not only be willing to speak on behalf of the protégé, but he must also have a sufficient amount of "clout" to be listened to. The vice president met both criteria, and Jan subsequently did get the job.

THE LEGAL SYSTEM

In 1964 the business community got a kick in its social consciousness with the passage of Title IV of the Civil Rights Act. Title IV, which deals with employment policy, prohibits discrimination on the basis of race, color, religion, national origin, or sex. It also made provision for the new federal agency, the Equal Employment Opportunity Commission, to investigate individual complaints.

In an attempt to comply with the letter, rather than the spirit of the law, several companies reacted in a manner which was blatantly discriminatory to many of their employees. This consequently gave rise to the "legal system," a manifestation of the conflict arising from a company's need to maintain its organizational homogeneity while simultaneously complying with the law.

The Legal System: Case Study A

Olga P. had been a supervisor at a large bank for 12 years. According to her department manager, she was "next in line" for promotion. The first opening occurred two weeks after members of the local N.A.A.C.P. met with the bank's president to develop methods of reducing the company's "historical pattern of racial discrimination." Olga was "next in line" *after* the black man who was hired for the available position.

Confrontation

When Olga P. questioned the credentials of the new department manager, she was told, "Well, I realize you are probably better qualified. However, we're getting so much pressure from the N.A.A.C.P., we *had* to hire a black manager — we already *have* a female manager."

Unfortunately, Olga P. had no external group pressuring for her promotion. No group was helping her company's president develop methods of reducing its "historical pattern of *sexist* discrimination." Undoubtedly, few within the company were even aware of the existence of such a pattern.

Adjustment

Olga P. is presently in the process of mobilizing the employment committee of her local chapter of the N.O.W. to act as her external pressure group. This group is composed of both men and women, black and white.

In an effort to maintain some semblance of organizational homogeneity, the law was read as "hire black men." The hiring of a black woman, two non-job-related characteristics previously defined as unacceptable, would have caused more heterogeneity than the organization could have tolerated. An unfortunate consequence of industry's attempt to compensate for years of racist hiring and promotional policies has been the white woman's tendency to blame her lack of advancement upon blacks as a group. What she, too, fails to realize is that blacks are both men and women.

Margaret Sloan, an organizer of the black feminist movement in Chicago, vividly retraced the steps in her life which led to her commitment to women's liberation *and* racial equality. She recalled, "I still had scars on my head and dust between my toes from Selma. Once I was left for dead. Then, when the revolution began, they asked me to make coffee — wherever you find sexism, racism is right around the corner. Wherever you see racism, sexism is creeping through the door. You can't have one without the other." It was more than coincidental that the "black" pressured for and hired was a black man — not a black woman.

The Legal System: Case Study B

Rita S., Terry U., and Vivian W. each had worked for R & S Manufacturing Company for 12 years. Each had come up through the ranks and held the position of research assistant, reporting directly to their respective vice president. They were the highest ranking women within their company, which had recently embarked upon a "progressive affirmative action program." The company's equal employment officer recommended to the company president that a woman be hired for the recently vacated director of marketing position. Although Rita, Terry, and Vivian were qualified for the position, the president personally hired a recent female M.B.A. graduate with no experience in marketing and no experience with the company.

Here the "legal system" was at work. Company officials, threatened with cancellation of government contracts, attempted to comply with the law. The nature of their compliance, however, detrimentally affected the female managers already working within the organization.

Confrontation

First, Rita, Terry, and Vivian should have more realistically appraised their situations. It is naive to suppose that a law can eradicate prejudgmental attitudes. At best, it can only encourage employers to evaluate prejudgmental behavior. According to Congresswoman Shirley Chisholm, the purpose of the recent civil rights legislation is to "shelter those most abused and to begin an evolutionary process by compelling the insensitive majority to reexamine its unconscious attitudes." [3]

Secondly, the women of this company could have encouraged the "evolutionary process" by pointing out to their equal-employment officer the effect that overzealous compliance has upon the morale of their qualified female executives.

Rita, Terry, and Vivian have allowed to happen within their organization the same type of thing which has happened within the political arena. Once the laws are on the books, women turn them over to men with the directive: Now *you* enforce them. Naturally, very little has been done. The assumption made by women both in the business world and the political world is that legislation passed is legislation enacted.

Adjustment

The passage of legislation is but one of a multiphased effort. Not only must employers be persuaded to reevaluate the conditions within their organizations; and not only must women plan for and accept the responsibilities which expanded opportunities bring; but also presently employed women must apply internal pressure to assure compliance with both the letter and the spirit of the law.

The above are some of the behavioral systems which sustain organizational homogeneity, the force which waves the "dead end" flag and sets invisible ceilings on a female executive's upward mobility within the business community.

Although many people are conducting valuable studies about the cultural conditions and historical base from which OH has sprung, today's executives, both men and women, are searching for more pragmatic courses of action. The question most frequently being asked is, "Once OH is recognized, must it be accepted as an organizational fact of life?" Probably not. OH can and is being beaten every day by men and women who, rather than withdraw from or withstand the negative pressures, have chosen instead to *identify*, *confront*, and *adjust* to each individual behavioral system. Identification and confrontation of a behavioral system within an organization requires courage and awareness — awareness that the adjustment required may be a personal as well as an organizational one. This process has often resulted in a great deal of introspection, leading to subsequent, often painful, personal adjustment.

PERSONAL ADJUSTMENTS

For many women, personal adjustment has often meant "getting rid of the albatross." For a long time, women have defined themselves so much in terms of the men in their lives — as mothers, sisters, wives, lovers, daughters — that they have fallen into the same traps as have many minority-group members. They have accepted much of the ideology of the dominant group. In other words, many women believe and perpetuate the myth that a *real* woman's place is, indeed, in the home. They still suffer pangs of guilt when an office becomes more appealing than a kitchen, or when an M.B.A. becomes more appealing than a Mrs. Now that women are clearly a numerical majority and many more job opportunities are being made available, they need no longer be burdened by antifeminist thinking. Rejection of the stereotyped woman plays a large part in a woman's personal adjustment.

For still another group of women, personal adjustment has meant avoiding the "I-made-it syndrome." Many successful female executives are very hesitant to acknowledge that discrimination exists within their organizations. Often, the mere mention of it sends them into a rage of denial. In effect, what they are saying is:

"There's no discrimination for any woman as smart as I am. Being the only woman good enough to make it in a man's world gives me power, prestige, and money which you don't have. I'm not going to jeopardize my status by helping more women into my select circle. I've had to fight every inch of the way with no one pleading my case before a Human Relations Commission." Gordon Allport might well see this response as "aggression against one's own group," an ego defense mechanism frequently found among members of groups that are discriminated against. [4] The tensions and frustrations resulting from being forced to "represent women," to carry both the negative and positive characteristics of all members of her sex, to be seen as "female executive" rather than "Mary Smith, executive," are released through an irrational hatred of "them." "Them" are those women who are not ambitious, who are not very bright or talented, who possess the despised qualities, real or imagined, of the female stereotype. "Them" are all those women who hold her back. Having achieved her own position of professional status, power, and prestige, the female executive bitterly resents giving help to other women since no help was given to her. She is encapsulated within the I-made-it syndrome.

The personal adjustment necessary to free herself begins with recognition of the victimization of women within organizational settings and the acceptance of the reality that she is a member of that group. Once this process has been completed, the female executive can objectively evaluate the "price" she has paid and will continue to pay for her successful but isolated position. Realization that she has been living in a marginal state within the business world — sometimes accepted, sometimes unaccepted — has led many female executives to drastically modify their negative behavior towards other women. They have successfully avoided and/or released themselves from the I-made-it syndrome.

Women are not the only members of the business community making personal adjustments designed to eradicate organizational homogeneity. For some men, personal adjustments have often meant "accepting job equality." More and more business executives, both male and female, are beginning to accept the push for equality of job opportunity as something more than a passing fad. Many view it as one phase within a larger context of social and civil dissatisfaction. Others see it as a cyclical occurrence — women demanding something which, in retrospect, everyone will agree they should have had a long time ago.

Both views reflect the reality of American women today. For the first time in our country's history, women are potentially in a position of control over their own lives. They have the potential to choose whether to marry or not; to choose to have children or not; to choose whom to marry; to choose how many children to have; to choose to complete an education; and to choose which education to complete. It is inevitable that women will want to fulfill their potential, that they will continue to demand life choices. And an occupational choice is, indeed, a major life choice.

The numbers of women recently hired and promoted within occupations formerly labeled "for men only" reflect the personal adjustments made by many male executives. Occupational doors are being opened by men who, after scrutinizing and reassessing their personal values, are responding sincerely and with a strong commitment to the task of making equality of job opportunity a reality. For other men, personal adjustment has meant "adapting to a new work force." Today's activist is more likely to be an intelligent, basically peaceful employee who feels the system is loaded against her and must consequently be changed. She can no longer be seen as a militant feminist, chronic malcontent, or social misfit. She is a female employee who has initiated action (often formalized and legalized) against a company which could not be made to listen by any other means.

Some male executives have waited until their backs were up against the wall, until suggestions became demands, memorandums became Magna Cartas, and incidents became crises before they began adapting their managerial styles and policies to meet the needs of their female workers. Other male executives have been deeply involved in the orderly transition from a white male-dominated organization to a people-oriented organization. The different postures reflect the personal adjustments each individual has been willing to make.

As the previous case studies illustrate, many business exec-utives, both male and female, are examining their organizational environments and becoming more aware of organizational homo-geneity and the behavioral systems which perpetuate it. Perhaps more importantly, they are becoming dissatisfied and are willing to *identify*, *confront*, and make the personal and/or professional *adjustments* necessary to change. When enough executives become concerned, we will see the beginning of a new behavioral system, one which encourages the utilization of the most talented individuals, regardless of race or sex. This new system will be based upon the concept that management considers ability a person's greatest attribute.

REFERENCES

1. Cynthia F. Epstein, *A Woman's Place* (Los Angeles: University of California Press, 1971), p. 167.

2. Carolyn Bird, *Born Female: The High Cost of Keeping Women Down* (New York: Simon and Schuster, 1969), p. 81.

3. Shirley Chisholm, *Unbought and Unbossed* (New York: Avon, 1971), p. 47.

4. Gordon Allport, *Nature of Prejudice* (Garden City, New York: Doubleday, 1958), pp. 142-145.

BIBLIOGRAPHY

Allport, Gordon. *Nature of Prejudice* (Garden City, New York: Doubleday, 1958).

Bird, Carolyn. *Born Female: The High Cost of Keeping Women Down* (New York: Simon and Schuster, 1969).

Chisholm, Shirley. *Unbought and Unbossed* (New York: Avon, 1971).

Epstein, Cynthia F. *A Woman's Place* (Los Angeles: University of California Press, 1971).

Fendrock, John J. *Managing in Times of Radical Change* (New York: American Management Association, 1971).

Mead, Margaret. *Culture and Commitment* (New York: Doubleday, 1970).

9

BANK OF AMERICA'S AFFIRMATIVE ACTION SEMINAR

by Suki Cathey

Ms. Cathey is an affirmative action officer in the personnel department at Bank of America in San Francisco. Prior to this, she worked closely with Bay Area high schools and junior colleges in developing career programs and teaching classes in banking. Suki's career in banking started several years ago as a management trainee at Chase Manhattan Bank in New York City. She was an employment interviewer and later counseled employees with personnel problems in an employee-relations function.

Aside from her banking experience, Suki was an on-campus recruiter and later a purser for Pan American Air Lines. While working for Pan Am she traveled extensively throughout Europe and Central and South America.

Suki received her B.S. from the University of North Carolina at Greensboro and attended the New School for Social Research and New York University.

Acknowledgements: Credit should be given to the following people who contributed time and ideas to the development of the seminar: Mae Bass Harper, Betty Browne, Joan Good, Marjy Joshel, and Jenifer Renzel.

Key Questions

1. What are the specific steps followed in one successful short session?

2. Why present a short seminar for managers and supervisors on affirmative action for women?

3. How can you select and develop leaders for these half-day seminars?

SEMINAR OBJECTIVES AND FORM

The seminar, "Exploring Your Staff's Potential," was developed for all supervisory personnel at the Bank of America as part of our affirmative action program for women. When designing the seminar, we kept the following objectives in mind. First, we wanted to provide information about the bank's philosophy regarding affirmative action and to explain recent governmental regulations (Revised Order 4) as they applied to the Bank of America.

Second, we wanted to educate supervisors about what equal opportunity is and what it requires. While it is not possible to change an individual's attitude within a 2- to 2½-hour time period, it is possible to deal with the company's expectations regarding its supervisors' behavior in the area of equal opportunity. These behavior changes can then lead to attitude changes at a later date. Finally, we hoped to create an awareness about women in business: their concerns, their rights, and their opportunities.

Keeping our objectives in mind, we wrote and revised the program several times. We conducted several pilot programs in which the participants added valuable input. In addition, outside specialists contributed helpful material, new ideas, and their own experiences. We particularly benefited from Dorothy Jongeward's advice on special techniques in dealing effectively with groups.

The outline of the seminar is designed to be flexible and adaptable to special concerns of a particular group. It represents only the framework of the seminar, which varied, depending on the participants' questions and responses. However, the seminar outline which appears later gives some consistency to our presentations.

GROUP PARTICIPANTS AND LEADERS

The group was small in size (usually under 25 individuals) and was a mixture of women and men. The style became relaxed and nonthreatening so that participants would be encouraged to have a free interchange of ideas. A horseshoe type table arrangement seemed to facilitate discussion. If one member demonstrated anger, for example, this was dealt with through feedback techniques and examining with others in the group the reasons for the anger. In many cases one participant dealt adequately with the concerns of another member. In the discussion of assumptions, group members often contributed information which exposed misconceptions about men and women. This had an even greater impact than if the leader had responded to the issues.

Before making the presentation, the leaders assumed that reactions to the seminar might be predictable. We thought, for example, that the younger officers in urban areas would be more "aware" and attuned to our subject than perhaps an older individual in a more remote area of the state would be. Our experience was, however, that assumptions relating to age, sex, position, or geographic location were entirely unfounded. Awareness and understanding of these issues seemed to be an *individual* matter — which was the message *we* were trying to relay to the group in our discussion of commonly held assumptions about men and women in business.

The individuals attending our seminar came with a broad spectrum of concerns and misconceptions about women in business. Some men and women were skeptical, uptight, and afraid. In some cases, young men showed anxiety when they believed their jobs would be taken away and filled by women.

Some women in entry-level official jobs felt they had "made it," but they hadn't even moved into middle management. Others felt that it was unfair to fill with a woman a position that could be filled by a man, because "after all, a man has to support a family." Some women did not like to be "singled out" and promoted "just because they were women." Both men and women were concerned that unqualified women would be promoted "just to make the numbers look good." There were many misunderstandings about the affirmative action program and why the bank had adopted the policy. It was this type of concern that the seminar addressed.

Another factor to consider when setting up such seminars is the careful selection of the leaders. The following qualities are necessary: commitment, tact, enthusiasm, objectivity, and responsiveness to individuals.

Our experience showed us that it is more effective to use two seminar leaders in each session. We have found it is important to keep the following points in mind when leading the group.

1. Leaders do not lecture; they interact with group members and control discussion.

2. As a representative of the organization, the leader should refrain from making personal comments or stating personal opinions regarding the subject matter.

3. The atmosphere should be informal and relaxed, and allow free expression of ideas.

4. All comments should be recognized, and differences of opinion acknowledged.

5. All questions should be answered or followed up.

6. The leader should respond to each participant (verbal and nonverbal cues).

7. *Active* listening is crucial.

COMMENTS ON THE SEMINAR

We received some interesting comments regarding the seminar which might be of interest. Responding to the question in a written evaluation, "What effect did the seminar have on you?" we received a variety of comments. For example:

"I was reminded that each individual is just that, an individual."

"Refreshed awareness."

"Hope!"

"Made me even more aware of these changing times."

"Reminder to look a little deeper for quality."

"Enlightening."

"Beautiful."

"There should be more talk concerning men — they are scared."

"Extremely mixed emotions."

"Causes an individual to search for facts instead of taking things for granted."

"Left me with an open mind."

"I have a better outlook toward evaluating the potential of both male and female."

"I now feel that the bank is sincere in regard to advancement for women."

"This gave me a better understanding of the affirmative action program and my part in it."

"It made me realize that I should go back to my office and talk to my staff about their goals and how I can help them."

"Shook this old man up."

SUMMARY

We hope that our approach to this seminar can be used in other business situations. We feel that we received as much from the participants of the seminars as we contributed to them. It has been, and continues to be, a rewarding experience for all concerned.

After completion of the seminar, we asked each participant to fill out the following questionnaire.

Evaluation of Exploring Your Staff's Potential

Male   Female

1. What did you think of the content of this seminar?

   Which part did you consider to be most worthwhile?

   Which part did you consider to be least worthwhile?

2. Did you think the discussion of the assumptions was helpful? If so, how?

3. Was there sufficient time spent answering questions regarding the affirmative action program?

4. What suggestions do you have for improvements or additions to the seminar?

5. How did you feel about the style of the presentation?

6. What effect did the seminar have on you?

Additional comments:

General rating _____ Excellent _____ Good
              _____ Fair   _____ Poor

EXPLORING YOUR STAFF'S POTENTIAL

    I. Introduction

   II. Why we have an affirmative action program

  III. Film *51%*

      Coffee Break

  IV. Discussion of common assumptions about the working woman

   V. Discussion of the affirmative action program

  VI. What you can do

 VII. Questions from the group

Introductions

Ask the participants to introduce themselves to the group (name, branch, and title).

I. Introduction

Today we are going to discuss our Affirmative Action Program for Women, sharing with you the reasons why the bank has this program, and our objectives. We will cover six basic points.

First, we will explain why we have an affirmative action program.

Second, we will explore some assumptions often made about women.

Third, we will explain the basic philosophy of our affirmative action program.

Fourth, we will answer some of the questions your employees may be asking about the affirmative action program.

Fifth, we will cover what you can do to help the bank.

Sixth, we would like to get comments and criticisms from you on our affirmative action program. Before going further, I would like to add that in the near future we will present a similar seminar on our minority program.

II. Why we have an affirmative action program

Let's consider why we have an affirmative action program for women. There are three basic reasons: a moral reason, a business reason, and a legal reason.

First consider the moral reason. Basically, it is simply this: it is *right* to utilize an individual's potential, and it is *wrong* not to do so. Every human being who has the desire and the potential should have the opportunity to grow in his or her job. Otherwise, it is an intolerable waste of a human being.

Next, there is a business reason for having an affirmative action program. It makes good business sense to maximize all of the potential of your employees. Employees will have higher morale, and they will take a genuine interest in the bank because of the challenges and responsibilities the bank has given them. This translates into concerned employees who will do their best to make the bank best. We cannot afford to let talent go unused — we should use all of the new ideas and developed skills that our employees have to offer us.

Finally, there is a legal reason for establishing an affirmative action program. As of April 2, 1972. Revised Order 4 issued by the Department of Labor requires that all corporations that do business with the government establish an affirmative action program for women similar to the affirmative action program established some years ago for minorities.

Note: Revised Order 4 was issued by the Secretary of Labor.

These legal requirements do not represent a change in our longstanding equal opportunity philosophy, but they do represent a change in some of the procedures used to insure equal opportunity practices.

Under Revised Order 4, the bank is required to

1. analyze its workforce at all levels;
2. set goals and timetables for the advancement of women which represent a good faith effort; and
3. develop programs to achieve our goals, and set up a monitoring system to measure the progress of our individual regions and departments in achieving their goals.

The Department of the Treasury can, at any time, audit our records to see that we are, in good faith, making every effort to achieve our goals and timetables. This is similar to our branches being audited by the National Bank Examiners and our own audit department.

What are the consequences if any unit of the bank is found not to be in compliance? If we were judged not to comply with Revised Order 4, we could lose all of our government business, including the sales and cashing of savings bonds, the loss of our substantial Federal deposits, and the loss of FHA and VA guaranteed loans.

For moral, business, and legal reasons affirmative action is vitally important to our bank. This is why we would like to spend some time discussing our affirmative action program for women with you.

III. Film: *51%*

And now the third point on our agenda is a film introduced by President Clausen which explores the changing role of women. While watching the film, see if any of the women remind you of someone on your staff.

Show film.   Film

As you have seen from the film, it is important that you see your employees as individuals. Also, you can see that the role of the supervisor is instrumental in the recognition and advancement of women.

Do you feel that "51%" represents a realistic situation?

Have any of you helped a woman advance in the bank, and if so, how did you do it? Did you encounter difficulties? What has happened to some of the women you have helped?

To the women:

What inspired you to pursue a career? Was it a difficult decision? When did you make the decision?

> The film pointed out some assumptions often made about women — we would like to explore some of these along with additional ones you may have heard.

Pass out worksheets.

> Here is a worksheet that won't be collected. Get into groups of four. Take about ten minutes and list as many assumptions (good or bad) as you can about both men and women in business. For example, under men some of you may say aggressive and under women some of you may say emotional. When you finish, we will break for coffee and discuss what you have written.

WORKSHEET

List below some of the commonly held assumptions about men and women in business.

Men	*Women*

Coffee break   Coffee break
10-15 minutes

IV. Discussion of common assumptions about the working woman

> We'll resume our session by discussing the assumptions you have listed. This is the fourth major

point on our agenda today. In this session, let's
consider men first.

*What are some of the assumptions you've listed
about men in business?*

Short discussion of assumptions.

Write comments on board or paper.

Keep it light! Laugh with the group if they can see
the humor in what they've written.

You have a very interesting list! I wish we had
more time to get into a discussion, but we are
working within time constraints. Since this is a
seminar on women, we'd like to discuss your
assumptions about the working woman.

The main purpose of this discussion is to
create an *awareness* in order

1. to show that many of us have accepted these
   role stereotypes and have applied them indis-
   criminately to all women,

2. to provide you with information with which
   you can carefully examine why you may
   believe these assumptions, and

3. to deal with the dramatic changes taking place
   in the role of women in America today.

Now let us discuss your assumptions about the
working woman.

Write down (on board or paper) as many as they
have.

Possible answers

Cultural:

emotional
belong at home, family responsibility
not aggressive enough or too aggressive
lose femininity
don't want careers

Job related:

pregnancy

absent a lot

high turnover

are poor supervisors

mobility

not accepted by customers

> Several of the statements you presented seem to indicate that women are not interested in or capable of higher level jobs.

Why do you think that women as well as men might have accepted these assumed limitations as real?

Sub-questions

How are average little girls raised differently from little boys?

> Examples: Toys that are made for children
>
>   dolls — girls
>   electric trains — boys

How does our educational system reinforce the trend of treating boys and girls differently?

> Textbooks traditionally show men going to the office and women as mothers caring for children. School curriculum encourages home economics courses for girls and mechanical drawing and shop for boys.

> In high school, teachers and counselors encourage girls to go into nursing, teaching, and secretarial studies rather than leave all options open.

What effect do you think mass media have had in reinforcing the differences between male and female roles?

$$\begin{bmatrix} \text{TV} \\ \text{Radio} \\ \text{Magazines} \\ \text{Newspapers} \end{bmatrix} \Bigg\} \quad \text{How are women portrayed in these?}$$

When working women are pictured, in what professions are they shown?

$$\begin{bmatrix} \text{Ads on TV show "the harried housewife."} \\ \text{TV programs and movies} \\ \qquad \text{doctors — usually male} \\ \qquad \text{nurses — female} \\ \qquad \text{executive — male} \\ \qquad \text{teller — female} \end{bmatrix}$$

From our short discussion, we can better understand what influences culture has had on the roles we play (both men and women have been affected). *Can we say that women cannot do certain jobs just because they are women?*

(Pause — let this statement sink in.)

Or should we say that women might not have been encouraged, or had opportunities, due to cultural stereotypes?

Now let's consider a few other assumptions which can be related specifically to Bank of America.

Let them guess.

What about *turnover*?

Let them guess the statistics and then compare with actual figures.

Turnover

Turnover seems to be more job related than sex related.

Mobility   *Mobility*

Women are less mobile than men as a general rule. Two things are important to note, however.

1. Mobility is less and less a factor in the progression of our officers. In 1971 only 8% of all official moves in the north were between regions. This figure dropped to 5.2% in 1972.

2. If mobility is the only avenue for advancement, it is important that the woman be *given the choice*. The decision should be between the woman and her husband if she is married.

Note: Stress the point that women should be given the opportunity to decide.

Supervision

Supervision

A high percentage of our operations officers are women and their performance reports are comparable to men. Many people who say they would not like working for a woman have not worked for one.

Length of service

Length of service

Compare length of service between men and women who are branch employees (grade 6+) with ten years of service:

        Women
        Men

Pregnancy

Pregnancy

The average woman nationwide has 35-40 working years available to her after her children are in school.

Note: You may not turn down a job applicant because of pregnancy. Recent EEOC guidelines state, "A written or unwritten employment policy or practice which excludes from employment, applicants or employees because of pregnancy is in prima facie violation of Title VII."

Summary

We could spend much more time discussing the assumptions you have listed, but we have to move on. I hope you will consider some of the things we've discussed so far when you return to your job. More and more women today, and men as well, are rejecting the limitations imposed upon them by cultural expectations.

What has brought about the changes in attitudes? One factor is the Civil Rights movement by many minority groups. Also, the number of women in the workforce has increased significantly. Women are in the workforce primarily out of economic necessity — not just to supplement their husbands' incomes. Attitudes about women in the workforce are changing

> because of higher educational accomplishments,
>
> because of technological advances freeing them from many household chores,
>
> because of earlier marriages and smaller families, and
>
> because careers for women are more and more acceptable.

Also, the life cycle of today's woman varies markedly from her counterpart in previous years. It is now psychologically impossible for most women to live the same lifestyle as women did at the turn of the century.

Show chart.

Comparisons of Mrs. Average 1900 and Mrs. Average today

	1900	Today
Marriage	20 yr	18+ yr
Last child	40-50 yr	26 yr
Children	6-8	2.7
Life expectancy	48 yr	75 yr

WOMAN'S LIFE TIME

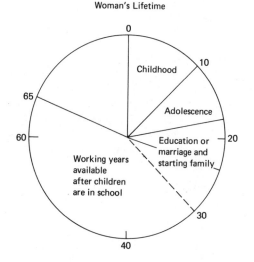

Woman's Lifetime

Included in the large percentage of women in the workforce are three basic types of women.

Group 1. Women who qualify for, and openly aspire to, positions in management. These should be easy for you to identify and promote when they are ready.

Group 2. Women who qualify for higher positions, but due to cultural conditioning do not *think* they can hold officer-level jobs.

The woman in Group 2 presents a challenge for you. She may want to advance, but she may be experiencing uncertain feelings about herself — she may have conflicts between what she wants and needs and what she feels is expected of her by her family and society. This type of woman needs to be asked if she wants to take a job with more responsibility. Your job as a supervisor is to recognize this person and give her the confidence and guidance she needs. Talk to her about her goals and aspirations, and give as much positive encouragement as you can, *if she has the potential.*

Group 3. Women who sincerely do not want to pursue careers.

The women in Group 3 who are honestly happy with their present jobs generally provide invaluable service to the bank, and we respect their decision about their life style. In no way should these women feel that the bank values them less because of their preference.

I hope we have created a new awareness of women in your offices who should be considered along with men on an individual basis, without regard to commonly held assumptions about their inabilities to hold official positions. With this awareness it is our desire that women will not be overlooked because of traditions, because they were never asked, or because of unexamined assumptions.

V. Discussion of the affirmative action program

Now we'd like to give you an explanation of the basic philosophy of our affirmative action program. As you can tell, the bank is firmly committed to equal opportunity for its employees.

1. The present goals of the affirmative action program for women have been established after analyzing where we are and where we can be with reasonable change.

2. Compare where the bank is now with the goals we have established. Individual goals for your branch or department will be established in the next few weeks.

3. We are going to be promoting many qualified women in the years ahead. It is important to note that *there will be plenty of openings in*

the bank due to promotions, retirements, turnover, and growth. There will be many opportunities for all employees.

4. We would like to stress that the emphasis of the program is on qualifying women for higher positions and on advancing women who want to advance. No pressure should be put on a woman who has considered advancement opportunities and prefers not to advance.

5. All of you should have had meetings with your staff on the program. Encourage your staff to read the affirmative action binder.

6. Discuss questions and comments on the affirmative action program from the group.

If your time permits, you may ask the participants at this point to refer to their handout entitled "Frequently Asked Questions About Affirmative Action Program."

(See handout A at the end of this chapter.)

VI. What you can do?

How can you help implement the affirmative action program? (See handouts B and C at the end of this chapter.)

1. The first thing you can do when you return to your office is to look around and try to identify the woman under your supervision who has potential for advancement. I'm sure that most of you have at least one woman in your office whom you rate highly. It is probably the one you ask to train the "trainees" and help them with their careers, the one you know is right there on the job when you need her. Perhaps she is Office Utility or Assistant Operations Officer, or perhaps Note Department Head.

2. The next thing we would like you to do is to *talk to your women employees at all levels.* Ask them what their interests and abilities are, as they see them. They need not name specific jobs, but try to find out if they like working with people, or supervising people; working with numbers, or writing or doing research work. There will be a new performance report for nonexempt personnel coming out shortly which will have a section on employee interests and development. It is important that each of the questions in this section be answered thoroughly. Included should be courses taken, special skills or talents, career goals within the bank, and, specifically, how you plan to help her attain her goals.

   Next, you should try to match the employees' interests to a feasible future job. The progression possibilities are quite clear in the branches, but are less clear in administration. You will soon have a valuable tool to help you with career information. It is a booklet entitled: "Training Opportunities at Bank of America."

3. We would also like to ask you to *encourage* (not pressure) *high-potential women to consider their careers with the bank.* Due to the role conflict discussed earlier, the immediate reaction of many women will be to say "no" to a change in job status. Your encouragement and support can be critical in helping a woman who is trying to determine the direction she wants to take.

4. *You might investigate getting those women who you feel are capable employees on relevant training programs* in your region, or in your department or another department. From the booklet "Training Opportunities at

Bank of America," you might get some ideas of how you can match your employees' interests with an appropriate training program. Procedures for enrolling employees in courses are described in the booklet.

5. Another area you might consider is *reviewing your part-time or prime-time staff to see if anyone in this group of employees qualifies for one of our training programs, especially those college or junior college students who will be getting their degrees.*

6. Finally, you should *bring to the attention of your district administrator or regional administrator any particularly well-qualified women.* They, in turn, might develop that employee in the region, or refer her name to our personnel relations officer for women for additional career counseling.

7. *You know your employees best.* If you feel you have a woman who could be officer material or who could be upgraded, get her started. We need your help!

VII. Questions from the group

HANDOUT A

Frequently Asked Questions About the
Affirmative Action Program

1. Is it only for college graduate women who are already bank officers?

   The program is *not* only for college graduates or for women who are currently officers; it is for all interested and qualified women.

2. Is the program primarily for newly hired and young women in the bank?

   The program will deal primarily with promoting our present staff, regardless of age.

3. Will the decision to advance women be removed from the supervisors' hands?

   Definitely not. The supervisor is still the key to advancement for his or her employees. Supervisors will be expected to treat women equally in regard to promotions, however.

4. Will women who don't want to advance be pressured into doing so?

   Women who are not interested in advancing should feel no pressure to do so as a result of this program. Individual life styles and preferences are very much respected by the bank.

5. What is the difference between the functions of the Equal Opportunity section and the functions of the Personnel Relations Officer — Women?

   The Equal Opportunity section will deal largely with the coordination of the various action-oriented programs of the affirmative action program for women and for minorities while the Personnel Relations Officers — Women will continue to work with individuals' career interests and plans.

6. When can we expect all of the action-oriented programs mentioned in the affirmative action program binder to be implemented?

   Within the next year most of the programs should be implemented.

7. What if we don't achieve our goals?

The goals represent aims to strive toward. The bank, and consequently its supervisors, will be judged on its good-faith effort to meet the goals. If we can indicate that you have made every effort to achieve your goals and have been unable to do so, this will not be held against us or the bank. However, the burden of proof falls on our shoulders to show that you have made every reasonable effort to promote or hire qualified women.

HANDOUT B

What You Can Do

1. *Talk* to your women (include part-time and prime-time staff).

   Suggest that your women prepare for a counseling session.

   The woman should have the opportunity to analyze her needs, career interests, and personal limitations before her discussion with you.

   Conduct a counseling session. Ask about interests, abilities, and goals. Determine the type of work she enjoys and what she does best.

2. *Identify* women with potential for advancement.

3. *Use performance report.*

   Note specific information about your employee, including courses taken, special skills or talents, and *her* career goals within the bank and how you plan to help her.

4. *Encourage* high-potential women to consider careers with the bank.

   Build up confidence by increasing responsibility.

   Help her to see herself as a successful business woman.

   Arrange for her to discuss various community office jobs with successful bank women.

5. *Training*

   Start preparing your qualified women for higher-level positions.

   Arrange for them to attend classes and seminars. Consider management development courses and Giannini Foundation grants.

   Encourage them to take advantage of the self-development program.

   The booklet "Training Opportunities at Bank of America" will be available shortly with information on all training programs.

The bank's Personnel Relations Officer — Women can provide information or additional career counseling.

Employment Checklist

Please note the following guidelines which reflect changes in hiring practices resulting from recent government legislation. One helpful reminder: *Do not* ask a woman a question which you would not ask a man!

- Marital status — may not be a criterion for hiring men or women.

- Do not ask about children or child care arrangements.

- You may not turn down a job applicant because of pregnancy. Recent EEOC guidelines state, "A written or unwritten employment policy or practice which excludes from employment, applicants or employees because of pregnancy is in prima facie violation of Title VII."

- Do not ask about contraception practices during an employment interview. This is an invasion of privacy.

- You may not refuse employment to an unmarried woman who has children. This has been found to be discriminatory against women.

- Be careful about using "stereotyped assumption" about women. Applicants must be considered as individuals. Ability to do the job in question should be primary consideration in your hiring decision.

When interviewing a college graduate, determine what type of job or career goals the applicant has. Refer those interested in management training to your regional office or management recruitment department.

The above changes will be incorporated into the Employment Guide which is presently being revised.

HANDOUT C

U.S. DEPARTMENT OF LABOR
EMPLOYMENT STANDARDS ADMINISTRATION

Women's Bureau
Washington, D.C. 20210

Why Women Work

More than 33 million women are in the labor force today because their talents and skills are needed by the American economy. The development of new industries and expansion of other industries have opened new doors for women in business, in the professions, and in the production of goods and services.

Decisions of individual women to seek employment outside the home are usually based on economic reasons. Most women in the labor force work because they or their families need the money they can earn — some work to raise family living standards above the low-income or poverty level; others, to help meet rising costs of food, education for their children, medical care, and the like. The majority of women do not have the option of working solely for personal fulfillment.

Millions of the women who were in the labor force in March 1972 worked to support themselves or others. This was true of most of the 7.5 million single women workers. Nearly all the 6.2 million women workers who were widowed, divorced, or separated from their husbands — particularly the women who were also raising children — were working for compelling economic reasons. In addition, the 4.1 million married women workers whose husbands had incomes below $5,000 in 1971 almost certainly worked because of economic need. Finally, about 3 million women would be added if we took into account those women whose husbands had incomes between $5,000 and $7,000 — incomes below the $7,200 estimated by the Bureau of Labor Statistics for a low standard of living for an urban family of four.

The marital status of women workers in March 1972 is given in the following table.

	All women		Women of minority races	
Marital status	Number	Percent distribution	Number	Percent distribution
Total	32,939,000	100.0	4,176,000	100.0
Single	7,477,000	22.7	920,000	22.0
Married (husband present)	19,249,000	58.5	1,991,000	47.7
Husband's 1971 income:				
Below $3,000	1,925,000	5.8	281,000	6.7
$3,000 - $4,999	2,194,000	6.7	394,000	9.4
$5,000 - $6,999	2,926,000	8.9	406,000	9.7
$7,000 and over	12,204,000	37.1	910,000	21.8
Other marital status	6,213,000	18.9	1,265,000	30.3
Married (husband absent)	1,500,000	4.6	538,000	12.9
Widowed	2,570,000	7.8	412,000	9.9
Divorced	2,143,000	6.5	315,000	7.5

Among the 4.2 million women of minority races who were workers in March 1972, slightly more than half (52 percent) were single, widowed, divorced, or separated from their husbands; about one-sixth (16 percent) were wives whose husbands had 1971 incomes below $5,000. In fact, only 22 percent of all women workers of minority races were wives whose husbands had incomes of $7,000 or more.

Women heads of families. Of the 53.3 million families in March 1972, 6.2 million were headed by women. About 3.3 million, or 53 percent, of the women family heads were in the labor force, and more than three-fifths of these women workers were the only earners in their families. About 1 out of 10 women workers was head of the family.

Nearly 3 out of 10 families (28 percent) headed by women had incomes below $3,000 in 1971. This was true for 4 out of 10 families headed by black women. More than one-fourth of all women family heads were black; the median income of such families in 1971 was $3,645, as compared with $5,842 for families headed by white women.

Mothers with husbands present. Of the 19.2 million married women (husbands present) who were in the labor force in March 1972, 10.5 million had children under 18 years of age. About 3.2 million of these mothers were helping to support their children. Included were 593,000 mothers whose husbands had 1971 incomes below $3,000, 1 million whose husbands had incomes between $3,000 and $5,000, and 1.6 million whose husbands had incomes between $5,000 and $7,000.

Of the 3.7 million working wives with children under age 6, 1.5 million, or 39 percent, had husbands whose incomes were less than $7,000.

Wives whose husbands are unemployed or unable to work. In the 45.8 million husband-wife families in March 1972, 1.3 million husbands who were in the labor force were unemployed and 6.6 million husbands were not in the labor force. Some 607,000 wives of unemployed husbands and nearly 1.5 million wives whose husbands were not in the labor force were working or seeking work. Many of these women were the sole support of their families.

Women whose husbands are employed in low-wage occupations. In March 1972 there were 607,000 married working women whose husbands were farmworkers; another 768,000 had husbands who were nonfarm laborers; and 1.1 million had husbands employed in service occupations. The median wage or salary income of men in these three major occupation groups was low in 1971. Among farmworkers it was below the low-income level, and among nonfarm laborers it was barely above.

Note. Figures are from the U.S. Department of Commerce, Bureau of the Census, and U.S. Department of Labor, Bureau of Labor Statistics.

Data for minority races refer to all races other than white. Negroes constitute about 90 percent of all persons other than white in the United States. Spanish-origin persons are included in the white population.

June 1973 (rev.)

10

SEMINARS FOR CAREER WOMEN: COMBINING AWARENESS TRAINING WITH TRANSACTIONAL ANALYSIS

by Dru Scott

Dru Scott's special achievements include solving problems in a number of areas using the transactional analysis (TA) method. Specific applications in the field of women and management include using TA in training for managerial communications, executive effectiveness, personal time management, and career development for women.

Before founding Dru Scott Associates, a San Francisco-based management consulting group, Dru Scott was associate director of the west-coast Communications Training Institute of the U.S. Civil Service Commission. She consults with corporate and governmental groups from Honolulu to New York and San Diego to Anchorage.

A specialist in ongoing, problem-solving seminars, Dru Scott has also designed and conducted numerous training courses. Three of her designs have been presented and adopted nationwide: Interpersonal Communication for Managers, Office Management, and the Career Women's Seminar described in this article.

Ms. Scott is a faculty member of the University of California Extension where she teaches Women in Management, Women at Work, Transactional Analysis in Management, Introduction to Transactional Analysis (a credit course), and Advanced

Transactional Analysis. She is a frequent speaker
for other private and governmental groups.

Dorothy Jongeward and Dru Scott are coauthoring
another book to be published by Addison-Wesley in
1975 on transactional analysis and the changing
roles of women.

Key Questions

1. What kind of job-related training can help women better understand what motivates their behavior?

2. How can transactional analysis be combined with special training for women?

3. How can a short course be organized?

4. What are the results of such training?

INTRODUCTION

Using transactional analysis (TA) in developmental training for women avoids the problem of only giving information and categorizing what's wrong. The Seminars for Career Women are a proven way of helping women be more effective in their jobs. Although the model I'm discussing is Federal, it can be adapted to any organization.

Many courses for women vividly present the plight of women. During such courses participants may learn about the earnings gap, the decreasing number of women in many professional jobs, and the cultural negation of women. In this training, women frequently get angry about what's wrong, and yet they return to their jobs repeating the same self-defeating patterns.

This training problem can be avoided, however. Using Seminars for Career Women is one way of presenting a problem and developing action steps for improvement. TA gives participants more options and workable tools for change. The main goal of the seminars is *more awareness leading to more choices*.

The theories of TA were developed by Dr. Eric Berne and popularized in his best seller, *Games People Play*. The awareness that comes as the result of this method enables people to see themselves more clearly so they can change what they want to change and strengthen what they want to strengthen. TA focuses on helping people better use their own mental resources to solve problems and make decisions.

Since the course design is written for trainers with a background in both women's studies and TA, a number of TA terms appear throughout the article. If you are just starting to work with TA, you may want to study the books suggested in the appendix. (See Appendixes A and E at the end of this chapter.)

The Seminars for Career Women are a proven way of helping women channel newly awakened awareness into constructive outlets on the job. The seminars have already done many good things for women in organizations. The following training model is designed to share the wealth.

THE COURSE ANNOUNCEMENT

SEMINAR FOR CAREER WOMEN

What's the approach?

This course is designed to help you answer these questions:

Do you discriminate against yourself?

Who are you at work?

How did you get that way?

What do you do with and to others?

How can you use the transactional analysis method to improve your interpersonal relations?

What psychological games are played at the office?

Where are you going with your job and your life?

What do you need to change to get there?

What should you know about the President's Federal Women Program?

Who may attend?

You, if you are a career-minded woman*

in a managerial, professional, technical, administrative, or clerical position

and work for a Federal, state, or local government

Purpose

To help you make a more effective contribution to your agency and get more job satisfaction

*The course has been expanded and is now open to men also.

The course announcement started the ball rolling. The immediate response was enthusiastic. We originally planned for 30 women in a seminar, and we had enough responses for two classes the first time the course was announced. Since the first seminar in the Spring of 1971, these notes have stimulated over 4,000 women to attend Seminars for Career Women. The notes also stimulated over 140 employers of these women to pay the course tuition and travel costs. Before leaving the Regional Training Center, I answered a lot of questions. This article includes the answers to some questions that may be coming to your mind also.

THE SEMINAR ANNOUNCEMENT STIMULATED A NUMBER OF QUESTIONS

Who sponsors the seminars?

These seminars were presented as part of the curriculum of the San Francisco Regional Training Center of the U.S. Civil Service Commission. The training center is one of ten similar operations across the country serving the training needs of Federal, state, and local government agencies. All courses operate on a cost-shared basis, with the sponsoring governmental agency paying tuition. The seminars, as well as other Training Center courses, are held in a number of cities in California, Nevada, Arizona, and Hawaii.

The original development of the seminars included input from Dorothy Jongeward and Muriel James, who have both been active in women's programs for many years.

Dorothy Jongeward and I later developed the seminar so that others could lead it. Most of the training aids are included in the course design section. Much of the material reflects Dorothy Jongeward's long involvement in the psychology and motivation of women and her experience in training over 6,000 women since 1960. Her training experience not only reaches many women (and men), but it also covers a wide range of levels. The levels extend from high school to university graduate school, from evening adult education to on-the-job training, and from beginning clerical training to corporate vice-presidential seminars.

Who is a career woman?

A career woman is any woman who sees working in paid employment as a significant part of her life. She is any woman who wants to achieve organizational goals, and who sees work as a way of expressing her potential as a human being.

Who comes to this seminar?

Women in the groups range from clerk-typists to district managers, from secretaries to engineering project managers, and from attendance clerks to mathematicians. The women range in experience from 1 to 25 years in their jobs. Organizations range from the City of Pleasant Hill to the U.S. Army in Hawaii to the Social Security Payment Center in San Francisco.

Although the seminars appeal to a diversity of women, they primarily attract women who are just starting to think through traditionally prescribed sex roles and new life and work possibilities.

Many different attitudes are represented in the seminars.

Some women come to the seminars knowing exactly who is responsible for the woman problem. They know that men cause the problem. And they know that their role is to fix blame and complain loudly about what men have done to them.

Other women come feeling that something needs to be changed, but they are not sure what or who.

Other women come ready to take positive steps to help themselves and other women better use their talents.

Still others wonder what the fuss is about.

Are the courses women's lib or people's lib?

Shortly after the seminars began they were nicknamed courses in "people's lib," and the nickname stuck. The term is a natural, since a goal of the course is women winning and men winning. Winning for men and women means both living and using their potential. Winning means all people getting what they want out of life without hurting themselves or others. [1]

Does the seminar teach that every woman should work?

The course stresses giving each woman a chance to make her own decisions. No one tries to cram one person's expectations down another person's throat. Each woman is encouraged to make her own Adult decisions and to take charge of her own life. She often uses the talents and ideas of other people in the seminar to help her, but the final decision is hers.

Many women decide to strive for higher-level jobs. Many women decide to take their work more seriously. On the other hand, some women decide they do not have to work, they really do not want to work, and they are working merely because of social pressures.

Other women feel better about continuing to do what they have been doing already. For example, some women, without consciously deciding, do things that are quite constructive and productive in their lives. However, they sometimes feel uncomfortable about these things because of vaguely felt pressures from society. By getting factual information and becoming aware of their decisions, they can deal with any of these feelings of uneasiness. Often, women are scripted to feel guilty about their accomplishments. The training often helps women feel better about things they have already achieved.

THE COURSE DESIGN

This section lists materials, a sample schedule, and a lesson brief keyed to each title in the sample schedule. The course design highlights practical guides that will help you as a trainer conduct similar sessions.

Materials

Using *Born to Win: Transactional Analysis with Gestalt Experiments* [2] speeds learning before, during, and after the actual workshop.

The first six seminars were presented before the book was published. The remaining seminars used the text. In the later seminars we had to spend two to three hours less on basic TA concepts. Also, participants having the advanced study assignment were immediately more confident about the usefulness of course material.

Before the course

Two or three weeks before the seminar, we send each woman a copy of *Born to Win* and "The Myth and Reality," an article by the Department of Labor's Women's Bureau. We ask each participant to study all of the four-page pamphlet and the first three chapters of the book. We ask them, as they study the book, to think about defining these terms: Parent, Adult, and Child ego states; complementary, crossed, and ulterior transactions; and psychological games.

During the course

Using the text in class makes Adult-Adult teaching easier. Participants have sources of information other than the workshop leader and each other, and using reference material in class helps sharpen the habit of actively seeking new information. During an agree-disagree exercise participants first jot down their individual decisions. They then come to a consensus in a small group. The consensus stage frequently involves checking out information in *Born to Win* or other books in the classroom. (See Appendix A at the end of this chapter.) The first evening we ask the women to study Chapter 4; the second evening, to study any chapter they are particularly interested in.

Afterwards

After the training session, the text serves (1) as a summary of the transactional analysis material covered in class; (2) as a means of sharing some of the information to co-workers; (3) as a guide to a study group; (4) as a study source of chapters not covered in class; and (5) as a quick reference for individual participants.

Other materials are helpful

You can give each participant a program schedule; a portfolio with notepaper, pen, and name plate card; and a roster of the persons attending the class.

Use of an overhead projector, chalkboard, or flipchart can add visual interest.

If you decide to use the Mass Media and Your Image of Women unit on the first afternoon, each participant needs one or two magazines. If you use the Putting It All Together unit on the second afternoon, the group needs 18 sheets of $2' \times 3'$ poster board, 6 bottles of rubber cement, and 6 pairs of scissors.

If you as a trainer are interested in participative TA teaching materials, look at *Winning with People: Group Exercises in Transactional Analysis* by Dorothy Jongeward and Muriel James. [3] It is full of workable involvement ideas.

SAMPLE SCHEDULE

Day One

A.M.   Program Objectives and Introduction

Four Growth Paths to Personality Development for Women

Transactional Analysis Overview

P.M.   Analysis of Personality: Winner or Loser Compulsions

Four Psychological Positions

Mass Media and Your Image of Women

Day Two

A.M.   Ego State Contamination

Women: A Historical Perspective

P.M.   The Midpoint Checkout

Putting It All Together: A Workshop

Day Three

A.M.   Time Structuring

Psychological Games People Play at Work

P.M.   Changing Back on the Job

Summary, Evaluations, and Presentation of Certificates

The seminars begin at 8:30 A.M. and end at 4:00 P.M. with an hour break for lunch.

LESSON BRIEFS

Day One, A.M.

Lesson Brief Title: Program Objectives and Introduction

Objectives

Demonstrate to participants they won't be embarrassed, talked down to, or bored.

Give participants a chance to get some Child-Child strokes.
Convey the importance of the Child getting strokes for better Adult functioning.
Give participants permission to take responsibility for their own learning.
Give participants permission to learn without hurting.

Time: 30 to 45 minutes

Lesson Brief

During the first part of the seminar we review the program objectives printed on the back of the schedule. These are the same questions that appear in the course announcement.

Throughout the seminar each participant can measure her own progress toward the goals of the course. This approach avoids the Parent-Child "I'll give you a test, and then I'll tell you how well you measure up."

Besides measuring her own progress toward clearly defined and accepted goals, each woman takes responsibility for her own learning. I usually say, "Most women in our culture learn over a period of years that the way to live is to be passive and wait for someone to come along and do things for you. Just as that rarely works on the job, it rarely works in training classes. Some time ago at the end of a three-day management course, a woman wrote me a note saying, 'I couldn't see very well the last three days. My chair was in an awkward spot.' "

I assure the current group that Mother Drusilla will not be around to move anyone's chair. The permission to take responsibility for one's own learning and to do something about any problem that blocks learning does work, but the results are sometimes funny. In one seminar in Los Angeles, immediately after talking about this permission, three people immediately stood up and left for the rest room.

In a group in San Francisco, one woman stood up and said, "I'm bothered by smoke. Can we use the airplane seating system? The smokers sit on the port side and all the nonsmokers on the starboard side." All of a sudden everyone started moving.

An introductory discussion of ego states and strokes tests how well the women understand the advance reading. The discussion also leads into the importance of making sure the Child is getting plenty of strokes.

Here is an opening exercise that provides Child-Child stroking and facilitates later Adult data processing. Two participants who don't know each other work through three one-minute steps. Before the steps begin, each two-person team decides which person will be an "A" and which will be a "B."

Step One: A imagines out loud what she feels the other person is like. For example, she might say, "I imagine that you hate Chinese food, you like to get up early in the morning, you like Hermann Hesse . . . ." During this step B has the hard job — staying quiet.

Step Two: The roles are reversed. B does the one-way imagining. A does the listening.

Step Three: A and B check how accurate their imagining was. [4]

At the end of this exercise the participants discuss what happened and how they felt. They find a collection of 30 stiffly sitting strangers taking a big step toward becoming a fully functioning learning group. They find a group that feels better and a group that has fewer not-OK Child feelings detracting from Adult learning.

Lesson Brief Title: Four Growth Paths to Personality Development for Women

Objective

Present a framework for understanding how people learn to see themselves.

Time: 40 to 60 minutes

Lesson Brief

Four paths to the development of personality serve as a framework for much of the material that evolves later in the seminar. This unit concentrates on bringing out special scripting American women often learn.

- *Personal identity* is how women identify themselves in nonsexual capacities. Some examples are the sense of ability, intelligence, competence, and personal worth.

- *Sexual identity* for many women comes from a relationship with a man and from taking care of others. Women are often first defined by their sexual roles, such as wife or mother, rather than as a person who is also a wife or a mother.

- *Life goals* for a woman are frequently in terms of getting married or having children. As we point out in the first part of the seminar, these goals are often achieved by the middle of a woman's life.

- *A value system* for a woman that is culturally approved is likely to revolve around taking care of someone else and getting satisfaction from others' achievements to the exclusion of her own achievements. Also, values women frequently adopt, such as being constantly submissive, are unproductive on the job.

This unit is largely lecture with some questions and answers. Information in the "What Do You Do When Your Script Runs Out?" article (in Appendix A at the end of the book) fits into this segment.

To conclude this section, you can ask participants to make up a list of what a little girl growing up in America today would likely hear about each path.

Lesson Brief Title: Transactional Analysis Overview

Objective

Make sure participants understand some basic TA terms.

Time: 45 to 75 minutes

Lesson Brief

This unit opens with a brief discussion of the functions of each ego state. Participants contribute ideas until there is a list of two to five functions for each ego state, written where everyone can see them. For example, the list for Parent would include criticizing and nurturing.

Women working in groups of two to four comprise the next step. They pick three situations and develop a Parent, Adult, and Child response to each situation. We ask them to be prepared to act out their situations and responses.

The time breakdown is about one-third to discussion of ego state functions, one-third to small group work, and one-third to role-playing and analyzing the examples.

You can follow the same pattern for transactions. A lecture-discussion brings out the characteristics of complementary, crossed, and ulterior transactions. The next step is diagraming some transactions and asking the small groups to prepare to role-play a transaction that fits each diagram. As a team is presenting one set of transactions, the other teams check to make sure the role-play fits the diagram.

The final step of this unit is a discussion of what characteristics must be present for a set of transactions to be called a game. This definition is brief, since games are discussed in greater detail on the third day.

Day One, P.M.

Lesson Brief Title: Analysis of Personality: Winner or Loser
Compulsions

Objectives

Establish the validity of the concept of script.
Present script types — winning, nonwinning, and losing.

Present examples of common nonwinning scripts for women. Have the women start identifying their own script.

Time: 45 to 60 minutes

Lesson Brief

"What goes into a dramatic script?" is a good opening question for this session. As participants suggest elements of a dramatic script, these ideas can be related to a psychological script. Developing this analogy helps define how a psychological script works. The next step is verifying the definition. One way to do this is to describe a person living out a destructive, or losing, script. Then ask the participants if they know anyone personally who seems to be living out this pattern. You can use the same approach for a winner, and then a nonwinner. By this time most people are nodding and saying, "Yes, that's really true." Although we don't directly ask for a personal assessment, many participants start figuring out what kind of a script they are living out.

This introduction generates high interest — more than enough interest to carry you through a 30- to 40-minute lecture. During this presentation we cover the ways in which scripts are developed and examples of common nonwinning scripts that women frequently adopt. Cinderella, Sleeping Beauty, and Mother Hubbard are all good examples. At this point it's useful to let participants pick out common threads in the sample scripts. Usually, most of the women quickly spot the passivity and the waiting for a magical rescuer. Some of the women will notice that all the samples portray women who give more strokes than they receive. Frequently, the discussion centers on the harmful implications of women constantly giving strokes to others and getting very few themselves.

The next step concentrates on helping the women think through their own scripting. One way is to ask each person to jot down the specific things she learned about key subjects such as mental ability, physical ability, personal appearance, education, woman's place, femininity, and sexuality. Before participants start jotting down script messages, point out that learning can be from verbal messages or nonverbal examples. I stress that answers are for their personal use only.

Lesson Brief Title: Four Psychological Positions

Objectives

Define strokes.

Discuss how positions are developed.

Summarize key characteristics of

I'm not-OK — You're OK,

I'm OK — You're not-OK,

I'm not-OK — You're not-OK,

I'm OK — You're OK.

Have participant think through how a person operating from each position acts.

Time: 30 to 90 minutes

Lesson Brief

The concept of strokes and their life and death necessity is a powerful opener for this unit. If you think someone may not clearly understand what a stroke is, you can briefly review some definitions. One definition that I find people grasp quickly is: A stroke is any way we let other people know we know they are alive.

Participants should have this concept, at least, firmly in mind at the end of this unit. There are both positive and negative strokes. Strokes may be either physical or symbolic. Without strokes, an infant will die. If an infant gets negative strokes, he will not die, but he will grow up emotionally ill in some way. A person intuitively knows that negative strokes are better than no strokes at all and will work to get negative ones if not enough positive ones are forthcoming.

At this point, the women will have some understanding of the importance of strokes. The film *Second Chance* extends the understanding to a feeling level. This fifteen-minute film shows how a lack of strokes has slowed the growth of 22-month-old Susan to the height and weight of a child less than half her age. Susan's retardation is temporarily arrested when, during her hospitalization, she is given stroking and loving care for over six hours a day for two months. [5]

The film also leads into a discussion of the development of psychological positions. You can mention the different ways the same position may be arrived at. For example, a child may learn to feel, "I'm not-OK — You're OK," if a parent frequently yells, "You dumb kid! You can't do anything right. Why, your sister Helen was toilet trained by nine months, and look at you at a year and a half." A child might arrive at the same position by frequently hearing, "Oh, don't bother your head with those old nasty shoelaces. I'll tie them for you."

Looking at the four psychological positions: I'm not-OK — You're OK; I'm OK — You're not-OK; I'm not-OK — You're not-OK; and I'm OK — You're OK is a useful framework for helping women examine their own self-image.

After discussing each position, you can ask the participants to work on the next project individually or in small groups. The worksheet grid includes a list of the four positions, with a number of characteristics that apply to all four. For example, how would a person with an I'm not-OK — You're OK position

> be described by close acquaintances?
>
> give and get strokes?
>
> collect feelings or stamps?
>
> deal with conflict?
>
> manage?
>
> receive supervision?

The small teams then answer the same questions for another position, until all four are discussed. [6]

Lesson Brief Title: Mass Media and Your Image of Women

Objectives

Point out how women are portrayed in magazines and how these portrayals may effect women's image of themselves.

Focus on using the insights to make positive changes rather than just fixing blame.

Time: 30 to 45 minutes

Lesson Brief

We use this lesson only when there is a low level of awareness of women's portrayal in the media. Before the course, we ask each participant to bring one or two magazines with her to the seminar. During the exercise on Mass Media and Your Image of Women, the participants look closely at how women are portrayed. They look for generalizations about how a woman should look to be OK in the eyes of Madison Avenue. What size? What age? What roles? What should she be doing to her body? How should she relate to other people? to men? to other women? to children?

Most of the women have not thought about the impact of the media on their own roles and how they picture themselves. This exercise ends with women saying, "No wonder I feel not-OK every time I look in the mirror. I'm not an 18-year-old size 5 with two spotless children, three-inch-deep carpets, and an impeccable house." Many of the women are vaguely aware of how women are stereotyped by the media, but they have not felt the force of this representation before.

A few words of instruction, plus a group of women with some magazines, equals an explosive, insightful exercise.

At the conclusion of the exercise you may want to stress, "What are you going to do about it?" This helps avoid the "If It Weren't for Madison Avenue" game. Again, the goal of this exercise is to develop insight that leads to action, and not just insight that leads to fixing the blame.

Day Two, A.M.

Lesson Brief Title: Ego State Contamination

Objective

Help participants identify cultural contamination relating to women.

Time: 20 to 30 minutes

Lesson Brief

A question that comes to many women's minds after the information on scripts and growth paths is that, with all of this information, why are so few changes being made? Looking at how Parent thinking may contaminate an Adult explains why change is so slow. It explains why "facts" may not change someone's mind, even though that person is a clear thinker in many other areas.

Here is an exercise that points out cultural contamination about the role of women. We ask each team to make up a list completing this sentence: "Women are . . . ," and another list for the sentence, "Men are . . ." In this exercise they don't ask, "Is this statement true?" but "Would a child growing up in our culture commonly hear these statements?"

The contrast between the "women are" and the "men are" lists jumps out when the lists are summarized on a transparency or chalkboard. Frequently, the first response women have is "The men have all the good things and the women have all the bad things." After looking at the lists a little longer, they may decide that it isn't that good to have cultural scripting to always be the leader, always be strong, never show emotions, etc.

After looking at how the Parent can contaminate Adult thinking and produce prejudice, we look at Child-contaminated thinking or delusion. A form of delusion women frequently have is waiting for a rescuer. The group discusses how a woman might live out the rescuer delusion.

Lesson Brief Title: Women: A Historical Perspective

Objectives

Spotlight the history of women acting from subordinate roles.

Create an awareness of the role of women played in the struggle for equal rights.

Time: 1 to 3 hours

Lesson Brief

At this point, most of the participants are aware of the importance of a sense of history. They realize that before you can get where you want to go, it's important to know where you've been and where you are.

The opening for this exercise is a six-question quiz. Just to get the feeling, you may want to answer the quiz yourself right now.

---

1. What happened to the women delegates who crossed the Atlantic to attend the World Anti-Slavery Conference in London in 1840?

2. What happened at Seneca Falls in 1848?

3. Who was Susan B. Anthony?

4. Who was Carrie Chapman Catt?

5. When were women given the right to vote?

6. Who was Sojourner Truth?

We ask the women to complete the quiz and, after doing this individually, to talk about their answers with other team members. One or two minutes of strained silence is usually followed by three or four minutes of embarrassed conversation. "I've never even *heard* of Carrie Chapman Catt," "I think Susan B. Anthony was a weirdo I saw in a history book someplace," and "I'm not sure when women got the vote." Suddenly, the realization of how ignorant most women are of their history as women hits the group. These few questions create an awareness of the need for more knowledge about the history of women, and a willingness to seek out more facts. Usually at this time, we show the film, *Women on the March: The Struggle for Equal Rights*, part I, by the National Film Board of Canada. [7] The film includes actual film clips of the feminist movement in England in the early 1900's. Although the film features England, the struggle there closely parallels the American struggle for "votes for women."

After the film, women in the class talk about their feelings and observations about the film. The reactions consistently are, first, a great deal of pride and appreciation for what has been achieved for women, and second, a new or renewed sense of the importance of women taking positive action. Usually at this time, the information we've covered on how women are scripted to be passive starts coming together with how the equality that has been achieved was won by women who were active and not passive.

Direct quotes and examples from the lives of outstanding women in history add feeling and power to this section. You may want to jot down specific ideas as you prepare for the unit. *The Century of Struggle: The Woman's Rights Movement in the United States* by Eleanor Flexner is an excellent source book on the history of the struggle for the right to vote in the United States. The "And ain't I a woman?" quote from Sojourner Truth is particularly moving. [8]

We conclude this unit by summarizing the Federal Women's Program. Part of this summary is a short report by participants who are involved with this part of the Federal Equal Employment Opportunity effort.

Day Two, P.M.

Lesson Brief Title: The Midpoint Checkout

Objective

Clear up some frequently misunderstood TA details.

Time: 30 to 60 minutes

Lesson Brief

Exercises in this section give participants a chance to do Adult-Adult self-teaching. [9] The Ego State Checkout list (Appendix B, Part 1 at the end of this chapter) and the

Agree/Disagree handout (Appendix B, Part 2) summarize and reinforce important transactional analysis concepts covered so far during the course. Participants individually complete the exercises, then discuss them as a team.

The most valuable part of the learning is in sharing and evaluating the ideas with each other. The terms *agree/disagree* further stress Adult learning, rather than the Parent *right/wrong* learning. This lesson also portrays women learning to facilitate other women's personal growth rather than competing with other women.

The Ego State Reaction Quiz (Appendix B, Part 3) closes this unit. Since participants generally can quickly identify the appropriate answers, the quiz gives a success at the end. (The Agree/Disagree Sheet takes more time to analyze and is more difficult.)

Lesson Brief Title: Putting It All Together — A Workshop

Objectives

Sharpen participant's ability to identify Parent, Adult, and Child ego states.

Sharpen participant's ability to see how women are portrayed in magazines.

Time: 60 to 75 minutes

Lesson Brief

During this exercise each five-person team builds three collages. One collage represents Parent ego state, another Adult, and the last, Child. The examples are taken from magazines the women brought with them to class.

This exercise reveals several different things. The team members find out quite a bit about their styles of leadership and followership. (We deliberately do not give any instructions on how to go about building the collage, so they have the chance to experience and examine the process.)

In addition to observations about process, the participants increase their ability to figure out which postures, positions, etc. represent which ego states. They also figure out that it's difficult to find examples in the media of women functioning from the Adult. The limiting implications of this on scripting women for Parent or Child roles comes through clearly.

During 1971 we used this unit in all of the seminars. As a result of an evaluation after that time, we dropped it from some. We now use it only when the group needs more work in recognizing ego states and in seeing how women are portrayed in the media.

Day Three, A.M.

Lesson Brief Title: Time Structuring

Objectives

Present enough information so that participants can

1. define each time structuring method,
2. estimate how much time they are investing in each method,
3. estimate what kind of strokes they're getting.

Time: 30 to 60 minutes

Lesson Brief

We use our time to give, get, or avoid strokes in these six ways:

Withdrawal	Games
Rituals	Activities
Pastimes	Intimacy

After discussing each method of time structuring, the women evaluate each method and decide which one provides the strongest intensity of strokes and which provides the most readily available strokes. For example, rituals provide easily available strokes but strokes of low intensity. Games provide easy-to-get strokes that are strong, although negative. And games are a two-for-one sale — twice the ego state involvement with the same number of transactions.

You can lead from this discussion with any one of a number of questions. Here are a few.

1. What percentage of your time do you spend in each time-structuring method?

2. What percentage of strokes do you get through each method?

3. What are your favorite pastimes?

4. Who gives you negative strokes?

5. Who gives you positive strokes?

6. What kind of strokes do you usually give to others?

7. Do you get more than 20% of your strokes from any one source?

8. When did you last experience psychological authenticity or intimacy? What feelings did you have from your Child ego state?

An excellent way to use this material is to give each of the participants a printed list of these questions. Ask them to pick one and concentrate for sixty seconds on answering it. Pick another for the next sixty seconds. Keep going for three or four questions. It's surprising how much people can figure out and jot down in sixty seconds. (I've tried this exercise for an unlimited time, and Parkinson's Law prevailed. Work did expand to fill the time available for its completion.)

These last two questions are not optional.

9. Is there anything you want to change?

10. What are you going to do about it?

Lesson Brief Title: Psychological Games People Play at Work

Objectives

Review general dynamics of games.

Give participants a chance to analyze an on-the-job game, identify roles and the payoff, and experience stopping the game from any role.

Time: 90 to 120 minutes

Lesson Brief

The first step in this lesson is to make sure all participants understand and can identify the requirements for a set of transactions to be a psychological game. Since some of the participants will already have a good TA background, this is usually done in teams, with the more advanced participants helping teach the less knowledgeable ones. Working in teams, the groups identify what the necessary characteristics are. They usually say there must be

1. a predictable payoff,
2. involvement of more than two ego states,
3. an ulterior transaction,
4. a repetitive pattern of transactions,
5. a period of discount.

A brief review of the Karpman Drama Triangle introduces the approach we take toward games. We stress the importance of understanding the roles in games, rather than being able to attach a name. Talking through two or three sample games shows how the roles are played and switched. To give the participants a better idea, you can have them play a practice round of *Why Don't You, Yes, But.*

After this, participants look at the game sheet developed by Dorothy Jongeward (See Appendix C at the end of this chapter). The sheet lists a number of games by predominant roles: Persecutor, Rescuer, or Victim. The people in the class then pick out any games they would like more information on.

The training class breaks into groups of three to five participants to discuss examples of games they observe on the job. After a few minutes of talk about game playing that they have observed or participated in, they select one example to concentrate on.

Deciding how to portray this example is the next step for the small groups. After the first role-play in front of the entire class, a group demonstrates how the game can be stopped. With the help of the entire class the group may run through the example two or three times, showing how the game can be stopped from any role.

This portrayal of games in front of the entire group is one of the most valuable parts of the seminar. Participants get practice in spotting roles in realistic situations. They also get practice identifying exactly what a game is.

The last game we discuss is *Psychiatry*. It's often tempting for participants to leave a training session and go back to their jobs as experts in the game of *Psychiatry*. This game uses TA information and terms to put down others. To avoid this, we role-play examples of how the information learned in the seminar can be communicated in a nonjargon, nongamey way. Rather than a participant going back to the job and saying, "Oh, you're always being Parent," we discuss ways to present the information. For example, "When you shake your finger at me when evaluating my reports, I feel put down." This ability to communicate the same information in a non-threatening way helps speed the transfer of skills to the job. It also eliminates the problem of people returning and creating more hostility with the techniques learned.

Day Three, P.M.

Lesson Brief Title: Changing Back on the Job

Objective

Show participants they can increase the usefulness of the course on the job by planning now how to start applying the material.

Time: 20 to 30 minutes

Lesson Brief

This session concentrates on the critical problem time — the two weeks immediately following the training. Former course participants from a variety of training subjects tell me the first two weeks after the course is the make-or-break period. If they do not apply the material on the job during those two weeks, they usually never apply it.

This unit helps bridge the gap between classroom and job performance and creates an Adult-Adult contract for taking action. It also creates a new positive stroke source to make up for a possible decrease in strokes from giving up old behavior.

"Two by two by two" is the subtitle for this unit. The unit takes two people two steps in two weeks. Here's how it works: Each person selects a partner she feels comfortable working with. The two people brainstorm together. From the ideas developed in the brainstorming, each woman picks two steps she can take during the next two weeks. The steps must be ones she can take on her own initiative.

Here are some sample steps participants have selected during this exercise:

"I'm going to level with John about my feelings toward the way he frequently gives me work at the last minute."

"I am going to play *Uproar* with subordinates not more than once a week."

"I am going to speak up in staff meetings rather than be quiet and collect feelings of resentment."

After selecting the two steps, most of the two-person teams make a contract to help each other achieve their goals. A major benefit of the contract is providing an alternative stroke source. For example, if a participant stops getting strokes from playing *Uproar* with her staff, she will need some strong strokes from another source. Her partner can give these strokes, and positive ones, to fill the new need.

I have found this two-person exercise more useful than having an individual participant decide on a plan of action and turn in a card to the instructor. The participant-participant contract emphasizes Adult-Adult, whereas the participant-leader contract tends to be more Child-Parent. (Since I have 90 to 120 new participants each month, I'm not going to be able to give many individuals strokes for change.)

Lesson Brief Title: Summary, Evaluations, and Presentation of Certificates

Objectives

Get a sense of closure on course material.

Get reactions of participants about effectiveness of training.

Time: 10 to 20 minutes

Lesson Brief

The summary is made by participants rather than the workshop leader. We sit around informally, and if a woman wants to mention what changes she is going to make, she just speaks out. The comments are typically brief, but pointed. They touch all aspects of the course from the history of women to time structuring, and from strokes to psychological games.

During the closing exercise, participants receive a certificate and a feedback form. On the form we ask the following questions.

1. In terms of how well the course objectives were achieved for you, how do you rate the course? Not at all achieved = 1. Fully achieved = 20.

2. What part of this training session will be the most useful to you on the job?

3. What part will be the least useful to you on the job?

Although this feedback does not measure on-the-job results, it does provide a useful guide to methodology or subject matter to be changed.

THE FOLLOW-UP SURVEY REPORTS SEMINAR SUCCESSES

This section outlines the manner in which the survey was conducted, the conclusions from seminar participants and their supervisors, detailed answers from the participants' survey, and detailed answers from the supervisors' survey.

How We Made the Survey

Participants in five classes held between October 1971 and early March 1972 received a follow-up survey two to seven months after they participated in a seminar.

This anonymous survey was divided into two parts: one for the participant to complete, and one for the participant to give to her immediate supervisor. Supervisors and participants were asked to return the anonymous surveys independently. Of 130 participants receiving the survey, 85 returned the forms. Seventy supervisors returned the questionnaires.

What We Concluded

Our conclusions summarize first the findings of the participants' survey, and then the findings of the supervisors' survey.

Highlights From the Survey of Participants

The survey findings agree that the seminar greatly benefited participants. The responses to the key questions were very enthusiastic. We found that:

> 72% of the participants agreed that they were more effective on the job as a result of participating in the seminar.
>
> 67% agreed that they now got more job satisfaction.
>
> 93% agreed that they now have more Adult control in their interpersonal relationships.
>
> 77% said they had stopped playing psychological games or played at a lighter degree. (Some believe that most people spend 50 to 90% of their waking hours playing psychological games. If so, this one area alone can result in major dollar savings.)

One group of questions deals directly with discrimination — men against women, women against women, and individual women against themselves. Here we found that:

> 88% agreed that they recognized subtle forms of discrimination more readily as a result of the seminar.
>
> 86% were more aware of stereotyping of women by women.
>
> 88% of the women agreed they were more aware of how some women learn not to succeed.

The last statement is probably the most significant. We found that:

> 85% of the women felt that the seminar had a great effect on their lives. (Several commented further on this point in the open-end questions.)

Highlights from the Survey of Supervisors of Participants

The statements on this survey were less emphatic than on the survey for participants. None of the statements ranked higher than 64%, while on the participant survey one statement ranked 93% and five ranked in the 80 to 90%'s.

Although none of the statements was as high on the supervisors' survey, the most important question ranked almost two-thirds. That was the following one.

> 64% of the supervisors said they believed their subordinate (a class participant) was more effective on the job as a result of the seminar.

Answers to the open-end survey questions were the most revealing part of the supervisors' survey. There were several concrete examples of major improvements. One problem in this part of the survey, however, was that the supervisors were not familiar with the seminar terminology and details. This, combined with the diversity of job classifications and levels represented by participants, made it difficult to get accurate supervisory feedback.

Survey Details in the Appendix

The survey questionnaires, and responses are included in Appendix D at the end of this chapter. [10]

SUMMARY

For many reasons, the need for special training for women is now. The need is great. Organizations need training that helps women make more of a difference back on the job. Using TA in special training for women avoids the problem of just giving information and defining what's wrong, but not giving a workable method for change. The evaluation survey of the Seminars for Career Women gave us evidence that we'd only suspected before. The seminars did help improve on-the-job performance. Participants and their supervisors alike recognized and reported the improvement.

FOOTNOTES AND REFERENCES

1. This definition of winners is developed in *Born to Win: Transactional Analysis with Gestalt Experiments*, by Muriel James and Dorothy Jongeward, (Reading, Massachusetts: Addison-Wesley, 1971), pp. 1-6.

2. The course tuition includes a copy of this book.

3. Dorothy Jongeward and Muriel James, *Winning with People: Group Exercises in Transactional Analysis* (Reading, Massachusetts: Addison-Wesley, 1973).

4. I first saw Kris Hayes, a training director at McClellan Air Force Base in Sacramento, use this approach.

5. Film, *Second Chance*, Hoffman-La Roche Laboratory, Nutley, New Jersey, 07110.

6. See also *Winning With People* by Jongeward and James. This book contains a similar worksheet and several other instruments that can be used in Seminars for Career Women.

7. Film, *Women on the March: The Struggle for Equal Rights*, Part I, by the National Film Board of Canada. We didn't find Part II of the film which features more contemporary women pertinent to the course.

8. Eleanor Flexner, *The Century of Struggle: The Woman's Rights Movement in the United States* (New York: Atheneum, 1971) pp. 90-91.

9. The Ego State Reaction Quiz is reprinted with permission from *Winning With People: Group Exercises in Transactional Analysis*. This quiz, the Agree/Disagree sheet, and the Ego State Checkout are in Appendix B of this chapter.

10. Sally Keen, a training officer with the U.S. Social Security Payment Center in San Francisco, contributed many valuable ideas when I was developing the questionnaire.

APPENDIX A: REFERENCE BOOKS

We have a copy of some useful reference books displayed in the training room. As the course progresses, participants borrow and add books to the collection. The following books (listed in recommended order) are a good start.

About Women

Flexnor, Eleanor, *The Century of Struggle: The Woman's Rights Movement in the United States* (Cambridge: Belknap Press, Harvard University, 1959).

Friedan, Betty, *The Feminine Mystique* (New York: Norton, 1963).

Morgan, Robin, ed., *Sisterhood is Powerful* (New York: Vintage, 1972).

Gornick, Vivian and Barbara K. Moran, eds., *Women in Sexist Society* (New York: Vintage, 1972).

About Transactional Analysis

Harris, Thomas A., *I'm OK – You're OK* (New York: Harper & Row, 1969).

Ernst, Ken, *Games Students Play* (Millbrae, California: Celestia Arts Publishing, 1972).

Berne, Eric, *Games People Play* (New York: Grove Press, 1964).

Berne, Eric, *What Do You Say After You Say Hello?* (New York Grove Press, 1972).

James, Muriel and Dorothy Jongeward, *Born to Win: Transac tional Analysis with Gestalt Experiments* (Reading, Massachusetts Addison-Wesley, 1971).

Jongeward, Dorothy and Muriel James, *Winning With People: Group Exercises in Transactional Analysis* (Reading, Massachu setts: Addison-Wesley, 1973).

Meininger, Jut, *Success Through Transactional Analysis* (New York: Grosset & Dunlap, 1973).

APPENDIX B: EXERCISES

Part 1: Ego State Checkout

Individually decide which ego states would be most frequently associated with the following behaviors. Then discuss your choices with your group.

1. Being affectionate
2. Automatically doing what you're told
3. Being self-centered
4. Passing on traditions
5. Worrying that people will be critical
6. Nurturing
7. Procrastinating
8. Quickly judging right or wrong
9. Being authoritarian
10. Testing current reality
11. Acting protective
12. Having fun
13. Being intuitive
14. Making decisions to change
15. Being seen and not heard
16. Making new decisions and acting on them
17. Rebelling
18. Estimating
19. Gathering facts

Part 2: Agree? Disagree?

Will you individually go through the list, marking each statement "Agree" or "Disagree." After everyone in your group has finished, discuss the answers.

Key: P - Parent ego state   A - Adult ego state   C - Child ego state

_____ 1. The main use of TA is to change the people around you.

_____ 2. An 8-year-old boy has only a C.

_____ 3. A depressive life position is based on I'm OK — You're not-OK.

_____ 4. I'm not-OK — You're OK is a hostile position.

_____ 5. It's bad to act from your C.

_____ 6. A person should never do what the P says.

_____ 7. The A checks out or validates current reality.

_____ 8. The natural C is self-centered.

_____ 9. The A makes new decisions.

_____ 10. You can change through your P.

_____ 11. The adaptive C is spontaneous.

_____ 12. Cultural traditions are passed on through the A.

_____ 13. The P is best at solving problems.

_____ 14. Script is based on a decision made in early childhood and is a compulsion to live life in a certain way. A script ends in a predictable manner.

_____ 15. You can become I'm OK — You're OK through A decisions and positive experiences.

Part 3: Ego State Reaction Quiz*

Identify each reaction to the situation as either Parent, Adult, or Child (P, A, C). There will be one of each in each situation. Naturally these will be educated guesses, since you can't hear the tone of voice or see the gestures.

1. A clerk loses an important letter.

    a. "Why can't you keep track of anything you're responsible for?"   _____

---

*   This quiz is from the Instructor's Manual for *Born to Win* (James and Jongeward).

b. "Check each person who may have used it in the last two days and try to trace it. Perhaps Mrs. Smith can help you."   _____

c. "I can't solve your problems. I didn't take your old letter."   _____

2. A piece of equipment breaks down.

a. "See if a repairman can come this morning."   _____

b. "Wow! This machine is always breaking down. I'd like to throw it on the floor and jump on it."   _____

c. "Those operators are so careless. They should know better."   _____

3. The boss is not satisfied with a letter his secretary wrote in reply to a memo from another department.

a. "Golly, Mr. Smith, I read that memo three times and it's so bad I just can't figure it out. He must be a jerk."   _____

b. "I found the memo contradictory, Mr. Smith. I'd appreciate your telling me what you see as his main question."   _____

c. "We shouldn't have to answer this memo at all. That man clearly doesn't know what he's talking about."_____

4. Coffee break rumors report a co-worker is about to be transferred.

a. "Boy, tell me more. I'd like to get something on George. He gives me a pain in the neck!"   _____

b. "Let's not spread a story that may not be true. If we have a question, let's ask the boss."   _____

c. "We really shouldn't talk about poor old George. He has so many troubles — financial, marital, you name it."   _____

5. The boss has had an important proposal rejected.

a. "Poor Mr. Brown, you must feel terrible. I'll fix you a little cup of tea to cheer you up."   _____

b.   "You think you feel bad! Just listen to what happened to me!"   _____

c.   "I'm sorry about the reversal, Mr. Brown. Let me know if there is anything you want me to do."   _____

6. A buxom secretary appears on the job in a very tight sweater.

a.   "Wow, look at that!"   _____

b.   "Tight sweaters should not be allowed in the office."   _____

c.   "I wonder why she chose that to wear to work."   _____

7. Someone unexpectedly gets a promotion.

a.   "Well, Mrs. White deserved it. After all, with all those children to feed, she needs that extra money. Poor thing."   _____

b.   "Oh brother! She got that for buttering up the higher-ups."   _____

c.   "I thought I was more qualified for the promotion than Mrs. White. But maybe I haven't given her enough credit."   _____

8. A reduction in personnel is announced.

a.   "What will I do if I'm laid off?"   _____

b.   "This damn company isn't worth working for anyway."   _____

c.   "I believe that all women should be fired first. They don't need the money. They're just taking jobs away from men."   _____

Participants may differ in responses. However, here are our suggestions.

1. PAC	5. PCA
2. ACP	6. CPA
3. CAP	7. PCA
4. CAP	8. ACP

APPENDIX C: THE GAMES PEOPLE PLAY

Games are played from the manipulative roles of Victim, Persecutor, and Rescuer. These roles switch as the game progresses. Also, these games can be played from different roles. This is a guide only.*

Victim games usually reinforce a psychological position of I'm not-OK. Inadequacy and/or depression stamps† may be collected.

Kick Me	*Poor Me*
Wooden Leg	*Ain't It Awful (about me)*
Harried Executive	*Love Me No Matter What I Do*
Lunch Bag	*(Schlemiel)*
Why Does This Always Happen	*See How Hard I Try*
to Me?	*Stupid*

Blaming games reinforce an I'm not-OK position by acting out a You're not-OK drama. Purity and self-righteous stamps may be collected, often covering up fear.

If It Weren't for You
See What You Made Me Do?

Persecutor games usually reinforce a psychological position of You're not-OK. Anger and/or purity stamps may be collected.

Blemish	*Making Someone Sorry*
Corner	*Uproar*
Now I've Got You, You S.O.B.	*Why Do You Always . . .*
Rapo	*Ain't It Awful (about you)*
Bear Trapper	*Mine is Better Than Yours*
Let's You and Him Fight	*Putting Someone Down*
Yes, But	*Psychiatry*
I Told You So	

---

*   Prepared by Dorothy Jongeward from *Everybody Wins: Transactional Analysis Applied to Organizations* (Reading, Massachusetts: Addison-Wesley, 1973).

†   Stamps represent feelings that are collected, saved up, and then cashed in, similar to the way we collect and redeem S&H green stamps.

Rescuer games usually reinforce the You're not-OK position. Purity, anger, inadequacy, and/or depression stamps may be collected.

I'm Only Trying to Help You
Let Me Do It for You

Games are played to avoid or regulate intimacy, to get strokes, to collect stamps, to reinforce psychological positions, or to reinforce psychosomatic illness. They are a bad habit and can be given up in favor of more honest, authentic, intimate human encounter based on the present rather than on what happened in the past. Winners try their best to give up destructive or hurtful games.

APPENDIX D: FOLLOW-UP SURVEY

DETAILS THE PARTICIPANTS REPORTED

Questionnaire for Participants

Seminar for Career Women Training Evaluation

For each statement, circle which of the positions at the right most aptly describes your present thinking.	
SA	Strongly Agree
TA	Tend to Agree
NSO	No Strong Opinion
TD	Tend to Disagree
SD	Strongly Disagree

As a result of participating in a Seminar for Career Women, I	Percent	Percent	Percent
	SA and TA	NSO	TD and SD
1. _____am more effective on the job.	72	26	2
2. _____ get more job satisfaction.	67	27	6
3. _____ have more adult control in my interpersonal relationships.	93	6	1
4. _____ find working with overly dependent persons increasingly frustrating.	27	27	45
5. _____ more effectively handle authoritarian or bossy persons.	75	20	5
6. _____ am less sure of exactly what is expected of me at work.	1	18	81
7. _____ act more often from the ego state most appropriate to the situation.	80	9	11

	Percent	Percent	Percent
8. _____ find myself in more "it was the only thing I could do" situations.	5	18	78
9. _____ have stopped playing, or play at a lighter degree, psychological games.	77	15	8
10. _____ have an increased consciousness of how some women are programmed to be losers and nonwinners.	88	8	4
11. _____ understand more clearly subtle patterns of discrimination.	88	8	4
12. _____ am more aware of stereotyping of women by women.	86	7	6
13. _____ see fewer psychological games played in the office.	2	25	73
14. _____ see less stereotyping of women by men.	12	15	73
15. _____ believe the seminar has had little effect on my life.	6	9	85

Participant Question

1. *Considering all training courses you have attended, how would you rate the seminar in terms of its value to your job performance?*

   61% of the participants ranked the seminar in the top 10%.

   87% of the participants ranked the seminar in the top 20%.

   97% of the participants ranked the seminar in the top 30%.

   4% of the participants ranked the seminar lower than the top 30%.

The following are typical answers to these open-end survey questions.

Participant Question

2. *What is your most important learning from this course?*

"The realization of the subservient role which women have accepted without question, and the fact that it can be changed, and that changes are taking place today. Becoming more interested and active in bettering the present conditions for women and myself."

"A new awareness of myself on the job and the roles that I play, and the things I can do that will give me more job satisfaction and advancement in my career."

"Learning to adjust to job situations and coping with demonstrative and unreasonable personnel."

"An awareness that people are programmed for certain behavior patterns, and that reprogramming is possible."

"Beginning of an awareness of people's problems — analyzing and understanding behavior. Realization of the power to direct one's own life."

"I am OK and women are OK. I have had a tendency to discriminate against myself. I am working on this problem."

"I was quite impressed by the statistics on length of time a woman works and this has definitely made me take my own job more seriously. Also, I think I will reeducate my daughter to place more emphasis on career choice."

"A more rational approach to my job performance. Analyzing myself and solving problems."

"My own smugness in thinking I was such a super manager came in for some critical analysis."

"I had begun to believe my own stereotype. I learned I could change myself — that there was no reason I couldn't be a leader in the organization, instead of a secretary, and to get off my duff and break out of the stereotype, instead of simply feeling frustrated."

Participant Question

3. *What is your least important learning from this course?*

"Learning about the psychological games people play."

"That there is prejudice against women by both sexes. I already knew that."

"Not applicable. The course was meaningful and well planned in its entirety."

"I felt the entire course was very informative and helpful. It was so well planned that I felt every woman left with a new awareness of her future as a career woman."

"Can't think of anything that fell into this category — all seemed succinct and important. The collage making didn't teach me much — I would have preferred more time to discuss."

Participant Question

4. *What subjects would you like added or covered more thoroughly?*

"How we as women put down ourselves and other women."

"How to have mini-classes in TA when we get back to work."

"A little more history of women perhaps."

"How much of our makeup is the result of upbringing."

"How women themselves discriminate against women."

"How to deal with discrimination against women."

"How women are their worst enemies in getting ahead in business."

"It was already very thorough."

"Life scripts — how to change."

"Games people play. More information about the female role in American society."

"Developing self-control and personality development."

"How one can change from a loser to a winner."

"We didn't have time to cover all the material in *Born to Win*. Also I was sorry I had not read the entire book before the beginning of the seminar. I would strongly urge that it be mandatory for attendees to read and thoroughly understand the material in the book before going to the seminar."

"Games and game thwarting and how to cope with other's games."

"More on games played and which ego states are involved."

"History of women was fascinating. Would have enjoyed more time spent on this part as a background for the course."

"Turning a 'man's world' into everyone's world is so much easier when everyone is trained for this."

"I can suggest no changes. The course could not be improved in any way. Let a good thing alone."

DETAILS THE SUPERVISORS REPORTED

Questionnaire for Supervisors of Participants

Seminar for Career Women Training Evaluation

For each statement, circle which of the positions at the right most aptly describes your present thinking.		
SA	Strongly Agree	
TA	Tend to Agree	
NSO	No Strong Opinion	
TD	Tend to Disagree	
SD	Strongly Disagree	

As a result of participating in a Seminar for Career Women Training Session, do you believe the participant	Percent	Percent	Percent
	SA and TA	NSO	TD and SD
1. _____ is most effective on the job? Please jot down any examples.	64	34	1
2. _____ gives evidence of getting more job satisfaction? Please jot down any comments or details.	61	34	4
3. _____ is less conscious of traditional and new roles for women at work? Any comments?	19	37	44

	Percent	Percent	Percent
4. _____ demonstrates less initiative on the job? Please list examples of actions that suggest this conclusion.	1	13	86

Here are some sample comments from the open-end questions on the survey of supervisors.

Supervisor Question

1. *As a result of participating in a Seminar for Career Women Training Session, do you believe the participant is more effective on the job?*

   "Appears to be less argumentative in presenting her opinions and making compromises where necessary, without sacrificing any of her ideas."

   "Assumes more responsibility."

   "More understanding with other people and understands their problems."

   "Used to have constant chip on her shoulder. Highly critical of everyone else. Much better attitude now. More compassionate towards fellow employees. Actually has some understanding for the boss, too."

   "Seems to get along a little better with people she supervises."

   "Participant uses a more relaxed and less defensive approach when working with others. Participant's self-confidence has increased."

   "Gets along better with subordinates, appears to understand their problems more. Doesn't overreact as much as she used to."

   "Is becoming more career minded and has a higher degree of dedication."

"Participant seems to be more receptive to points of view other than her own."

"More prone to acceptance of more responsibility and personal career planning."

Supervisor Question

2. *As a result of participating in a Seminar for Career Women Training Session, do you believe the participant gives evidence of getting more job satisfaction?*

"Have noticed she initiates more actions on her own and with less skepticism."

"Seems to be more eager to get the job done pronto. Has launched a couple of new projects on her own."

"Volunteers readily for additional assignments."

"Enjoys accomplishing assigned tasks to a greater degree."

"Her attitude has improved, as evidenced by a decrease in her complaints and a willingness to tackle more complex assignments."

"Present position is designed for women and fulfills their satisfaction needs."

Supervisor Question

3. *As a result of participating in the Seminar for Career Women Training Session, do you believe the participant is less conscious of traditional and new roles for women at work?*

"If she has been conscious that there is a traditional role for women, she hasn't transmitted it to me. We both believe that if there are traditional roles for women, it's because of the organization and its hierarchy."

"Freely counsels women employees within the organization. Has prevented/settled some minor gripes. Feels free to discuss things with boss, knowing her ideas will be considered on merit."

"Participant focuses on work accomplishment and ability and not on past traditional male/female roles to evaluate a situation."

Supervisor Question

4. *As a result of participating in a Seminar for Career Women Training Session, do you believe the participant demonstrates less initiative on the job?*

   "She works more independently and with a minimum of guidance."

   "Appears to seek more responsibility."

   "With increased confidence she has increased initiative in her own job, but does not feel the need to solve other person's problems outside her job."

   "In spite of the fact that she is overworked, she still exercises a great deal of initiative."

   "After training, I observed several instances of looking for opportunities to help others with backlog."

   "Always has demonstrated high initiative."

APPENDIX E: TA TRAINING FOR TRAINERS

In addition to individual reading, there are several other avenues you can follow.

For special classes that integrate TA with training for women, contact:

Dru Scott, President
Dru Scott Associates
106 Point Lobos
San Francisco, California 94121

Dorothy Jongeward, Director
Transactional Analysis Management Institute
487 Malaga Way
Pleasant Hill, California 94523

For general information, referrals on TA, and a list of affiliates, contact:

International Transactional Analysis Association
3155 College Avenue
Berkeley, California 94705

11

WHAT DO I WANT
TO DO NEXT?

by Janice A. Kay

Janice Kay is president of her own firm, Career
Information Systems, in Oakland, California.
After extensive research in career fields, she created
her own system of vocational assessment which she
has used extensively for the last five years. She
holds California teaching credentials in group guidance, vocational counseling, psychology, and
administration.

She travels to conduct lectures and seminars for
business, industry, and government and is currently on the faculty of Holy Names College and
College of Notre Dame. Ms. Kay was educated in
Africa, Europe, and the United States, receiving her
B.S. degree from the University of Maryland. She is
a Master's Candidate at Holy Names College, spe-
cializing in career planning and continuing education for women.

She is a member of the Bay Area Consortium on
Continuing Education for Women and the Bay
Valley District of Business and Professional Women
which selected her Outstanding Career Woman
of 1972.

Key Questions

1. What can a woman who has been a capable
   executive secretary for 15 years, with a B.A.
   degree, do next?

2. What can a housewife in her forties who
   hasn't worked outside the home for 15 years
   do next?

3. What can an office manager concerned about
   the affirmative action program for women
   do next?

WOMEN'S VOCATIONAL PROBLEMS

My vocational planning system helps women like those in the key questions, plus many more. The system has been applied to schools, businesses, and individuals, and to all ages and socio-economic levels. The age range has been from 16 to 67, and the salary range from $3,000 to $70,000. I have discovered that the problem of vocational planning has a universality; it merely comes in different shapes, sizes, ages, and sexes.

I have found that many people feel they are standing in a deep, dark tunnel, looking into it with no end in sight. They have not learned how to mobilize themselves, turn around, look out of the tunnel, and then move forward.

Women's feelings of being immobilized in the world of work are traceable to the early years, when much of their training was to be smart in school — up to a point — but not to pass the boys. This is confusing. Instead of being taught or allowed to value their minds in anticipation of appropriate and meaningful expression in fulfilling work, women are taught that marriage and family are the ultimate goals. They are influenced to repress any natural feelings of mental superiority and/or desire for a career. The romantic notion of "marry and live happily ever after" is perpetuated in the world of work by the concept of "stay with one employer, and he'll take good care of you."

Men change their jobs every three to five years — and they get ahead. Ambition and aggressive desire to advance in women are called objectionable. Society's denial of female intelligence forces many women into highly restrictive and limiting jobs that require minimal effort and function. The job often becomes a protective vacuum within which the woman withers. It is no wonder that many women have little ambition and, in fact, fear movement. These attitudes, perpetuated by society and then turned into the many popular myths used by employers for not promoting women, help keep women in the same circular pattern.

Women have for so long settled for second best that it is extremely difficult for them to keep their focus on what they might want. I am convinced that a woman, far more than a man, needs to scrutinize her motives before she plans her life choices. I say "more than a man" simply because men are not subjected to those family or social influences which condition women to accept their life role as that of "serving others." Clearly, my chosen career is evidence that I am not, in principle, adverse to serving others; but I have found that women tend to belittle their "rights" to choose what they want, to underrate themselves and their abilities, largely because society has urged them to do so. Let us hope that our younger generation will reach adulthood without such conditioning. The following example from a mother in one of my groups illustrates the magnitude of the problem.

> "My little girl, who is five, is convinced that she can't be a doctor, that she can only be a nurse, because she is a female. To try and counter this, I have made appointments with every female doctor I can find in the area, so she can talk to them and see they exist. I'm not too sure how successful I have been, because the child is still convinced that the women aren't 'real' doctors; but I felt I had to do something to help her realize that her sex doesn't spell 'limited outlook'."

In spite of these self-image problems, women are entering the world of work in ever increasing numbers, and they come to work from all kinds of backgrounds. Some are divorced, some widowed, some married, some single, and they all have different problems, but with an underlying commonality.

To illustrate the difference and the commonality, I have surveyed more than 200 working women I have had in groups or seminars or as private clients. Please keep in mind that this represents a sample taken in the San Francisco Bay Area in the first half of 1972. The sample cuts across several industries to include banking, heavy industry, manufacturing, insurance, and retail. Other variables are as follows:

The age range was 22 to 58 years.

Two-thirds of the women were head of household, i.e., widowed, divorced, or single.

One-third had one or more dependents, either children or parents.

All were high-school graduates and about one-fourth were college graduates; another one-fourth had some college.

The salary range was between $5,000 and $10,000 per year with a cluster at about $7,000. It is clear that the more education she has, the more money a woman earns.

PROGRAMS TO HELP WOMEN

The future of the working woman has been significantly brightened by the reawakening of women's rights after a forty-year sleep, and the passage of Executive Order No. 4 in March, 1972.* Because of the pressures from these two developments, it is not surprising that many employers are working on affirmative action programs in order to

1. Establish seminars expecially for women and aid them with professional growth,
2. Implement vocational counseling for women,
3. Place women in positions of responsibility,
4. Encourage women to apply for promotional positions,
5. Develop programs expecially designed to motivate women toward career development, and
6. Encourage a management awareness of these needs.

It seems relevant, however, to stress that employers also need to grasp the concept that career growth requires an organizational climate in which individual growth is valued. Without this climate, the kind of training being discussed is of no value. I will discuss later what several firms in the Bay Area are doing in this regard.

Training programs are integral parts of career growth, but historically, women's participation in them has been nonexistent. The average male spends one month per year attending in-service training on company time. Women's participation has been less than a day per year. Not only do we need to include women in training programs that exist, but we need to develop new training programs aimed at the special needs of women.

The last five years of experience have proved the effectiveness of this vocational assessment system. I want to stress that I do not see my method, nor any other, as the magic answer. The answer lies within the person who has the problem and can apply the necessary tools to obtain an acceptable solution. I see my method as one way of providing these tools.

---

*   Executive Order No. 4 requires all companies doing business of more than $50,000 annually with the Federal government (as prime or subcontractors) to establish affirmative action programs.

SEMINAR OUTLINE

I will begin by giving a general outline of the seminar. I say "general" because the seminars often need to be tailored to the needs of a specific group or employer.

GENERAL SEMINAR OUTLINE

I.   *Focus on True Capabilities and Strengths*

The typical woman worker of today never completes a thorough vocational assessment. She is therefore unaware of the vocational qualities used and not used, and the compatibility of the demands of her job and leisure. She is unaware of life patterns which can help or hinder her career development. She also may not see the relationship of individual wants and needs to achieving satisfying career goals and life goals. Therefore, the seminar begins with an individual assessment of each participant to identify, integrate, and built new concepts of professional change and growth. Each participant receives an individual, computerized assessment.

II. *Identification of Professional Life-Style*

What is professionalism for a woman?
Marriage and professional life: either/or/compatible
Decision-making habits

III. *Exploration of Professional Self-Identity*

Teamwork with others
     Peer group relations
     Supervisory relations
     Subordinate relations

Formalization of professional goals
     Organizational potentials and limitations
     Personal potentials and limitations
     Alternatives to minimize limitations

Methods: Lectures, small groups, role-playing, individual work, simulation games, and audio-visual aids

Suggested texts/readings
    Born Female by Carolyn Bird
    Woman's Place by Cynthia Epstein
    Future Shock by Alvin Toffler

Participation in the seminar should be voluntary and should involve some sense of commitment on the part of the participant. A person who wishes to succeed must want career development and growth. Therefore, participation is useless if the sessions are not a chosen activity.

Role of the Trainer

The seminar is set up to engender participation and to produce a maximum of career growth through learning and information gathering. The role of the trainer is to establish conditions for professional self-development and to serve as a resource for the participants. Her role is *not* to determine goals, assess the participants, or tell them what to do. Nor should the trainer be a "laissez-faire" leader who explains the exercises and leaves the group to its own devices. The trainer is explicit in giving directions for each section. She carefully discusses seminar objectives with each participant. She begins each session with a short introductory presentation which is followed by one or more directed experiential exercises that actively involve all of the group as full participants, and then a discussion period led by either herself or one of the group members.

Time Basis of Seminar Varies

The seminar is taught on a flexible basis. It can be held on a three-day basis or a weekly meeting basis, or can even be extended over several weekends. There does, however, seem to be a minimum amount of time needed, within the range of 21 to 30 hours. I find that the working woman manages well with the minimum time, but the woman who is returning to work after an extended absence needs the extra hours. I do not run the three-day seminar for women who are returning to the world of work, as, in their own words, it is simply "not satisfactory." Most commonly, however, the seminar is taught on the three-day or weekly basis.

Three-Day Seminar

With regard to the different methods, all of them have advantages and disadvantages. The advantages of the three-day seminar are (1) it loses no momentum, and little time is lost in terms of stops and starts and warm-up time; and (2) it fosters dependence on self. I do, however, use a "buddy system," so that later, when a woman needs support, she can talk to someone with whom she has worked in the class and someone who has had the same seminar experience.

The disadvantages of the three-day seminar are (1) it is extremely concentrated and therefore leaves much of the growth and assimilation and integration to be done on one's own, and (2) it is exhausting for the trainer.

Weekly Seminar

Some advantages of the weekly meeting seminar are (1) long-term support from the group and the trainer. (The group itself is a significant factor, and this should be kept in mind. The support the women get from each other is one of the most important things that happens.) And (2) the ability to grow and then be able to return and ask questions, verify, share, and test reality.

The disadvantages of the weekly seminar are (1) dependence on the trainer can develop; (2) time is lost in getting started and in warm-ups; and (3) weekly continuity can be lost unless the trainer has bridges carefully planned and uses them for each session.

Content of the Seminar: Life Style

I begin the seminar by explaining my belief that a person must deal with vocational planning within the framework of total life planning. None of us can separate our lives into compartments neatly labeled "work," "family," "play," "friends," etc. I think the life style of a person can be diagramed (see Figure 1) in order to take into account her need for balance and integration.

What do I mean by these terms? First of all, by "life style" I mean the boundaries within which one chooses to live. "Work" is that part of meaningful activity which one does for money. "Play" is that part of meaningful activity one does not do for money. Play also includes what I call "maintenance activities," those

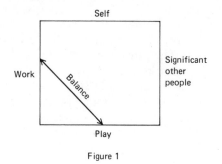

Figure 1

activities that we have to do, like cleaning the house or washing dishes. I don't mean to imply that anyone will love to wash dishes when she gets her life style together, but certainly the activities can be fitted in her program in such a way that she will dislike them less.

Work and play make up the two parts of meaningful activity and should serve to balance each other. By "balance" I mean the interplay between task demands that serve to refresh us, the release of one demand because of the need for another. Perhaps a personal example will serve to clarify this. My career as a vocational consultant deals with people and the communication of ideas, and it engenders prestige. In my leisure I am mainly involved in two other kinds of activity, which I label "things and objects" (washing dishes, knitting) and "machines and techniques" (cooking, sewing, tinkering with the car). These activities afford me tangible, productive satisfaction. I look at my work and leisure as two opposites which complement each other: people and ideas versus things and objects; prestige versus tangible, productive satisfaction. If I do not balance my leisure activities against my career demands, I become awkward at things that I normally do well — I am out of balance.

The other two sides of the life-style diagram are the "self" and "significant other people" (see Figure 2). By "self" I mean the concept of who I am, what I want, what I believe, where I am going. By "significant other people" I mean those in our lives whom we care about — our family and friends.

It should be reasonably clear that in working on this life style, the self has input into the choices we make about what we will, can, or aspire to do, and that our choices in these areas will affect the other people in our lives.

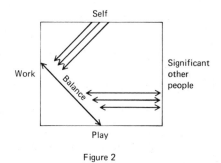

Figure 2

When the four aspects of our life style — work, play, self, and significant other people — are not seen as integral parts of a whole, we inevitably develop internal conflict. A typical reaction is to concentrate on a couple of the areas to the detriment of the rest; and this increases vulnerability and self-doubt, for when new and attractive challenges arise, we often lack the confidence of an integrated personality. A very real danger in this narrow approach is that we may become lulled into losing sight of our own identity. This trap is most often sprung in marriage, when a woman begins to think she no longer has to care for her "self" because she now has someone else to do it. She may have so many other people to care for that there seems to be no time left for herself. But if "self" is neglected, others are neglected also; and self-neglect can become the first step toward the destruction of one's nature.

This danger is equally relevant if a woman "buries herself" in her career. An example of this was Mary Lou. She came to me intending to change jobs. On investigation, I found that her current job was well-paid, she was efficient and thoroughly competent in her work, enjoyed excellent company benefits and working conditions, and got along well with her co-workers. The company was even willing to train her for advancement within the organization. She was not attracted. Her problem? All she could express was a vague "need to change." Deeper assessment revealed that her job function was not the only area basically lacking in satisfaction to her. Her whole life had revolved around the office. Her life style was work (see Figure 3).

Whenever I explain the life-style concepts in class, I see bobbing heads and know that people are at least hearing me. But I know the material isn't integrated until the same people actually do the exercise.

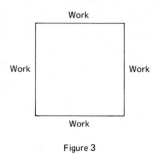

Figure 3

Life-Style Exercise

You have had the explanation — why not do the exercise now? Set up your boundary box and fill in the sides.

Is it balanced? If not, ask yourself "why?" Then take the four concepts from the balanced life style and fill in what would make up a uniquely balanced you. Here are some suggested questions to ask yourself first.

Work

> What do I really do?
> What needs are met?
> What needs are not met?
> What demands are made?
> Are these demands challenging enough?
> How do I feel about all this?

Play. Ask the same questions, but also ask:

> Is play something I do because I want to or because I'm trying to please others and their likes?

Ideally we should have play that is our own and which we share with someone we care for. This can be one and the same, or different.

Now ask:

Do work and play balance?
Do they refresh each other?
Do I let work skills rest and use different skills at play?

If things are not balanced:

What can I reorder to achieve a balance?

Significant Other People

Who are they?
What demands do they make?
What needs do they have?
What demands do you make on them?
What needs do they meet for you?
Are there overlaps in work?

If there are overlaps of needs and demands from job and significant other people, you need to ask:

Can I handle all that?
Have I enough to give?

An example seems helpful here.

One woman in my seminar had her terminally ill mother and father-in-law living with her. Also in the house was her daughter, who had just been through a traumatic divorce, and the daughter's child, as well as the woman's own husband. The woman wanted to return to work to help defray expenses but she also felt the need to get away from the house. In terms of balance, what sort of job should she seek? Right. One that had a minimum of people contact, one that gave her some routine and stability and dealt with things. She chose a job in a typing pool (she had this skill) and is quite happy. She will, however, have to reinventory her balance when her home situation changes.

Now consider:

Self

> What makes up my self-image?
> Who am I?
> What do I believe in?
> What will I take risks on?
> How does my self-image limit or motivate me?

You can put your life style together in any combination you like, as long as the total equals a balanced, integrated person. Balanced not because all contributions are equal, but because they supplement and refresh each other. Our life styles should serve as the boundaries within which we function, encompassing our need to expand our energy creatively, to relate with people, and to attend to ourselves. Inside our chosen precincts we should live and thrive to the fullest of our own capacities. The choice of activity reflects the total person, and the essence of growth is that it be directed.

Construct your own value system in terms of what is for you positive and negative. It is important for you to understand the effect of your attitudes, both positive and negative, toward yourself and your ability to function. Understanding these attitudes helps neutralize the harmful effects and maximize the positive effects. However, understanding is not enough.

Personal History

After the initial understanding of the conceptual framework of life style, each person in the seminar fills out a Personal History Composite, which includes questions about the person's work, training, and leisure time. I ask questions about her work that cover what she has done, how the jobs changed, what the impact of each job was, what she liked or disliked about each, how long the jobs lasted, why she took each job, and so on. All work is important, and this is stressed. Most people tend to put aside any activity they don't like or that was short term. I try and break this thought pattern because everything we do is important as we learn something from it. It is also important to analyze something we didn't like to be sure we will recognize it and not put ourselves in that situation again.

The questions are simple, but they make each seminar participant actually write down a history of her life spontaneously, and in an orderly fashion. The exercise initiates an evaluative process, and this is reinforced by the trainer's putting the answers into a tangible form. The information given on the personal history sheets is analyzed onto a computer printout which each participant receives. Formally, I call this an "Analysis and Comparison" — an analysis of past experiences compared with a set of constant criteria. These charts serve as the foundation for the rest of the seminar.

Since the computerized "Analysis and Comparison" isn't available to you who are reading, I have included samples of the Personal History Composite (on the following pages) for you to use. (Make up as many as you need.) These are helpful in thinking through past experiences — even without the charts.

Employment Information Instructions:
Personal History Composite

You will need about 2 1/2 hours to fill out these history forms. They are the foundation of the thinking pattern we are going to work on during the seminar. You will probably take about 20 minutes to get settled; but once you do, it will go quite smoothly. Please be specific and detailed.

1. Begin with your last or current job and work back.

2. Be specific about what you did.

3. If you need more sheets, Xerox the sheets you have, continuing to number in sequence.

4. Jobs that were the same may be lumped together, even if they were for different employers or departments.

5. Jobs that were different should be listed separately, even if they were for the same employer or within the same department.

6. List all your paid employment.

7. Be sure and list jobs you didn't like so you can think through why you didn't like them.

Personal History Composite
Employment

No. _____ employer name _____

Pay beginning _____ Pay ending _____ Date began _____Date left _____

Why did you leave?_____

_____

Job title _____

What were your duties? _____

What was the job's impact on you? _____

_____

Machines-equipment used? _____

_____

How did the job change? _____

_____

Supervise?_____ How many?_____Why did you take this job?_____

_____

What did you like?_____

_____

What did you dislike?_____

_____

Additional comments you wish to make about this job.

_____

_____

Leisure Information Instructions: Personal History Composite

By leisure I mean *all unpaid activities*. Leisure includes hobbies, clubs, sports, movies, and all unpaid activities. These activities can be current, but you should also include activities which you have done in the past. A good way to get into this is to ask yourself, "How do I fill my time when I am not working or sleeping?" You could also organize your thoughts around an activity pattern of current before marriage, before children in school; or current, before moving to this job, school, etc. — whatever pattern your life has taken and the elements that made it up.

1. Start with current activities and work back, including activities which may not be current.

2. All similar activities can be lumped together on one sheet — for example, sports, or sewing, knitting, crochet — but be sure and say how long you've been doing each and how good you are at each.

3. A minimum of five leisure sheets should be filled out, otherwise there will not be a balanced picture to work with.

4. You may draw a blank when you first start on the leisure sheet, but you fill your time with something. What is it?

Personal History Composite

Leisure

Leisure activity name _____

Was it with a club or group?_____Give name _____

_____

What was done? _____

When began?_____When stopped?_____

Machines or equipment used? _____

_____

Leadership positions held?_____

What did you like about the activity?_____

What did you dislike about the activity?_____

Why did you begin the activity?_____

Why did you leave the activity?_____

Additional comments you wish to make about this hobby.

_____

_____

Personal History Composite
Training

What is your highest degree completed? _____

What was your major in college? _____ minor in college?_____

What was your major in graduate school? _____

Average grades?   High School ____ College____Graduate_____

List your major courses in high school and how long you took them.
(I realize that high school may be a while back and most of the time majors were either business or college preparatory, but state which you had and list the courses you can remember.)

_____

_____

_____

_____

List your college courses that were *not* in your major or minor and how long you took them.
(These will probably be mostly electives — the few courses you took because you really wanted to or had a choice about.)

_____

_____

_____

_____

List other courses taken and how long you took them. Through what school were they taken?
(This will include in-service training, adult school, technical school, or private lessons.)

_____

_____

_____

_____

Personal History Composite
General

What limitations do you have that might limit your choice of activity?

_____

_____

_____

DREAMS

If time, money, and education were no problem, what would you do for a career?

_____

If time and money were no problem, what would you do for a hobby?

_____

What is the minimum salary you need? _____

Additional comments you wish to add.

_____

_____

_____

Function of the Charts

The nonjudgmental function of the charts is an important factor in the seminar. I try to maintain this attitude by staying away from the concepts "good" and "bad." Being locked into stereotyped ideas, such as considering change as good or believing that not working to help others is bad, can get in the way of making realistic decisions. I also encourage the participants not to use the qualifiers "just" and "only." I playfully say that these are not allowed. When the class members catch someone saying I am "only a wife" or "just a mother" or "I did it for only a year, and it was just a simple job," they usually can understand why it is important to stop this habit.

In working with the personal history charts, it is necessary to develop an accurate idea of the woman's philosophy and past life style. When we do vocational counseling, we are dealing with people's lives, and what we must sift through are the patterns of past behavior, and the bits of information that are productive or nonproductive. A well-developed history brings out a person's attitudes, values, feelings, and expectations, or the lack of these. To understand the aura of a person's work, training, and leisure is to understand her work attitudes as well.

We analyze the data collected on the history sheets not from the angle of trying to standardize people, but rather trying to standardize tasks. The participants are directed and encouraged to change, clarify, and modify their histories as needed. The history is never considered complete – it is a starting point – but the hope is that it will help to break the habit of relying on outside, frequently artificial methods for decision making. It enables the person to see herself objectively and to realize the relationship between self, activity tasks, activity environment, and activity industry. Thus the attitudes and values, while different for each of us, can develop from a factual data beginning.

Once the person agrees that the information on her history sheets is reasonable, logical, and true, she is unable to rationalize it away. It becomes real, and she can work with it. It is experiential, not verbal; it is participatory. The charts serve to make life experience a tangible thing. A woman in one of my classes had come to this country trained as a teacher in another country. She came with little English, and during the time she was learning

English, she had to take a job scouring pots and pans as they came off an assembly line. She had been very unhappy at this time and with this job. In one session, after discussing it somewhat emotionally, she took a large magic marker and obliterated the whole section from her charts. She said confidently, "You know, now I feel as if I have *really* taken care of *that*!"

Some participants express their feelings about the charts by saying: "I may not like what I see, but if I agree that it is me, then I can't run away from it like I can abstract thoughts or concepts," or "Since it is written down, the only way I can get rid of it is to throw it away — and who is going to literally take their whole life and pitch it in a waste can?" Other typical responses are:

"I've never organized my life before. Now I've started."

"I already see some patterns developing. They're so obvious — why didn't I notice them before?"

"I've done more than I thought."

"I've never spent that much time — all together — thinking about myself."

"I've spent some time thinking about myself, but it never made any sense — now I have the feeling I can begin to make it mean something to me."

and frequently:

"I'm drained."

Draining is meant in the emptying sense — to make room for a new way of thinking. It also begins to get some of the baggage unloaded. I often say in class, "What we want to do is take the bag we are lugging around off our backs, set it on the floor, open the draw-string, and take everything out. Then pitch the things we don't want and keep the things we do want." But instead of putting the things we choose to keep back into the bag, we must integrate them into ourselves. We need to open the seams of the bag and turn it into a cape we can wear with comfort — our way of nurturing ourselves.

At this point we can express what women are doing for themselves by a diagram such as Figure 4.

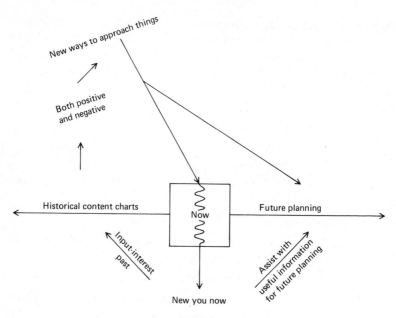

Figure 4

All the information is funneled from the past into the present, digested, and then utilized for now and for future planning.

Charts Lead to Planning

One of the questions on the personal history chart is, "What limitations do you have?" I had originally said, "List any physical or mental limitations you feel will restrict your choice of occupation or activities." I was thinking mainly of physical disabilities, like back fusions or varicose veins. Often, however, I got responses like "four young children and a grumpy husband," or "a waistline and other female accouterments," or "being single," or "being a minority," or "not enough education." Since the word that obviously clicked with the women was "limitation," I dropped the words "physical" and "mental." The trainer needs to be open to the possibility for change just as much as the participants in the seminar.

Women must realize that the patterns which they have set and which they become aware of in the seminar are reversible. The first step in this is to build confidence in their own capabilities. A woman in a group I had two years ago, who was at that time reentering the labor market after raising four children and after being widowed when they were small, wrote me a very personal and moving letter, in part as follows:

> "I'd like to be able to tell you that I've got everything together and am all set. However, things aren't that simple. I am working and have been since last October. I am Assistant Manager of _____ Book Store. Started out as part-time and within six weeks the Assistant Manager quit and I was offered the job, just in time for the Christmas rush. It was devastating — I have *never* been so tired. I have mixed feelings about the job, so I know I won't stay in this work. But it did do something really important for me — I realized I could do a job right and cope in emergencies. (I know you said that anyone who has brought up four children can do all this, but proving it to myself was very important to me!)"

I do not demand that each woman, while in the seminar, grow, develop, and become on schedule. Typical procedure is to set up specific criteria for success and then require each person to fit into them, but I don't do this. I say that as long as there is *some* growth and decision making, success is being achieved. Once the woman adjusts to the openness of this approach and accepts responsibility for her own growth, great strides are made.

Most vocational work in the past has been heavily oriented to "what is or will be available, and how the person can be fitted into it." I approach the problem from the other end and say, "Let's see what the person is and has available, then worry about the fitting." Another problem which should be considered is, If what a person wants can't be worked out, what is the most closely related alternative? People forget that many different activities and jobs will satisfy the same interests and temperaments. For example, take the woman who was going to be a doctor. All during her childhood when someone said to her, "And what are you going to do when you grow up, little girl?" she would answer, "I'm going to be a doctor." Well, schools were not that easy to get into, and several other problems got in the way, but the biggest was a health problem which limited strenuous situations like the life of an intern. An alternative for her might have been dentistry, which offers many of the same task demands as being a doctor does. The problem of schooling would still be there, but a taxing internship would not.

There are also questions on the personal history sheets about what careers and/or hobbies a person has thought about doing. These ideas are usually put aside because of unfeasibility, marriage, children, lack of confidence, and many other reasons, including poor counseling. But the dreams are still there. And very often, with a little modification, they are entirely within the realm of possibility, especially if we realize that leisure time offers a great untapped way to realize dreams. Ever since I can remember, I have wanted to play the harp. Since concert harps start at about $3,000, it was too expensive a dream. Also I assumed, because someone once told me, that all harp teachers first required you to play the piano well. I also assumed — for no reason I can think of that has any validity — that harp lessons, if you could find a teacher, would be prohibitively expensive. However, after twenty years of wishing, I *am* learning to play the harp. It is not a $3,000 concert harp, but I have a lovely teacher who puts up with my wanting to play both the ballet music from "Prince Igor" and "Eleanor Rigby," when I'm really at the "Mary Had A Little Lamb" stage. I'll never be a great harpist, but that isn't the point, because I don't aspire to that. What I am doing is fulfilling a dream.

Many people ask me, "Do people really tell you the truth on the history composite?" I believe they do. However, I don't worry about this because there are checks and balances built into the system. Also, I value a person's right to privacy, and I firmly believe that the person has the right to share with me, or not share with me, the growth taking place. As long as it takes place — that is what is important. And I found my knowing about it doesn't change whether it happens or not.

What about people making wrong decisions? Given the information of the seminar and the analytical pattern it develops, few people make such bad decisions that they are going to be devastated. The whole point of the seminar is to give people mental tools with which to work and enough knowledge of their personal resources to avoid this kind of error. Plus, there is the hard fact that a trainer has to accept: you cannot completely protect people from mistakes.

We all know that vocational planning for women is traditionally very limited in the area of occupations. Nursing, teaching, sales, and secretarial are the common clusters. This limited aspect also includes a heavy emphasis on the "right" plans for the additional assumed roles of wife and mother. It is no wonder that women have serious questions, and guilt, about who they are professionally and what their identity is in the role of worker. The work done up to this point in the seminar, using the analysis and comparison charts as a guide, has served to explore a lot of misconceptions women have about their lives. However, it is still necessary to explore and evaluate specific difficulties.

Professional Life Style and Self-Identity

After the initial discussion of life styles, and work with the personal history charts, the later phases of the seminar deal with "Professional Life Style" and "Self-Identity," as noted in the outline. Even though the seminar outline has the Professional Life Style and Self-Identity sections separated from discussions of "Strengths and Capabilities," the three areas are actually interwoven in a framework that is meaningful and appropriate to each person. The framework varies somewhat, since each group has its own unique personality. One woman's comment, "I felt that I was getting individual attention even though I was in a group," expresses the effectiveness of the flexible concept of having certain material to cover, but not in a rigid manner.

In dealing with the problem of professional life style and self-identity, I have found the combination of participatory and thought exercises to be quite effective. Such ideas need to be explored as: setting priorities, making decisions, taking risks, recognizing the sediments of feeling about past learning experiences, facing difficulties with teamwork, setting up action steps, developing concepts of minimizing weaknesses or difficulties, and coping with multifaceted roles. Various exercises are used during the seminar to work on these concepts.

One which produces positive feedback for each woman is the self-image representation. Why don't you try this for yourself. Get some glue, scissors, colored construction paper and crayons, and any other things that will help you represent graphically, using no words, how you see yourself now. Figure 5 is an eloquent example.

At the beginning —

And at the end —

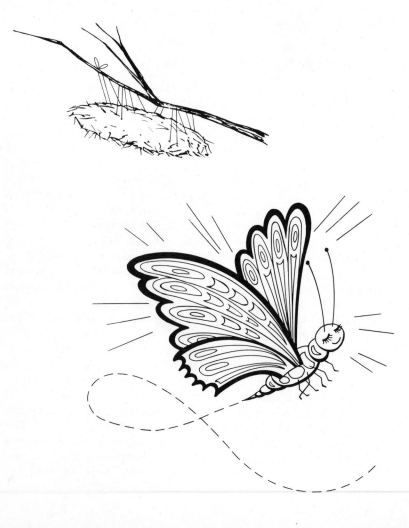

This exercise is not intended to convey a psychoanalytic message, but rather to have the women in the seminar find their commonality. There are always similar themes in the pictures. The drawings the women make at the beginning of the seminar are displayed; the women then choose those with which they empathize most; and small discussion groups are formed on this basis. The groups discuss the feelings and ideas portrayed in the picture. Finding out that other women have the same feelings is an extremely liberating experience.

A Learning Analysis

A "learning analysis," another seminar exercise, has also proved valuable. Again, do you want to try this? It's more fun and useful for you to do it yourself than for me to talk about it.

Sit down and analyze yourself and your unique needs in a learning situation. Ask yourself the following questions to help discover your ideal learning situation.

Who —	is the kind of person you learn best from?
What —	is the subject matter you learn best? — have the hardest time learning?
When —	is the best time for you to learn? We all have a time clock within us. Do we listen to it?
Where —	do you learn best? This is the physical setting. We have all been taught to sit at a desk, feet on the floor, etc., when studying. Some recent research has discovered that mathematics and science are in fact best learned in this manner, but subjects that have some relationship to our own personalities and that need to be integrated are better learned in a more comfortable position. I suggest that most seminar exercises be done in a comfortable position.
Why —	do you want to learn?
How —	do you learn best? This is methodology which includes any combination of reading, touching, seeing, hearing, and so forth.
Emotional state —	Is anxiety paralyzing for you? Or do you need some anxiety to get moving? If so, how much?

> Can you put aside worries about family, friends, and job to settle down to study? How does your emotional state affect your actual performance?

Inevitably there are variables in the learning pattern. For example, some teachers are better than others. Some methods work better than others. Variables such as these need to be taken into account as part of the sorting-out process in getting to know the learning self.

Once you have sorted out your ideal learning experience, try analyzing four past learning experiences, comparing and evaluating them according to the ideal example. These learning experiences can vary from a school course to marriage, birth, death, or solitude. Two of the four experiences chosen should be negative — abject failures which you still feel strongly about — and two should be positive — ones which you remember happily and which exhilarate you. Most of the time the positive ones follow closely the ideal. If they don't, there is probably an extra variable involved. The negative experiences usually do not follow the ideal. It is important for you to note why these negative experiences don't follow the ideal and to understand how you could have minimized your learning difficulties.

This exercise is useful when learned insights can be applied to any current learning situation. For example, one woman, after taking the seminar, returned to school at night to get her degree, and she was doing very poorly in a required course. She analyzed the situation and found several things amiss for her; she then moved to minimize these difficulties. She was not able to drop the required class, but she arranged with another professor, who taught the same subject, to audit his class. She learned well in the class she audited, and she attended and took exams in the class in which she was registered, thus managing to pass the course creditably.

OTHER PROGRAMS IN THE BAY AREA

In addition to an overview of my method of vocational planning, here are some ideas about how this method can fit into an organization.

In alphabetical order here are some of the Bay Area firms that are doing developmental programs for women: the American Institute of Banking, Levi Strauss, and the University of California at Berkeley.

American Institute of Banking

The San Francisco Chapter of the American Institute of Banking serves all bank employees in this area with educational opportunities particularly pertinent to banking needs, especially classes which are specialized and/or not offered elsewhere.

The seminar, as outlined earlier, is offered with the San Francisco American Institute of Banking and has helped to answer some of the questions women in banking are asking themselves about "What do I want to do next?"*

Wells Fargo Bank has a particularly good method for implementing internal planning. They assist their women in setting up a road map from *Now* to *Success*, ascertaining what has to be done in terms of a time frame, to achieve this success. For example, a high-potential woman is asked: "Where do you want to be in two years?" She is then asked to identify the training experiences and skills she thinks she needs to get from where she is *Now* to *Success*. Those drafting this road map are the "Woman on the Move," the "Task Model Counselors," and the "Process Skills Counselors." These counselors are drawn from the entire Wells Fargo system, as needed, which avoids placing the total burden on the direct supervisor. The opportunity includes a clear understanding that the woman can turn away from this road map, or drop out, at any time she feels she is unsuited for the accelerated program. Should she make this decision, she would then continue in the regular promotional path.

What makes this program different is that placement, training, and evaluation are done concurrently. The woman is placed in her new job, and, at the same time, gets training and relevant feedback in the form of evaluations. This gets high-potential people and the job together simultaneously. Wells Fargo, in the words of their training officer, is seeking "success, not visibility, so we are

---

* Further information on the AIB program may be obtained from the American Institute of Banking, 58 Sutter Street, San Francisco, California 94145.

implementing this with limited numbers of women to make sure we have a workable product."*

Levi Strauss

Levi Strauss also uses the seminar, as outlined. It is given on site after work, and college credit is available for those who want it, from Notre Dame in Belmont, California. Tuition reimbursement is also available.

Concurrently with the course for women, a different seminar was designed for the direct supervisors at Levi Strauss. The objective of this was to give these supervisors some time to consider and brainstorm their needs as hirers, counselors, and trainers. This triple and overlapping role was discussed by the supervisors, and they defined the following areas as ones in need of development: (1) clarifying their own feeling about their roles as internal counselors, (2) training and experience in handling vocational problems, (3) establishing cross-fertilization of vocational information between departments, (4) developing personal flexibility in approaching problems, and (5) budgeting time to handle personal and/or vocational counseling — the press of everyday business seemed to get in the way of individual attention. One supervisor summed it up when he said, "The only time counseling gets done is when someone walks up to you and says, 'I've got a problem,' and that doesn't happen too often." †

University of California at Berkeley

The University of California at Berkeley's plan, "Upward Mobility for Women," is a comprehensive idea. The basic steps are (1) personal introspection for the women. Using the transactional analysis model, participants review their personal needs and commitments in the light of their own perceived readiness for career development. (2) Concurrently, direct supervisors receive training to inform them of the program goals, sensitizing them to

---

*   More information about this program may be addressed to: Wells Fargo Bank, Organization and Management Development Section, 475 Sansome Street, San Francisco, California 94145.
†   Further information may be obtained from Levi Strauss Company, Affirmative Action Manager, 98 Battery Street, San Francisco, California 94106.

the crucial role they play in the success of the participants, and confronting their fears that the participants may be "thinking of leaving." Then the participants move into step (3) which provides a modification of the outlined seminar, incorporating some specific needs of the university. The next step is (4) the "University Administration Modification of Policy Negotiation Simulation Game," to be played to reality test the woman's decision about going into management. The simulation game has been specifically designed for this program at the University of California at Berkeley. The last two steps are (5) a curriculum development which is discussed with each participant (subjects/ functions/skills commonly accepted by managers will be integrated into a training concept individualized to each person), and (6) curriculum implementation which will vary in time for each individual. Included here will be an extra piece from my career program. It will include training in preparing promotional resumes and applications as well as practice in taking promotional interviews. Evaluation of the program will be done by participant, trainer, and supervisors, and follow up will be done on each participant.*

All of these employers recognized that it was unrealistic to try to turn their direct supervisors into professional vocational counselors, and they sought external help in answering their women employees' questions about "What do I want to do next?" But they have also realized that after external assistance is given, there needs to be an internal commitment to implementation by the companies' direct supervisors, personnel department, and department managers.

This gives an overview of what I am doing and how some companies are applying the program in ways unique to their needs. I hope these ideas may spark your interest in thinking of creative ways you can become a part of the exciting world of women today — as they struggle to emerge from the cocoon of traditionally imposed roles.†

---

* Further information may be obtained from the University of California, Personnel Training, 250 Sproul Hall, Berkeley, California 94720.

† My thanks to Anne Homan for her steadying hand, and the many other women who are making this system work.

BIBLIOGRAPHY

Books

Beauvoir, Simone. *The Second Sex* (New York: Bantam Books, 1961).

Bird, Carolyn. *Born Female, The High Cost of Keeping Women Down* (New York: Pocket Books, 1969).

Epstein, Cynthia F. *Woman's Place, Options and Limitations in Professional Careers* (Berkeley: University of California Press, 1971).

Friedan, Betty. *The Feminine Mystique* (New York: Dell, 1964).

Glasser, William, M.D. *Reality Therapy, A New Approach to Psychiatry* (New York: Harper & Row, 1965).

Gornick, Vivian and Barbara K. Moran, eds. *Women in Sexist Society, Studies in Power and Powerlessness* (New York: New American Library, 1972).

Hall, Richard H. *Occupations and the Social Structure* (Englewood Cliffs, New Jersey: Prentice-Hall, 1969).

Hole, Judith and Ellen Levine. *Rebirth of Feminism* (New York: Quadrangle, 1971).

Jackins, Harvey. *The Human Side of Human Beings; the Theory of Re-Evaluation Counseling* (Seattle, Washington: Rational Island Publishers, 1965).

James, Muriel and Dorothy Jongeward. *Born to Win* (Reading, Massachusetts: Addison-Wesley, 1971).

Jourard, Sidney M. *Disclosing Man to Himself* (New York: Van Nostrand Reinhard, 1968).

Jourard, Sidney M. *The Transparent Self; Self Disclosure and Well Being* (New York: D. Van Nostrand, 1964).

Lewis, Edwin C. *Developing Woman's Potential* (Ames, Iowa: Iowa State University Press, 1968).

Lewis, Howard R. and Dr. Harold S. Streitfeld, eds. *Growth Games; How to Tune In Yourself, Your Family, Your Friends* (New York: Pocket Books, 1972).

Luft, Joseph. *Group Processes; An Introduction to Group Dynamics* (Palo Alto, California: National Press, 1963).

Maltz, Dr. Maxwell. *Psychocybernetics; A New Way to Get More Living Out of Life* (New York: Pocket Books, 1969).

Neff, Walter S. *Work and Human Behavior* (New York: Atherton Press, 1968).

O'Neill, William L. *Everyone Was Brave; A History of Feminism in America* (Chicago: Quadrangle Books, 1969).

O'Neill, William L., ed. *Women at Work* (Chicago: Quadrangle Books, 1972).

Perls, Frederick F. *Gestalt Therapy Verbatim* (Lafayette, California: Real People Press, 1969).

Peterson, Severin. *A Catalog of the Ways People Grow* (New York: Ballantine, 1971).

Russo, Sabatino A., Jr. *Women! Business Needs You; A Back to Business Guide for Modern Women* (New York: Popular Library, 1968).

Smuts, Robert W. *Women and Work in America* (New York: Schocken Books, 1971).

Pamphlets and Reports

Advisory Commission on the Status of Women, *California Women 1971*, Documents Section, Sacramento, California, 1971.

Bem, Sandra L. and Daryl J. Bem, "Case Study of a Nonconscious Ideology; Training the Woman to Know Her Place," in D.J. Bem, *Beliefs, Attitudes, and Human Affairs* (Belmont, California: Brooks/Cole, 1970).

California, State of, Human Relations Agency, *Women Workers in California*, Part A: 1966-1970, State of California, January, 1971.

Citizens Advisory Council on the Status of Women, *Women in 1970*, Superintendent of Documents, Washington, D.C., 1971.

Mills, Rebecca, ed. *Personnel Practices Related to Women; Summary and Recommendations Based on an Exploratory Study of the Berkeley Employment Office* (Berkeley: University of California, Office of Equal Employment Opportunity, December, 1970).

Missouri, State of, Department of Labor and Industrial Relations, *Counseling Girls and Women; Awareness, Analysis, Action*, Superintendent of Documents, Washington, D.C., 1966.

President's Commission on the Status of Women, *American Women* (Washington, D.C.: Government Printing Office, 1963).

United States Government, Code of Federal Regulations, *Title VII, Equal Employment Opportunity Civil Rights Act of 1964*, Superintendent of Documents, Washington, D.C., 1964.

United States Government, Code of Federal Regulations, 41 Part 60-2, *Office of Federal Contract Compliance, Affirmative Action Programs*, Federal Register, Vol. 36, No. 169, Tuesday, August 31, 1971.

United States Government, Department of Labor, Manpower Administration, *Dual Careers, A Longitudinal Study of Labor Market Experience of Women*, Monograph 21, Vol. I, Superintendent of Documents, Washington, D.C., 1970.

United States Government, Department of Labor, Manpower Administration, *Years for Decision; A Longitudinal Study of Labor Market Experience of Young Women*, Monograph 24, Vol. I, Superintendent of Documents, Washington, D.C., 1971.

United States Government, Department of Labor, Women's Bureau, *Background Facts on Women Workers in the United States*, Superintendent of Documents, Washington, D.C., 1970.

Conferences

Equal Opportunity for Women: Corporate Affirmative Action Programs, San Francisco, California, October 21-22, 1971, Urban Research, Chicago, Illinois.

Midwest Conference on Women's Studies; Milwaukee, Wisconsin, October 22-23, 1971, Research Center on Women, Alverno College, Milwaukee, Wisconsin.

12

WOMEN
IN PSYCHOTHERAPY

by Nanci I. Moore

Dr. Moore received her Ph.D. in Clinical Psychology from the University of California at Berkeley in 1970. Since then she has been employed as a staff psychologist at the Veterans Administration Hospital in Martinez, California. Her major responsibilities are as the program coordinator for the Drug Dependency Treatment Unit and as the director of the Group Therapy Training Program.

She has taught a number of courses in psychology, most recently "Concepts of Femininity in the Psychological Literature" through the extension school of the University of California at Berkeley. She has given lectures before such groups as the San Francisco Chapter of the National Organization of Women and appeared on several radio programs where her topic was "Women in Psychotherapy."

Dr. Moore is licensed to practice psychology in the state of California. Her private practice currently consists primarily of psychotherapy with individuals and couples, although she has also done group psychotherapy and multiple-therapist couples therapy.

Key Questions

1. How can a woman pick a therapist who will not discriminate against her because she is a woman?

2. Would it be better for a woman to go to a woman therapist?

3. Should a woman go to a psychiatrist, a clinical psychologist, or a psychiatric social worker?

4. Would it be better for a woman to go into group psychotherapy or individual psychotherapy?

5. Does psychology really discriminate against women, or is it just a reflection of the general cultural bias?

There are many reasons why a person might seek personal counseling or psychotherapy. One reason would be when the person had thoughts such as the following:

1. I do not feel that I am operating efficiently in some important aspect of my life (job, family, marriage, etc.);

2. I find myself having thoughts and feelings which I do not understand and which frighten me; or

3. I find myself doing things or wanting to do things which would not be healthy for me or for those around me.

Normally, a person has talked these things over with a spouse, or friend, or supervisor, and that person has suggested professional counseling. Often, too, the person who suggests counseling may be asked to follow it up by making a definite referral.

Unfortunately, most people do not know how to go about suggesting counseling, let alone how to make a definite referral. When the spouse or friend or supervisor has been to a psychotherapist himself or herself, and it has been helpful, the idea is liable to occur to him/her more quickly. Also, such a person is likely to refer to his/her own therapist. But often this is not successful.

More often than not, however, the person consulted has never had occasion to seek psychotherapy. How does one recognize when a person needs professional counseling? How does one recommend it? How does one make a referral?

Illustration

Barbara B. has received several reprimands from her supervisor for coming in to work late. Her reaction to these reprimands has been to make excuses or to promise to do better. Her supervisor also notices that her work has dropped off and that she often sits at her desk apparently daydreaming. When this is mentioned to her, she gets angry and tearful and asks her supervisor whether she doesn't have anything better to do than to spy on her.

Barbara's supervisor responds that if her work continues to fall off, they will have no choice but to get someone to replace her. Finally, Barbara admits that she is having personal problems at home. She continues by saying that she feels her work is meaningless and that she just isn't getting anywhere and that maybe they ought to replace her anyway.

At this point, Barbara's supervisor realizes that she may be losing a valuable employee. She asks Barbara if she thinks she might like to discuss these problems with a professional counselor. The firm will let her use sick leave for this purpose. Barbara responds that she would like to talk to someone but that she doesn't know anyone to talk to. She asks her supervisor to recommend someone.

Like most other people, Barbara's supervisor does not know how to go about finding a psychotherapist for another person. Yet, she feels obligated to do so.

What she may also not know is that many psychotherapists may not be able to give Barbara the most effective psychotherapy because they are prejudiced against women. It is toward this issue that this chapter is directed.

WOMEN VERSUS MEN IN PSYCHOTHERAPY

The Key Questions listed at the beginning of the chapter are a few of the questions I have been asked most frequently in the last several years of teaching and practicing psychotherapy. Before giving specific answers, I would like to give an overview of women in the history of psychotherapy. It is all too easy to fall into a general condemnation of male psychotherapists, traditional individual verbal psychotherapy, or psychology in general. [1] A discussion of these subjects often leads to a condemnation of our society and to the conclusion that social institutions (e.g., marriage and psychotherapy) will not change until the whole capitalistic, imperialistic, racist, sexist foundations of our society are overturned. [2] Perhaps this chapter might be entitled "What to do until the revolution comes." Women are going to continue to become emotionally distressed and seek help. Many of them are too disturbed to gain much benefit from consciousness-raising groups or reality-oriented, problem-solving groups. Many women seeking help with emotional problems are too upset to actively confront their psychotherapist about possible sexist biases in his/her practice.

Accepting Dependency

It is true, as Chesler and others have remarked, that psychotherapy involves a dependency relationship. Any time one person goes to another person to seek help with a problem, particularly an emotional problem, the relationship established can be characterized as a dependency relationship. Psychotherapists are viewed as experts, authorities, saviors, and lovers. However, physicians, ministers, lawyers, nurses, scientists, automobile mechanics, computer programmers, and income tax specialists are also placed in these roles.

It is difficult for most people to accept the idea that anyone can be an expert or an authority in such areas as human behavior and human relationships. Somehow, though, it is not so difficult to accept the notion that a person can be an expert in the workings of the body, in spiritual or legal matters, in the mysteries of the universe, in machinery, or in the workings of the Federal government. Yet, the way a person comes to be an expert or authority in any of these fields is pretty much the same. The person goes to a school where this expertise is taught and studies what is known, thought, theorized, and speculated about in the chosen field.

Unfortunately, the subjects mostly known about in the field of psychology are white rats, college students, and white middle- and upper-class males. Inasmuch as generalizations from these groups are valid for other groups, psychologists can claim to know about those other groups.

There is a prevalent, and largely unfounded, assumption that women can be understood by first making men the standard and then comparing or contrasting women to this standard.

A more reasonable approach would be to study women on a largely atheoretical basis, but this has yet to be done. As a result, it is true that psychology in general is often less than understanding of the nature and problems of women. Where men and women share the same problems, psychology can be of some help.

There is some evidence to suggest that many of the problems of men and women are not the same, or at least that the ways that men and women react to their problems are not the same. For example, more of the criminals in this country are male than female, while more of the emotionally disturbed are female rather than male. Part of the reason for this difference may be due to the fact that men are encouraged to be active. Men are encouraged to do something about their feelings of frustration and anger and hurt. Women are not only discouraged from acting out against society, but they are also encouraged to seek the support of society and the agents of society.

Women are not discouraged from being dependent. They are encouraged to see themselves as weak, helpless, and inferior. The sources of their problems are to be found within themselves, either in their own bodies or in their own emotional inadequacies.

Difference in Seeking Help

The differences between the sexes make it easier for women than for men to enter psychotherapy. Men seem to be more reluctant to seek help in general. They feel they should be able to deal with their own problems, particularly emotional problems. Therefore, if they do enter psychotherapy, they are more likely to disguise their asking for help. They are more likely to put the therapist in the "expert" role. They do this by asking for "expert" advice on vocational problems or for explanations on how people's heads work. The message to the therapist is something like: "I will help myself if you will tell me how to do it, but don't ask me to admit that I have any emotional problems."

Women are not discouraged from turning to others for help. Seeking help fits in very easily with the "helpless" role they are taught to assume, particularly toward males. The difficulty for the therapist in this case is in getting women to help themselves and to give themselves some positive reinforcement for doing so. Often, if women do try to solve their problems themselves, they run the risk of losing societal support. Men, also, may be given negative reinforcement if they do seek help with their emotional problems.

The symptoms that female clients present to psychotherapists are not the same as the symptoms presented by male clients. Male clients are likely to complain of difficulty in dealing with unacceptable thoughts or in inhibiting unacceptable impulses or antisocial behavior. Female clients are more likely to complain of depression and feelings of inferiority (low self-esteem) — symptoms which are characteristic of oppressed people. A therapist who fails to consider the possibility that the depression presented by his/her female client is due to the societal oppression of women is likely to overlook other important factors in the life and being of his/her client.

WOMEN AND PSYCHOLOGICAL THEORY

The tendency to ignore what it is like to be a woman in our society is general to the whole field of psychology, not just to psychotherapy. Within the narrower field of psychotherapy (which includes clinical psychology, psychiatry, and psychiatric social work), there are more specific sources of bias against women.

Women and Freud

The entire concept of modern psychotherapy is based on the theories of Sigmund Freud. He was the founder of "talk therapy," the idea that a therapist could "cure illnesses" by having the patient talk. Freud's theory continues to be important to this day, although unfortunately, in many ways, his theory may be seen as the legitimizing of a Victorian stereotype through the process of theory building. In other words, if you embody a stereotype in a theory, the very fact that it is called a theory makes it legitimate.

One of the major elements in Freud's theory is the idea that anatomy is destiny. What this essentially means is that a person's body structure, to a large extent, determines the personality of the individual. For example, Freud has referred in various places to women as "the poor creature without a penis" or "a receptacle." [3,4] Any form of protest on the part of a woman was considered to be "penis envy."

Freud himself, in later years, felt that his ideas about women were not particularly well developed or that they might not necessarily be sound; he left it up to subsequent psychoanalysts, particularly women psychoanalysts, to come up with a better theory. [5] Helene Deutsch probably did make an effort to do this, but she still found herself bound to the anatomy-is-destiny notion. [6] Further, her writings about women painted a picture of women as naturally and inherently passive, masochistic, and narcissistic.

Eric Erikson is a contemporary psychoanalyst and therefore is not necessarily saddled with Victorian stereotypes. [7] While he very much de-emphasizes the anatomy-is-destiny point of view, he still maintains that a woman's personality and her fulfillment are wrapped up in making herself attractive in order to interest the right kind of husband, in order to get married, in order to produce children. Again, therefore, essentially her identity is bound up with her physical being.

Women and Behaviorism

After Freud, the second major force in clinical psychology — which came into being around the thirties — is behaviorism. Behaviorism is very much opposed to the notion that anatomy is destiny, and is, therefore, in many ways kinder to women. The behaviorist is more likely to say that, rather than anatomy predetermining a person's personality, early training more or less predetermines a person's personality. [8] If early training is destiny, then the question becomes, Is it any easier to change the patterns established by early training than it is to change anatomy? Or, are the patterns established by early training so firmly entrenched that even years of psychotherapy and retraining can change only a small portion of them? If all women are reared a certain way, does this therefore mean that they should learn to live with it?

Because of the behavioristic point of view, a lot of research has been generated on early training. Much of this research turns out to be descriptive. One of the problems, then, is that when someone does a descriptive piece of research to point out the way that women are, such a statement is often read as, "it is natural for women to be this way." For example, there are two ways to read the statement "women are passive." One, reading it in terms of "most women are found to be more passive than most men by experiment," or two, reading it in terms of a demonstrable fact that women are ordained by nature to be more passive than men. Both readings leave the researcher with the question, What does this mean?

When reading words like "passive" and "aggressive," it is important to know how these terms are defined. For example, in some studies what is meant by the word aggressive is kicking, biting, running, jumping, and grabbing. And yet we find that in many studies, girls are found to make more verbally aggressive statements. So when researchers are talking about aggression, it is important to find out whether "aggression" means aggression toward others in terms of gross motor activity.

Women and Humanists

The third major force in clinical psychology is represented by the humanists — notably the late Abraham Maslow, who, in talking about the third force, includes Jung, Adler, Rogers, and others. It is very difficult in the humanistic theory to put your finger on possible prejudices. I urge you to read Appendix I in Maslow's *Religion, Values, and Peak Experiences*, [9] because there you will observe the danger in legitimizing a stereotype through histori- cal perspective.

Jung, for example, mentions numerous "archetypes." [10] You can think of archetypes as essentially prototypes or models. These are universal ideas, universal ways of looking at people and looking at relationships between people. The way that researchers uncover these archetypes is by looking at legends and myths, stories, art works, and artifacts, and seeing the consistent themes that emerge. Obviously the themes that emerge are likely to be cultural stereotypes, so if persistent cultural stereotypes occur independently in a number of cultures, they are called archetypes. There is danger in this kind of classification if a researcher begins to see that one culture after another has had consistent stereo- types, and he begins to think that somehow these archetypes are natural and are ordained by the very nature of man, or by God, or something like that. In other words, stereotypes *are* that way, so the researcher assumes that the stereotypes *must* be that way.

Jung mentions numerous archetypes. He has whole lists of archetypes. Some of the feminine archetypes that he includes in his lists are earth mother, witch mother, and goddess. It is interesting to note that in his lists of archetypes, he fails to account for such legends as Diana, the huntress; Athena, the warrior; and Minerva, the goddess of wisdom.

Many people may think that legitimizing these sterotyped cultural ways of viewing women through historical perspective is not a serious approach. Yet Jung would say that any professional woman, particularly if she is not married or does not have children, is probably an "animus woman," which is to say that she is overemphasizing her masculine side to the detriment of her feminine side. It should be equally true, from Jung's theory, that a woman who is failing to use her mind, who is failing to be logical and rational, has an underdeveloped "animus." She is failing to become a complete, integrated person.

It would also follow that a man who does not develop his gentle, nurturant, loving side, his "anima," is not a whole person. Unfortunately, these aspects of Jung's theory are almost never used to support liberation, while the notion of the "animus woman" is often used to condemn women's liberation. In any case, Jung implies that it is not "natural" or healthy for a woman to have no children; just as it is not "natural" or healthy for a man to fail to be a "breadwinner."

WOMEN AND THE TRAINING OF PSYCHOTHERAPISTS

Aside from these three major forces in clinical psychology, which all clinical psychologists must become acquainted with, there are other sources of prejudice and bias which can creep into the training of psychotherapists. For example, just about all the training of psychotherapists occurs in the universities (and in medical schools). There is a good deal of documentation that universities, at least until quite recently, have practiced discrimination in hiring, promoting, and retaining women faculty members. This definitely includes departments of psychology. [11] Where, then, are women students to find acceptable models?

During my training as a psychotherapist, I was presented with numerous instances of sexual discrimination. The sex of the therapist was not ignored. The "fact" that women, because of their nature and upbringing, were more suited to be child psychologists was brought up often. The "fact" that women were more easily manipulated by their clients, because they would become emotionally involved, was mentioned from time to time. And particularly the "fact" that it is impossible to be an intellectual, analytical, competitive, aggressive graduate student, and still play a female role with male professors, was also brought up from time to time, usually by female students.

It was recognized that a female therapist had to recognize the impact of her sexuality on the therapeutic relationship, *just as a male therapist* does (i.e., it was assumed that a female's sexuality has the same impact on the therapeutic relationship as a male's sexuality does and therefore it should be handled in the same fashion). For example, one of my first clients in the university psychology clinic, a fellow about the same young age as myself, said he wanted to go to bed with me because I was the only woman who understood him, etc. I found myself caught between a humanist supervising therapist and a more traditional, neo-analytic type. The humanist was pleased that I had done the following: I first told the young man that I was pleased and flattered by his feelings. I then said that I did not think it would be helpful to the therapeutic relationship, and he agreed.

The analyst was rather upset that I had not immediately moved to an "analysis of the transference" and commented that I sounded like a young girl who had just turned down a proposition and said "but we can still be friends."

Also, of course, most universities emphasize research. Until quite recently, most research in the area of psychology was done by males. The majority of research ignored such variables as the sex of the experimenter, or, in such areas as research in psychotherapy, failed to report information as to the sex of the therapist and the sex of the client. Therefore it makes it quite difficult for us to be able to say much about women in psychotherapy, women in psychotherapy with male psychotherapists, or women in psychotherapy with female psychotherapists. Although, given the similarity in training and the selective factors operating, there probably isn't much difference.

There has been a movement to correct the training of psychotherapists and other professionals, since there has been much criticism of traditional university training. The result has been the development of professional schools of psychology.

I urge you to read an article by Nick Cummings, who is the founding president of the California School of Professional Psychology, on "Exclusion Therapy." [12] This type of therapy was developed for working with delinquent adolescents, and it essentially has to do with establishing a firm contract with the adolescent and enforcing this contract with consistency and firmness. You should attend particularly to his remarks on the necessity of the "strong father figure" of the therapist (it is very unclear in the article whether both boys and girls need this "strong father figure," but I assume he means both) and how the female therapist is perceived as "Jewish mother" when she tries to imitate this model. I know that at the time the article was written, and for some time after that, the women students were asking for a course in the psychology of women. As of the date of this writing they still do not have such a course.

WOMEN AND THE VALUES OF PSYCHOTHERAPISTS

Besides theoretical biases and training biases, there is a third source of prejudice and bias in psychotherapy, namely, the personal values of individual psychotherapists. It is obvious that people cannot consider themselves to be totally free from the biases that exist in their society at large.

An article by Broverman, Broverman, Clarkson, Rosenkrantz, and Vogel illustrates the concept of mental health as it is held by many clinicians. [13] To summarize briefly, an adjective checklist was given by the experimenters to a number of people, including therapists and college students. The researchers asked the college students to check off those adjectives which they thought were desirable in a normal, healthy adult. Then the researchers split the group of therapists into three smaller groups, each group balanced in terms of amount of experience and proportion of male to female. Using the same questionnaire as used with the college students, they asked

- the first small group of therapists to check the adjectives they thought were desirable for a *healthy adult male* in our society;
- the second small group of therapists to check the adjectives they thought were desirable for a *healthy adult female* in our society; and
- the third small group of therapists to check the adjectives they thought were desirable for a *healthy normal adult* in our society.

The research team then compared the adjectives checked by male therapists with those by female therapists and found there was essentially no difference in any of the groups. They then compared the therapists as a group with the college students. The only difference they found was that therapists thought it was all right to show emotion, sometimes at least, whereas the college students were not as likely to endorse that.

Therapists didn't think it was all right to value security too much or to be too religious, whereas college students seemed to think that valuing security and being religious were all right. It appears, then, that what the layman considers to be desirable qualities in a healthy adult are essentially the same thing that trained psychotherapists see as being criteria for positive mental health. This suggests that psychotherapists are strongly influenced by cultural values.

When the researchers compared the adjectives that the therapists checked for a healthy male with those of a healthy normal adult in our society, they found essentially no difference. However, when they compared adjectives that were checked for a healthy female adult in our society with a healthy normal adult in our society, they found a significant difference. *Healthy adult women, as seen by clinicians, are expected to be more submissive, less independent, less adventurous, more easily influenced, less aggressive, less competitive, more excitable in minor crises, more emotional, more conceited about their appearance, and less objective, and they have their feelings more easily hurt than healthy adult men.*

It is not surprising, then, that a "healthy adult" in our society is almost synonymous with a "healthy adult *male*." This study shows that it may be quite difficult for a woman in our society to be perceived by a psychotherapist as both a healthy normal adult and a healthy woman.

In one course I taught, several of my students interviewed therapists in the Bay Area, and these therapists maintained that their goals in therapy were the same for men and women and that essentially these goals were some concept called "self-actualization." Some did say that they did not feel that a woman could be fulfilled or self-actualized unless she had children. They did not say this for men.

By and large, and granted these are generalizations, therapists agree they can be pinned down in their values in some sort of general sense. For example, they do say that they value independence or they think that independence is better than dependence, that realism is better than romanticism, that being rational (or rationality) is better than being overly emotional (or emotionalism). But if a woman strives toward being the sort of person the therapist values — being independent, realistic, and rational — she then runs the risk of losing societal support. And beyond that, she risks being put down by the therapist for being an animus woman, or having a masculinity complex.

What Women Need and Value

Some psychological literature reports evidence that women have a greater need to be loved than men do, [14] that they show more fear of loss of love and loss of approval than men do. This is very interesting, and I think it requires some explanation. It's possible that the differences might be biological, but if you look at the nature of a women's role, at how little girls are taught their sex role, you can see that a women's role is defined by the reactions of others. [15]

Think for a moment about sex roles and the types of things women are taught to value. For one thing, women are supposed to be attractive. Now being attractive is not something that a woman can define for herself. She can't look at herself and know that she is attractive. She has to gauge whether she is attractive or not in terms of whether she attracts anyone. Thus, a woman's role is being defined by the reactions of others. She can't define whether she is being nurturant by looking at herself; she has to look at the object of her nurturance — is that person being nurtured?

This is just one example. As a personal experiment, make a list of the kinds of things, values, sex roles, and sex characteristics that women are taught (are supposed to develop in themselves). After making the list, see how many of the items it is possible to develop without looking to someone else to validate.

In contrast, little boys are taught to be competitive. Little boys are taught such things as to see who can kick the football the furthest. That can be measured objectively. They are taught to see who is smarter. That can be measured objectively. And so on. Who can get the job? The answer is the one who *does* get the job.

The interesting thing about this contrast is that it causes women to pay a great deal of attention to the reactions of others, in terms of just validating themselves as women. It makes them more sensitive to societal demands. Women are more likely to be able to tell you what a situation demands and how to behave in response to it. Women are more attentive to interpersonal relationships. There is evidence in psychological literature to indicate that women make better predictors of behavior in a social setting than men do. The unfortunate aspect is that women are not taught how to self-validate. They are not taught how to judge themselves. They are taught, in fact, to turn to others to judge them. [16]

For example, one woman worker in an office needs to be given instructions on the same task several times and is constantly seeking approval for doing it correctly. Another worker can be given instructions once and seeks further instruction only when he/she is experiencing difficulty. This does not necessarily mean that the first worker is slower or more stupid than the second worker. It may simply mean that the first worker is not able to judge her own performance as well as the second worker. The first worker is not as capable of self-validation. She has probably never been trained in that respect.

A therapist cannot totally ignore the societal pressures that are placed on women clients any more than a therapist can ignore the prejudices in our society against black clients.

Illustration

David S., a 24-year old, black male, enters therapy because he is failing in school and is very anxious. He is married and has a 2-year-old son. The therapist is a 35-year-old, white male who is married and has several children. David is very quiet and has difficulty talking; he alternates between calling the therapist "sir" and getting angry. The therapist is aware of the difficulty David is having and points out that David is playing games, such as *Putting Whitey On* and *Tell the Man What He Wants to Hear*. The therapist understands why David feels he has to play these games, and he gets David to talk about how he feels about being in therapy with a white male therapist.

Illustration

Joan S., a 24-year-old, white female, enters therapy because she is failing in school and is feeling anxious and depressed. She is married and has a 2-year-old son. The therapist is the same as in the preceding illustration. Joan alternates between weeping quietly and explaining her problems in a calm, objective tone. The therapist makes comments like, "You seem to be feeling that life is hopeless, that you aren't getting anywhere. Is that right?" He is warm, gentle, and supportive. Joan leaves the session feeling that he understands her.

In fact, the therapist demonstrates that he shows more understanding of the sociological aspects of the black-white relationship than he does of the male-female relationship. Because of his understanding, he is able to treat the male patient like an adult. His lack of understanding of the male-female relationship leads him to treat the female patient more like a child. His attitude certainly does not challenge his female client to explore her own behavior in the light of the societal pressures and expectations which are being placed on her.

All of this information and speculation allows us to return with a better perspective to the questions raised earlier.

1. *How can a woman pick a therapist who will not discriminate against her because she is a woman?*

   a) Check with your local chapter of the National Organization of Women to see if they have a list of therapists who do not discriminate against women.

   b) If she is not too desperate and has the time and money to shop around, a woman should set up initial interviews with several male and female therapists recommended by friends, her local medical society, or a nearby university. She should try to assess whether they make her feel like a child, or an inferior person, etc., or whether they treat her like an adult.

   c) She should ask her therapist whether he/she believes the routes to self-actualization, self-integration, and self-fulfillment are the same for men and women.

   d) She should ask her therapist whether he/she prefers working with male or female clients, and why.

2. *Would it be better for a woman to go to a woman therapist?*

   Inasmuch as male and female therapists receive essentially the same training, it makes no difference. A male therapist who has recognized and dealt with his own sexism is better than a female therapist who has not. However, a female therapist has probably had more of an opportunity to become aware of the problems that women encounter in our society and may, therefore, have a better understanding of a woman's problems.

3. *Should a woman go to a psychiatrist, a clinical psychologist, or a psychiatric social worker?*

A psychiatrist is more likely to have a strong Freudian background than are either of the other two, although this is not always true. A psychiatrist is the only one of the three who can directly prescribe medication and is probably more likely to recommend it. Currently, trained social workers may be more aware of relevant social pressures; but often, when trained as individual therapists, they are even more traditional than recently trained psychologists or psychiatrists.

There are more women social workers than women psychiatrists or women clinical psychologists. Therefore, if a woman wants a female therapist, she would have a wider range of choice from psychiatric social workers; theirs is traditionally a "woman's job."

As for fees, psychiatrists are likely to be the most expensive, and psychiatric social workers the least expensive. However, various health plans will not pay for a person to see anyone other than a physician (i.e., psychiatrist) unless a physician refers her to that person. Psychologists usually have more academic training in psychology and psychotherapy than either of the other two.

4. *Would it be better for a woman to go into group psychotherapy or individual psychotherapy?*

From the point of view of avoiding discrimination, group psychotherapy may well be better than individual psychotherapy, particularly if a woman is unsure of the attitudes of the therapist. For one thing, having other people around sometimes makes it easier to confront the therapist. Also, watching the therapist interact in the group with other women, and with men, allows a person to see the therapist's practices somewhat more objectively.

Finally, group psychotherapy is usually less expensive than individual psychotherapy. However, sometimes in group psychotherapy, particularly when one is the new person in an established group, the other group members will not allow the new person to confront the therapist and may attack the person for attempting to do so.

Furthermore, if the group has a number of sexists in it and the therapist is also somewhat sexist, or even unaware of the sexism in the group, a woman may be worse off than she would be with the same therapist in individual psychotherapy.

5. *Does psychology really discriminate against women or is it just a reflection of the general cultural bias?*

Yes, on both counts. But more than simply reflecting the cultural bias, up until the last three or four years, psychology has actually supported and strengthened that cultural bias. Many psychologists have fought against racial prejudice; have fought for the rights of hospitalized psychiatric patients; have fought for rehabilitation rather than punishment of criminals, drug abusers, and alcoholics, and so on. Yet, for many of these same psychologists the concept of sexism was a joke, something to be ignored or scoffed at. Several steps definitely need to be taken in the area of psychology and psychotherapy:

a) feminists need to educate therapists about sexism and help the psychotherapist recognize his/her own sexual prejudices;

b) more qualified women need to be hired to teach and train psychotherapists; and

c) a new psychology of women needs to be developed in which women constitute their own norm and are not compared with men as the norm.

REFERENCES

1. Phyllis Chesler, "Patient and patriarch: Women in the psychotherapeutic relationship," in Vivian Gornick and Barbara Moran, (eds.) *Women in Sexist Society*, (New York: Basic Books, 1971), pp. 362-392.

2. For example, see articles in *Rough Times* (formerly *The Radical Therapist*) 3 (No. 1, September, 1972).

3. Sigmund Freud, "Some psychological consequences of the anatomical distinction between the sexes," *Int. J. Psycho-Analysis* 8 (1927): 133-142.

4. Sigmund Freud, "Female sexuality," *Int. J. Psycho-Analysis* 13 (1932): 281-297.

5. Sigmund Freud, "The psychology of women." In *New Introductory Lectures on Psychoanalysis* (Sprott, trans.), (New York: Norton, 1933), pp. 153-185.

6. Helene Deutsch, *The Psychology of Women*, Vol I-II, 1944-45, (New York: Grune & Stratton).

7. Eric Erikson, "Inner and outer space: Reflections on womanhood," *Daedalus*, 93 (No. 2, 1964): 582-606.

8. A. Bandura and R. Walters, *Social Learning and Personality Development*, (New York: Holt, Rinehart, & Winston, 1963).

9. Abraham Maslow, *Religions, Values, and Peak Experiences*, Columbus, Ohio: Ohio State University Press, 1964). (paper, New York: Viking, 1970).

10. Carl Jung, "Archetypes and the collective unconscious." In *Collected Works*, Vol. 9, (New York: Pantheon, 1953).

11. L. Fidell, "Empirical verification of sex discrimination in hiring practices in psychology," *Am. Psychologist*, 25 (No. 2, December 1970): 1094-1098.

12. Nick Cummings, "Exclusion therapy: An alternate to going after the drug cult adolescent." Paper presented at APA convention, September 7, 1970, Miami, Florida.

13. I. Broverman, *et al.*, "Sex-role stereotypes and clinical judgments of mental health," *J. Con. and Clin. Psychol.*, 34 (No. 1, 1970): 1-7.

14. J. Bardwick, *Psychology of Women* (New York: Harper & Row, 1971, pp. 114-134.

15. J. Kagan, *Personality Development*   (New York: Harcourt Brace Jovanovich, 1971, pp. 78-79.

16. Bardwick, *op cit.*, pp. 168-178.

OTHER SUGGESTED READINGS

Gall, M. and Mendelsohn, G. "Effects of facilitating techniques and subject-experimenter interaction on creative problem-solving." *J. Pers. and Social Psychol.* 5 (No. 2, 1967): 211-216.

Horner, Matina, "Women's fear of success." *Psychol. Today* 3 (No. 6, 1969): 36.

Rosenkrantz, P., *et al.* "Sex-role stereotypes and self-concepts in college students." *J. Cons. and Clin. Psychol.* 32 (No. 3, 1968): 287-295.

13

HOW TO ELIMINATE SEXIST LANGUAGE FROM YOUR ORGANIZATION'S WRITING: Some Guidelines for the Manager and Supervisor

by Robert M. Wendlinger and Lucille Matthews

Robert M. Wendlinger is Assistant Vice President, Communications at Bank of America World Headquarters, San Francisco. He is coauthor of *Effective Letters* (McGraw-Hill, 1973), among other books and articles. He is a board member of the Industrial Communications Council and a Fellow of the American Business Communications Association. A member of the International Transactional Analysis Association, he conducts workshops in business writing using the principles of transactional analysis.

Lucille Matthews is a San Francisco-based writer and language specialist who has written for *San Francisco Magazine*, and *Queen Magazine* in London. She has also been a senior fashion copywriter at Bonwit Teller in New York.

Key Questions

1. What is sexist language?

2. How can the language in writing, perhaps unknowingly, restrict equal opportunity for women?

3. What are some guidelines for eliminating sex-biased language?

WHAT IS SEXIST LANGUAGE?

What's wrong with this paragraph?

> When recruiting your new manager, be sure he
> takes a strong view on absenteeism. He has
> to keep a close monthly check so he can take
> action quickly and decisively. (From a
> memorandum to an executive)

And this one?

> The nurse deals swiftly with an emergency.
> She takes certain measures that mark her as a
> trained and helpful individual. (From an
> instruction manual for nurses)

Until recently, most of us would have answered that both of these statements were high-quality communications. By one set of standards, both are clear, concise, and readable. Viewed another way, both are sexist and discriminatory. Through the use of the male and female pronouns related to job categories, it is assumed that the new manager will be male, and that the nurse (or secretary, or bank teller) will be female. Statements like these, found in memorandums, manuals, instructions, forms, textbooks, and conversations throughout our society, encourage a stereotyped role for women. They discourage choices and encourage the entry of women into certain low-status occupations and activities.

During the past few years, the government's Equal Employment Opportunity Commission has criticized many companies which, probably without awareness or intent, have allowed job-related sexist statements to circulate freely within their organizations. The commission is committed to the principle that work and sex are not related; whoever has job skills or can acquire them must be allowed to compete for jobs for which he or she is qualified. Companies like Bank of America, Mobil Oil, Westinghouse, Pitney Bowes, Scott Foresman, and McGraw-Hill have taken steps to eliminate sexist language from their official documents and publications. They have issued "style" manuals covering the subject; included awareness segments on sexist language in training sessions for letter writers and report writers;

and developed programs to remove sexist language whenever a publication is written, revised, or reprinted.

Is *this* an OK statement?

As a human being grows, he should have the
opportunity to experience life in diverse and
meaningful ways.

And this?

In order to clarify individual responsibilities
for a worker who is not new to the organization,
it may be helpful for both you and your subordinate
to write out in detail what each of you considers
to be the responsibilities and duties of his job . . .

One might argue that both of these statements *are* OK and that the use of the male pronoun in these contexts does not mean to exclude women from the type of experience described. It is true that in our society the word "man" is traditionally used in a generic sense — to apply to both men *and* women. And one can certainly read both of the above statements in that light.

While this is possible, the use of "man" and "he" in the generic sense is likely to be misinterpreted because they are so often used to signify the so-called male qualities *specifically*.

With this on her mind, the historian Mary Beard has written:

Men who discuss human affairs frequently do so with an ambiguity amounting to double talk or half talk, or talk so vague that I cannot be sure in every case whether they are referring to men only or to both men and women. This gives them a peculiar advantage of self-defense if the charge is made that they are not remembering women at all when they speak of "man" or "men," for they can often claim that they are using these words in their generic sense. [1]

Can we be certain that those who wrote about experiencing life and clarifying individual responsibilities really meant to include men *and* women? Can we be certain that the statements will not be interpreted by sensitive women as an intentional or unintentional slur on their sex and potentials? Is there a better way to handle this kind of communication problem?

FIFTEEN GUIDELINES FOR WRITERS

De-sexing business writing begins by becoming aware and tuned-in to habitual biases in usage. Editing begins with awareness. Ideally, sexist words will stand out immediately in the editor-writer's mind every time they appear.

1. *Before releasing a letter, memorandum, or report within your organization, ask yourself whether the document has sexist implications. Does it, for example, use "man" or "he" in the generic sense?*

   Biased   Man works to utilize his skills to the fullest extent. *He* takes pride in accomplishment.

   Recast   People work to utilize their skills to the fullest extent. *They* take pride in *their* accomplishments.

2. *Use the word "he" to refer only to a specific man being discussed.*

   Biased   If a manager suits *his* department well, *he* is sensitive to the needs of *his* staff.

   Recast   Henry Wilson suits the department admirably. *He* is sensitive to the needs of *his* staff.

   Never use "he" to lump everybody, regardless of sex, generically together.

   Biased   In public dealings the employee should use extra courtesy. *He* should build solid relationships with *his* clients.

   Recast   In public dealings all employees should use extra courtesy. *They* should build solid relationships with *their* clients.

3. *Drop the male pronoun "his" (and "he") altogether.*

> *Biased*   The director holds on to *his* ideas about modernizing the company's equipment.
>
> *Recast*   The director holds on to ideas about modernizing the company's equipment.

4. *Use the all-inclusive wording "he or she."*

> *Biased*   The manager has a large responsibility to *his* staff. *He* must keep himself fully informed at all times.
>
> *Recast*   The manager has a large responsibility to the staff. *He or she* must keep fully informed at all times.

5. *Use job titles and functions instead of a pronoun.*

> *Biased*   The new officer is doing well in training seminars. *He* gained in technical ability from attentive study and is turning out to be a highly skilled *man*.
>
> *Recast*   The new officer is doing well in training seminars. This *employee* gained in technical ability from attentive study and is turning out to be a highly skilled *trainee*.

6. *Omit pronouns when the sense is not changed.*

> *Biased*   Reports must be written by the field representative *himself*.
>
> *Recast*   Reports must be written by only the field representative.

7. *Use the plural collective structure.*

> *Biased*   An engineer functions well in an atmosphere of multiple discussion. *He* finds varied opinion stimulating, opening up *his* alternatives.

Recast   Engineers function well in an atmosphere of multiple discussion. *They*
find varied opinion stimulating,
opening up *their* alternatives.

8. *Use the genderless "one," "person," "individuals."*

Biased   A political candidate should be well
versed in *his* country's history. *He* is
someone who should fully understand
the background of the positions *he*
seeks.

Recast   A political candidate should be well
versed in the country's history, *one*
who should fully understand the background of the position sought.

Biased   The sooner a flaw has been discovered
in the work of a new performer, the
sooner the assistant can help *her* with
corrective measures.

Recast   The sooner a flaw has been discovered
in the work of a new performer, the
sooner the assistant can help this
person with corrective measures.

Biased   The division head is well liked, a *man*
of fine character and long experience.

Recast   The division head is well liked, an
individual of fine character and long
experience.

9. *Rephrase the sentence to eliminate pronouns.*

Biased   The architect draws *his* building's
details with care as *he* knows *his* overall plan must be well coordinated.

Recast   The architect draws the building's
details with care, knowing the overall
plan must be well coordinated.

10. *Use the indefinite article "the" in possessive pronoun situations.*

    Biased   A lawyer's predicament can be awkward. *His* first consideration should be *his* client.

    Recast   A lawyer's predicament can be awkward. *The* first consideration should be *the* client.

11. *Wherever possible, find up-to-date substitutions for words with "-man" or "man-" suffix or prefix.*

    businessman   — business person
    businessmen   — business people
    salesman   — salesperson
    salesmen   — salespeople
    chairman   — chairperson
    workman   — worker
    manpower   — workforce

12. *Omit the use of the word "girl."*

    To some women this reference is offensive. For this reason, it is better not to use the terms "girl" or "girls." The definition of "girl" is a female child. (One proposal is to eliminate the use of the word "child" altogether in favor of "young woman" or "young man" to suggest a continuum through life.)

    Discriminatory   The *girls* in our bookkeeping division make up the most efficiently operating department of the company.

    Recast   The staff (or the employees, or the clerks) in our bookkeeping division make up the most efficiently operating department of the company.

13. *Eliminate courtesy titles.*

When you do not know whether a person's preference in courtesy title is Miss, Mrs. or Ms., omit
the title altogether. Use the full name alone.

14. *Omit salutations in correspondence when in doubt.*

When writing to a company without knowledge of
a person's name to direct the letter to, the best
solution to date is to omit the salutation altogether.

15. *Reverse the order some of the time.*

Female and male terms are usually expected to
be used in a certain order — he and she, his and
hers, man and woman, Mr. and Mrs. Jones,
Nichols and May. Reverse them sometimes.

Those who have studied the rise of language will find it
difficult to disagree with the women activists who have claimed
that:

"the very fabric of our language reinforces male supremacy," [2]

*"it is unjust to be forced to think in a language that denies or
limits human existence,"* [3] and that

*"our present language enforces both male chauvinism and female
inferiority."* [4]

Men who wish to test the effects of linguistic exclusion on
their own personalities may try using only "she," "her," and
"woman" when the generic "he," "his," or "man" has been used
and a person of either sex seems to be intended.

It seems clear that efforts to diminish the use of male
pronouns in job-related matters will be an important step toward
eradicating discriminatory attitudes toward women, and in encouraging women to explore their own nonstereotyped potentials.
Most important, relatively simple changes in our language habits
could profoundly improve day-to-day transactions between men
and women.

EXERCISES

The exercises represent the source of the deepest bias against women in our language: the books our children read when they are forming their opinions and attitudes about women and men.

Apply the 15 guidelines and remove the sexist implications from the following examples. [5]

1. In New England, the typical farm was so small that the owner and his sons could take care of it by themselves.

   a) Your revision _____

   _____

   b) Possible alternative: In New England, the typical farm was so small that the family members could take care of it by themselves.

2. Children had once learned about life by listening to aunts, uncles, grandparents, and the wise men of their town or neighborhood.

   a) Your revision _____

   _____

   b) Possible alternative: Children had once learned about life by listening to aunts, uncles, grandparents, and the wise people of their town or neighborhood.

3. Personal symbols are small, personal objects or possessions that have particular associations for their owner. To a woman, for example, a pressed flower might recall a dance she attended many years ago. A boy might keep a cracked baseball bat because it reminded him of the time he hit the winning home run.

   a) Your revision _____

   _____

   _____

   b) Possible alternative: Personal symbols are small, personal objects or possessions that have particular association for their owner. To a grown man, for example, an old yearbook might serve as a reminder of a boy he used to be. A girl might keep a broken tennis racket because it reminds her of a hard-won championship.

4. Write a paragraph about what you expect to do when you are old enough to have Mr. or Mrs. before your name.

   a)   Your revision _____

   _____

   b)   Possible alternative: Write a paragraph about what you would like to do when you grow up.

REFERENCES

1. Mary R. Beard, *Woman as Force in History* (New York: Collier Books. 1971, second printing. © 1946 by Mary R. Beard), p. 57. Reprinted by permission.

2. Tish Sommers, *The Not So Helpless Female*. Prepublication draft (New York: David McKay, January, 1973).

3. Wilma Scott Heide, "Feminism: The sine qua non for a just society," *Vital Speeches*, **38** (April 15, 1972): 403.

4. Emily Toth, "How Can a Woman Man the Barricades?" *Women: A Journal of Liberation*, **2** (No. 1, 1970): 57.

5. The exercises are adapted with permission from Scott, Foresman & Company's "Guidelines Improving the Image of Women in Textbooks."

APPENDIX A: "What Do You Do When Your Script Runs Out?"

Dorothy Jongeward, M. Ed.

Many hundreds of students go through my TA courses designed especially for women.* Nearly two-thirds of these women (primarily suburban housewives) exhibit what I've analyzed as the Sleeping Beauty Script. [1]

A typical Sleeping Beauty is one who bases her script identity and destiny almost exclusively on feminine identification and Parent-programmed, traditional female roles. She lacks a strong dual identity as described by Virginia Satir, [2] negating her sense of personhood and strengthening her sense of femaleness.

Script messages are sent through her first toys which are likely to be baby dolls and play household-gadgets at the exclusion of other possibilities. Parents' strokes determine her adaptations. They frown, discounting aggressive or scientific play, and smile when she is clean, quiet, and motherly. Her feminine scripting may be reinforced with verbalizations such as: "Isn't she the cute little mother." "See how sweet she is with her baby doll." The little girl begins to think of herself as "little mother," and her other possibilities are discounted.

She generally achieves well in grade school. Teachers like her. Her main adaptive pattern is compliance, which gains her much approval.

As she reaches age 12-14, her interests begin to center around her appearance to an *extreme* degree, often to the detriment of having fun, competing, or achieving. For example, she may not swim with the gang because her hair and eye make-up would be spoiled.

From *Transactional Analysis Journal*, 2 (April 1972):2. Reprinted by permission from the International Transactional Analysis Association.

Dorothy Jongeward, M.Ed. is a consultant and lecturer in business, education, psychology of women, sex education.

* Since 1962 such classes as: Psychology Of Women, The Nature of Women, Seminar for Career Women, Transactional Analysis of Women.

By age 14-16, she adapts her infantile script to adult life and firms up her script destiny as "I'm going to get married and have children" (often the sequence is reversed). When this script goal firms up, she "goes to sleep." Sleeping Beauty sleeps instead of developing her own unique talents and intellect. She sleeps instead of self-actualizing her full potential. In fact, she may play *Stupid* or practice martyrdom, playing the Victim role.

Her sleeping state is easily diagnosed when she makes such statements as:

"I don't need to know math. I'm just going to be a housewife."

"Why should I struggle in college? I'm just going to get married."

At this point marriage and children are the goal, the end in life, not a beginning. She thinks ahead to marriage but is deluded about the realities of marriage and child rearing. These delusions are reinforced by the mass media, which eagerly offers her help to reach her goal. She is encouraged to clean up her breath, sweeten her arm pits, remove the hair from her legs, and to spray away offensive feminine odors. Her script compulsion contaminates her Adult reality-testing function; her Parent contaminates her Adult with prejudicial messages about male/female roles and goal expectations.

If she goes to college, she takes the easy course and/or drops out when Mr. Right, her script complement, comes along with a kiss. (He may want her to help him fulfill his vocational scripting.) He is likely to come on authoritarian and prejudicial, reinforcing her Parental messages about a woman's place and function. She may play *If It Weren't For Him* and/or *See What He Makes Me Do?* As one Sleeping Beauty complained, "Why, Edward would have a fit if I went to night school!"

Sleeping Beauty maintains a sense of OKness as long as she follows her script compulsion and is caring for children. However, as her last child approaches age 15-16, she begins to feel lonely, her time is less structured, and depression becomes her main negative stamp collection. By the time her last child leaves, she is around forty years old and may have been to a doctor who prescribes anti-depressants or tranquilizers. If not tranquilizers, she may turn to alcohol.

At this point, her Open End script [3] runs out. She has completed her script and now faces an existential vacuum. No scripting messages come to her rescue to tell her what to do with her time. Some women, in desperation, have another baby to fill up the next ten years. This kind of temporary solution only structures time until the script runs out again and the Script Vacuum re-occurs. Then there is only death to wait for. I see many cases in which an authority figure — doctor, nurse, parent, counselor — has suggested another baby as a solution, perhaps not realizing that in the long run this will not solve the problem. As Eric Berne advises, "The moral of this is that a script should not have a time limit on it, but should be designed to last a whole lifetime, no matter how long that lifetime may be." [4]

It is interesting to compare how the Script Vacuum has evolved as more of a problem for contemporary women than for women at the turn of the century. Compare the pie diagram of Mrs. Average today (which follows) to what it would have been in 1900.

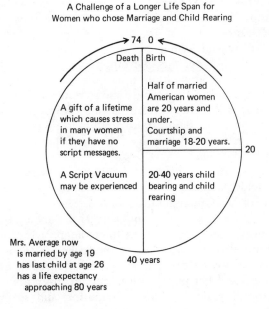

A Challenge of a Longer Life Span for
Women who chose Marriage and Child Rearing

74 0

Death | Birth

A gift of a lifetime which causes stress in many women if they have no script messages.

Half of married American women are 20 years and under. Courtship and marriage 18-20 years.

20

A Script Vacuum may be experienced

20-40 years child bearing and child rearing

Mrs. Average now is married by age 19 has last child at age 26 has a life expectancy approaching 80 years

40 years

Mrs. Average today marries by age 19, has 2.7 children (this continues to drop), gives birth to her last child at age 26, and has a life expectancy of 74 years.

Mrs. Average at the turn of the century married at age 22, had a large number of children, gave birth up to her menopause, and had a life expectancy of only 48 years! She had no time for her script to run out and might be hard put to understand what the fuss is all about with many women today.

When a modern woman suffers a Script Vacuum, she is likely to feel lost, finished, depressed, and useless in what is actually the prime of her life. Her drama is over and a new lifetime stretches before her that nobody told her about or prepared her for. As one woman put it, revealing the power of her delusions, "When my last kid went out the door, my whole sense of self went with him and a terrible feeling of not knowing what to do fell over me. I guess I expected babies to last forever. Here I am 43 and finished. I've never even thought of doing anything else."

Important to the treatment of Sleeping Beauty is the Adult in-put on the Open End script. She needs to become aware of the physical and mental symptoms of having no script and of the futility she faces waiting for inner messages to tell her what to do. I have had the best results with this if her previous roles of housewife and mother are not discounted. Otherwise, her resentments may be displaced as her children take the blame for her having "sacrificed" her personal development for them. Resentment toward husband and children is common when Sleeping Beauty "wakes up" and realizes where she is in her life. Her energy is better used if it is directed toward solving the problem. At this point, she can begin to understand and better cope with her uncomfortable, sometimes depressive feelings. Often a woman will start helping other women.

Eventually, to effect a cure she must begin to examine her life styles and set goals. Constructive goals are essential for developing a winner script for her remaining life's time.

Goals are more likely to be winner goals if they are based on the reality of talents and potentials of the woman. Vocational and educational counseling are often necessary to help establish these data. She needs to work hard gathering realistic, Adult information about herself and her possibilities. Her therapy "homework" is centered around gathering this information and setting and reaching goals.

To effect a cure, social changes may be necessary. [5] The commitment of the counselor may be directed toward seeking this change, as was mine. When I first became aware of the high number of women who had Sleeping Beauty or some other Open End script, there were few places available for them to fulfill the educational goals they set. As a result, I was able to develop curriculum for the local Adult School District which was picked up by other school districts, begin courses for women at the university level, instruct high-school counselors on how to break up this script earlier in life through my Family Life Education courses for educators, and testify before the California Status of Women Commission on behalf of continuing education for women.

An exercise that is useful is to have the client set goals for specific periods of time. For example, the first six months she may set goals monthly. (For some, daily goals may be necessary.) She deals with the questions: "Where do I expect to be one month from today?" and "What do I expect to be doing?" Gradually, the time is extended until she learns to think in these terms. It is important to have this second script go well into old age planning for realistic and satisfying activities for late life. (This is very similar to the kinds of programs that are developing for men whose scripts end at retirement.)

I have seen hundreds of women begin to take responsibility for their own life direction: Some by returning to school, some by developing a community project, getting a job, or developing a talent they were aware of at 10 years old. These are the women who choose getting on with life over waiting for the final curtain, or, as Berne wrote, "waiting for the Promised Land." [6]

REFERENCES

1. Cf Hogie Wycoff, "The Stroke Ecomony in Women's Scripts," *Transactional Analysis Journal*, Vol. 1, No. 3, July 1971, pp. 16-20. See also, Hogie Wycoff, "Radical Psychiatry and Transactional Analysis in Women's Groups," *Transactional Analysis Bulletin*, Oct. 1970, Vol. 9, No. 36. pp. 128-133.

2. Virginia Satir, *Conjoint Family Therapy*, Science and Behavior Books, Palo Alto, 1964, pp. 19, 48-53.

3. Eric Berne, *Sex in Human Loving*, Simon and Schuster, 1970, pp. 167-170.

4. Ibid., p. 170.

5. Cf Eric Berne, "Editor's Page." *Transactional Analysis Bulletin*, Vol. 8. No. 29. Jan. 1969, pp. 7-8.

6. Berne, *Sex in Human Loving*, p. 167.

APPENDIX B: What You May Not Know About Women

ABOUT THE EMPLOYMENT OF WOMEN, DO YOU KNOW THAT

_____ Nine out of ten girls under 18 will be employed some time in their lives?

_____ Almost half (49%) of all women 18 to 64 are in the labor force?

_____ 33 million women are employed, yet 2/3rds are in dead-end, menial jobs?

_____ Half of all employed women earn less than $5,323 as compared to $8,966 for men? (59.4%)

_____ Most women work for compelling economic reasons?

_____ Title 7 of the Civil Rights Act of 1964 prohibits private employers, labor unions, and employment agencies from discriminating on the basis of sex?

_____ Since the Act went into effect, the U.S. Dept of Labor has found 113,000 employees, nearly all of them women, underpaid by more than $47.5 million? Uncounted thousands of unequal pay situations still exist.

_____ The Federal Equal Pay Act of 1963 prohibits employers from discriminating on the basis of sex in payment of wages for equal work?

_____ By Executive Order 11375, government contractors (this includes many colleges and universities) are required to develop and implement affirmative action programmes to eliminate sex discimination or face the cancellation and future loss of government contracts?

_____ Only 7% of women earn over $10,000, as compared to 40% of men?

Prepared by the Unitarian Universalist Women's Federation. Reprinted by permission. This report was issued June 1, 1973.
(Information on the employment of women was compiled largely from material supplied by the Women's Bureau, U.S. Dept. of Labor)

ABOUT THE PLIGHT OF THE MINORITY WOMAN, DO YOU KNOW THAT

_____ About one-eight of all working women are Negro or minority women?

_____ 57% of all Negro women 18 years or older were in the labor force in 1969?

_____ One-fourth of all black families are headed by a woman?

_____ The median wage of the minority woman is lowest of all major groups?

_____ 62% of black families headed by women are poor?

_____ Most minority women have to work at unskilled jobs?

ABOUT WOMEN IN THE FAMILY, DO YOU KNOW THAT

_____ The wife's earnings often lift the family above the poverty level?

_____ 10% of all families are headed by women? Over 1 million of the families headed by women live in poverty?

_____ Day care centers are available for only about 5% of the children under 6 years whose mothers work?

_____ 40% of all employed women are single, divorced, widowed, separated, or deserted? They do _not_ work for pin money or out of boredom!

_____ The number of families headed by women is increasing more rapidly than the total of all families?

ABOUT THE OLDER WOMAN, DO YOU KNOW THAT

_____ Aged women are among the most impoverished? Half of aged women have an income of less than $1,888?

_____ Low wages during employment mean inadequate social security on retirement, thereby condemning millions of retired working women to a life of poverty?

_____ 2 out of 3 of the elderly are women? 10.5 million women aged 55 or older are "on their own?"

_____ 5 out of 8 older women are classified as poor or near poor?

THE JOBS WOMEN HOLD

_____ Women are 76 percent of all clerical workers, but only 4 percent of all craftsmen and foremen.

_____ Only about one-sixth of all nonfarm managers and administrators are women.

_____ Less than 10% of all doctors are women; less than 1% of all dentists.

_____ About 3% of all engineers; 3% of business executives are women.

_____ Only 4.2% of employed women earned over $10,000 (23.9% for men) . . . only 4/10 of 1% earned over $15,000 (8.2% for men) (1969 statistics).

_____ About 1.6 million women are private household workers; the median wage of full time year round household workers was $1,981 in 1971. In only 4 states are they protected by minimum wage legislation; there is no federal law.

EDUCATIONAL LEVEL MAKES LITTLE DIFFERENCE FOR A WOMAN

_____ Median income of women with college degrees ($8,156) is little more than men with grade school educations ($7,535). Men college graduates have a median income of $13,264. (1970)

_____ Women Ph.D.'s get few college faculty jobs.

_____ Educated women at all levels are sadly underutilized.

_____ Nearly 7 out of 10 women 45 to 54 years of age with 4 or more years of college are in the labor force.

WOMEN ARE LOSING GROUND

_____ The wage gap between men and women has been increasing for 25 years.

_____ In 1955, women's median earnings as a proportion of men's was 63.9%; in 1970 it was 59.4%.

_____ Men have been steadily taking over "women's jobs" (librarians, social workers, teachers, etc.)

_____ While more women than men are teachers, in public and elementary schools, less than 20% of principals and other supervisors were women in 1970-71.

_____ In 1970, only 1 in 10 Ph.D.'s was granted to a woman — fewer than in 1940.

ABOUT WOMEN IN RELIGION

_____ Some major denominations prohibit women from serving as rabbis, priests or ministers.

_____ In denominations where women are ordained, there are almost no women ministers serving in the pulpit.

_____ Women are seldom found in the paid executive echelons of religious institutions.

_____ They are employed in great numbers as clerical workers, with few opportunities for advancement.

_____ (For an account of the status of women in the Unitarian Universalist movement, read, *Does the Liberal Church Liberate Women?* in the March-April 1972 BRIDGE, available for 25¢ from the UUWF — address on page 334.)

ABOUT THAT MYTH THAT WOMEN CONTROL
THE NATIONAL WEALTH, DO YOU KNOW THAT

_____ Individual women own 18% of total shares of stock of public corporations; individual men, 24%? (Remaining 58% is held or owned by institutions, brokers, dealers, etc.) Since corporations are almost entirely managed by men and boards of directors are often entirely male, women have little actual control over the uses of their 18% of holdings.

LAWS DISCRIMINATE

_____ In the U.S., there are hundreds of state laws that discriminate against women.

_____ Four of eight states with community property laws still permit the husband exclusive rights to manage and control community property, even though it includes money contributed by the wife.

_____ In the 42 states without community property laws, when the husband is the wage earner and holds family savings in his name, he is free to manage, control, or dispose of savings without consulting his wife.

_____ The inheritance rights of widows differ from those of widowers in some states.

_____ Grounds for divorce for men and women are not the same in all states.

_____ Under the law, longer prison sentences are imposed on women than men for the same crime in some states.

_____ There is no federal law forbidding discrimination against women in housing or public accommodations.

_____ In most states, women are not protected by law from discrimination in granting credit.

_____ Laws in various states restrict a married woman's ability to conduct business.

_____ Some states permit women to be excused from jury duty solely on grounds of their sex. Predominantly male juries raise the question whether women can get a fair trial.

_____ State restrictive work laws, purporting to be protective on hours, weightlifting, etc. actually result in discrimination in employment of women by making it burdensome upon employers, and by giving prejudiced supervisors an "out."

_____ The Equal Rights Amendment, introduced in 1923, was passed by the Congress on March 22, 1972. It must be ratified by 38 states. When ratified, it will in effect void many discriminatory state laws.

FEWER WOMEN IN POLITICS

_____ No woman has served in the President's Cabinet since 1955.

_____ In 1973, only 14 women served in the U.S. House of Representatives, no woman in the Senate. In 1960, there was a total of 17 in Congress.

_____ Very few women serve in state legislatures or in positions of responsibility in the administration of their local communities.

WOMEN MAY BE DENIED THE HUMAN RIGHT TO CONTROL OVER THEIR BODIES

_____ In spite of the Supreme Court ruling allowing a woman the right to decide to terminate an unwanted pregnancy, many hospitals deny women the right to abortions.

DO YOU CARE? WANT TO TAKE ACTION?

WHAT YOU CAN DO TO UPGRADE THE STATUS OF WOMEN

Educate Yourself on the Facts

In your state or province,

_____ Acquaint yourself with the laws applying to employment of women, their property rights, laws on inheritance, ability to conduct business.

_____ Are there laws forbidding discrimination against women in housing and public accommodations? In education?

_____ Does your state have an active Commission on the Status of Women? What recommendations has this body made?

_____ In Canada — study the report of the Royal Commission on the Status of Women.

_____ Check your area's district office of the Equal Employment Opportunity Commission, which is charged with implementing Title 7 of the 1964 Civil Rights Act. Learn the process for filing a complaint. Gather facts on the complaints they have handled based on discrimination because of sex.

_____ Does your state have a human rights commission or equal employment opportunity commission which is working hard to end discrimination against women?

_____ What are the current unemployment percentages for women and men in your state?

_____ Are there equal opportunities in training, education, and employment for women and girls in poverty? Are women and children on welfare receiving adequate support?

_____ Does your community offer opportunities for continuing education for women that will help those who want to find employment?

_____ What kind of vocational courses are given for women and girls in your public schools or in other centers in your community? Will they lead to wider employment options?

_____ Is the private household worker paid a fair wage in your community?

_____ Are guidance counselors in schools encouraging girls to broaden career horizons?

_____ Does your community provide adequate and quality child care?

Select Area(s) for Action

_____ Plan meetings with other women.

_____ Look for allies and resources in your community. Urge church and civic groups to offer programs focussing on women's needs.

Learn About the Ideas of the New Feminism

_____ What is the new feminism all about? What are its ideology, goals, and problems?

_____ What new life styles are developing? What does it have to say to the individual woman who feels she has no problems? Read and discuss VOICES OF THE NEW FEMINISM, sponsored by the UUWF, available in paperback at $2.45 at your bookstore or from Beacon Press. ($2.00 to UUWF women when ordered from the UUWF) This book examines the situations of women and discusses the forces that will bring radical change in the lives of men and women alike. Included are articles by Congresswomen Martha Griffiths and Shirley Chisholm, Betty Friedan, Elizabeth Koontz, former Director Women's Bureau, and eight other women leaders. "*Voices* is neither radical nor shrill ... well reasoned, intelligent, carefully thought out and accurately presented." *Toronto Daily Star*

For more information, you may write to:

UNITARIAN UNIVERSALIST WOMEN'S FEDERATION
25 Beacon Street, Boston, Massachusetts 02108.

ABOUT THE AUTHORS

Dorothy Jongeward, coauthor of *Born To Win* (Addison-Wesley, 1971), is President of the Transactional Analysis Management Institute, Inc., and a prominent lecturer, author, and educator. She has traveled widely as a consultant to business, industry, and government. Dr. Jongeward is a pioneer in the fields of transactional analysis, careers and education for women, the psychology of women, family-life education, and the problems of organizations.

Dr. Jongeward earned the B.S. degree in psychology, the B.Ed. and M.Ed. degrees in educational guidance at Washington State University, and the Ph.D degree in applied psychology at California Western University. She is a teacher member and trustee of the International Transactional Analysis Association, a faculty member of the University of California Extension since 1963, and a life member of the California Association of Marriage and Family Counselors.

Dr. Jongeward is author of *Everybody Wins: Transactional Analysis Applied to Organizations* (Addison-Wesley, 1973), selected as one of the 10 best business books of 1974 by Library Journal. With Muriel James, she is coauthor of *Born to Win: Transactional Analysis with Gestalt Experiments, Winning with People: Group Exercises in Transactional Analysis*, and *The People Book: Transactional Analysis for Students*.

Dru Scott develops new ways of using transactional analysis to solve the problems of women and management. A specialist in ongoing senior management group development seminars, she consults with corporate and governmental organizations in the United States and in Europe. During the past seven years Ms. Scott has helped more than 12,000 people use T.A. on the job.

Now President of Dru Scott Associates, a San Francisco-based management consulting group, Dru Scott was formerly Associate Director of the West Coast Communications Training Institute of the U.S. Civil Service Commission.

She is a featured authority in the new *Psychology Today* CRM Productions film "Transactional Analysis." She is also a faculty member of the University of California-Berkeley Extension, where she regularly teaches courses on women and management, interpersonal communications for managers, transactional analysis, and executive team development.

Ms. Scott is coauthor with Dorothy Jongeward of a new Addison-Wesley book, *Women as Winners*. Her other publications include an article in *Personnel* on "Motivation from the TA Viewpoint" and an article in *Everybody Wins* (Addison-Wesley, 1973) on "How T.A. Helps People Manage Their Time."